ENCYCLOPEDIA OF
AQUARIUM
PLANTS

ENCYCLOPEDIA OF
AQUARIUM
PLANTS

Peter Hiscock

BARRON'S

Above: *The arching crinkled leaves of* Aponogeton boivinianus *dominate this aquarium display and provide sanctuary for the shoaling fish.*

First Edition for the United States and Canada published in 2003 by Barron's Educational Series, Inc. First published in 2003 by Interpet Publishing. *Encyclopedia of Aquarium Plants* © Copyright 2003 by Interpet Publishing.

All inquiries should be addressed to:
Barron's Educational Series, Inc.
250 Wireless Boulevard
Hauppauge, New York 11788
http://www.barronseduc.com

International Standard Book Number 0-7641-5521-0
Library of Congress Catalog Card Number
2002101225

Printed in China
9 8 7 6 5 4 3 2 1

Author

Peter Hiscock began keeping fish and aquariums as a child, inspired by his parents, both accomplished marine biologists. He was appointed manager of a retail aquatics outlet at just 17 years of age and went on to complete aquatic studies at Sparsholt College in Hampshire, UK. He entered publishing with contributions to the aquatic press. His main interests include fish behavior and the interaction of fish with their environment, as well as aquascaping and the natural habitats of aquarium species.

Publisher's acknowledgment

The publishers would like to thank Tropica Aquarium Plants a/s, Hjortshøj, Denmark for supplying plants for photography.

Left: Echinodorus uruguayensis, one of many echinodorus species and cultivars available for aquarium use. They provide bold shapes and contribute an elegant style to planting displays.

Contents

Part One: Practical section

Comprehensive practical guidance on all aspects of creating a stunning planted aquarium, from how plants work to the value and techniques of regular maintenance. The topics of water quality and filtration, choosing substrates, and correct planting methods are all featured in detail. Lighting, feeding, and propagation are also key areas to receive attention, followed by a major section on aquascaping.

Introduction	10
The natural biology of plants	12
Water quality and filtration	26
The right substrate	38
Choosing and planting	48
Lighting the aquarium	56
Feeding aquarium plants	66
Propagating aquarium plants	78
Maintaining a planted aquarium	84
Aquascaping	94
Fish for the planted aquarium	118

Part Two: Plant profiles

A wide-ranging survey of more than 150 popular aquarium plants presented in A–Z order of scientific name, including a brief review of nonaquatic plants suitable for temporary display in the aquarium. The majority of the featured plants are shown in color photographs, many with accompanying detailed views. Full botanical, practical, and growing information is provided for each plant, including common name, origin, height, growth rate, suitable aquarium zone, lighting requirements, optimum temperature range, propagation techniques, and difficulty rating.

Introduction	122
Plant Profiles	124
Index and credits	198

Part One
Practical section

Over the past 30 years or so the aquarium industry has boomed, and it is now easier than ever for aquarists to obtain the equipment, treatments, and fish and plant species they require to create a stunning aquarium. Experienced, long-term hobbyists will often tell of the difficulties they encountered when trying to obtain species and maintain aquariums in "the old days." Much of our success today is due to these pioneering enthusiasts, who were forced to experiment with various aspects of plant and fish care to find the best methods of maintaining planted aquariums. The knowledge they passed on and the methods they devised for aquarium maintenance and keeping plants healthy are now standard practice.

For beginners and newcomers to keeping aquarium plants, there is an increasing amount of information available relating to plant care, and at first glance, it can appear quite daunting. It is not uncommon to find conflicting advice from different sources regarding methods of cultivation or solutions to problems. However, a basic understanding of the requirements of aquatic plants and how to care for

them is essential for you to set up and maintain a successful display. Thankfully, a complete understanding of all the aquatic processes that govern good plant care is not required from the start. It is possible, and probably more useful, to learn as you go along.

The first part of this book focuses on practical matters, beginning with the biological processes that occur within plants and the systems they use to thrive in the aquatic environment. Understanding how plants work and why certain conditions are required for healthy growth are vitally important topics. If you acquire a basic understanding of the biology of plants and their requirements, the rest will follow.

Water quality dictates much of the aquarium environment, and in the water quality and filtration section, the properties of water are examined, along with the processes that occur in the aquarium that alter water quality. Filtration and the types of filter suited to a planted aquarium are also discussed.

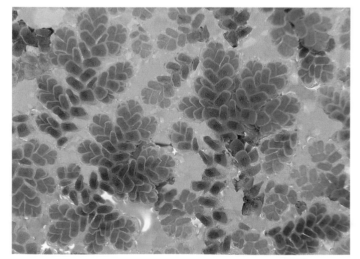

Azolla caroliniana

The successful health of plants depends largely on the environment they are kept in, and preparing this begins well before any plants are introduced. For example, the substrate provides much more than a simple rooting medium for plants. A whole chapter in this part of the book is dedicated to the choice of substrates, the vital role they play, and how to prepare, install, and care for them properly.

Other sections in this part of the book focus on choosing aquatic plants and preparing them for planting, lighting the aquarium, and feeding plants. In the feeding chapter, all the nutrients required by plants are examined in detail, including the role they play in plant health and growth. Fertilization methods are explained and applied to aquarium situations. Once planted, you must

Trimming plants in the aquarium

keep your aquarium display looking its best, so ongoing care and maintenance are discussed next, as well as the correct methods of dealing with pests such as algae and snails.

In the final chapter of Part One, we embark on the exciting prospect of aquascaping – how to design a superb aquarium display, using not only plants, grouped for maximum effect, but rocks, wood, bark, and other decor. And if you need further inspiration, take a look at the individual aquascaped display tanks that reflect different environmental conditions and a range of natural biotopes. We end with a brief look at some of the fish that will complete the display. Above all, this part of the book forms a vital resource of practical guidance that you can refer to at every stage of setting up and maintaining your aquarium. With a little time and patience, a stunning display aquarium is not difficult to achieve. You will find the result and rewards are well worth the effort involved.

*Microsorium
pteropus 'Tropica'*

Planting ludwigia

The natural biology of plants

Although there are a few exceptions, plants in general do not consume other organisms to obtain the energy and the basic elements they need to live, grow, and reproduce. Instead, they use the processes of photosynthesis to obtain energy, and absorb vital elements directly from the surrounding environment. This simplified way of life has allowed plants to thrive and spread in many habitats, becoming the basis of support for more complex organisms and food chains. Plants are producers rather than consumers; they "produce" biological material rather than "consume" it. Plants themselves are eaten by herbivorous animals, which in turn are consumed by predatory animals. Clearly, plants have an important place in the natural world as a provider of food sources; without them, the diverse range of animals would not survive.

Plants developed on land before venturing underwater and although aquatic plants are highly adapted to the underwater environment, many of their physical attributes can be traced back to their terrestrial ancestry. Other attributes have been lost in the course of evolution; fine hairs used to trap moisture and stiff, strong stems to support leaves are not needed underwater. Conversely, aquatic plants have developed certain less noticeable attributes to aid underwater survival. Many of these are based on the production of chemicals that "condition" the substrate so that plants can take up

Above: Oxygen produced during photosynthesis can be clearly seen on this Echinodorus sp. leaf. The oxygen is a waste product and is released back into the water and used by other organisms.

Left: Without the plants and other vegetation found in and around this river, there would be very little life beneath the surface. Plants provide the basis for most complex ecosystems.

How photosynthesis works

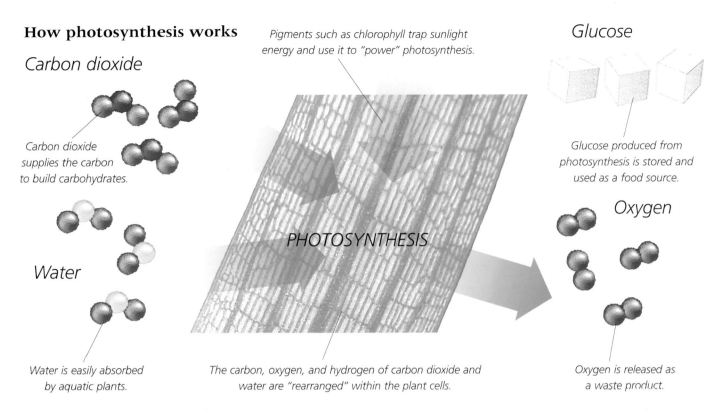

Carbon dioxide

Pigments such as chlorophyll trap sunlight energy and use it to "power" photosynthesis.

Glucose

Carbon dioxide supplies the carbon to build carbohydrates.

Glucose produced from photosynthesis is stored and used as a food source.

Water

Oxygen

PHOTOSYNTHESIS

Water is easily absorbed by aquatic plants.

The carbon, oxygen, and hydrogen of carbon dioxide and water are "rearranged" within the plant cells.

Oxygen is released as a waste product.

nutrients, and chemicals used to protect against consumption by animals and competition from other plants (see page 88). Physical changes can also be seen in the development of complex leaf structures designed to maximize the amount of light received by the plant, allowing it to survive in harsh conditions underwater.

Looking at the biology and structure of aquatic plants helps us to understand why certain conditions are needed in the aquarium if we want to keep aquatic plants successfully. A greater understanding of the functions of aquatic plants will also help to identify the causes and solutions to problems encountered when keeping plants in the aquarium.

Photosynthesis

The unique function that plants possess is the ability to obtain energy from sunlight, carbon dioxide, and water, using the process of photosynthesis. Photosynthetic cells within the leaves and stem tissues contain pigments that trap light energy to break down the molecular structure of water (H_2O) into hydrogen and oxygen. The hydrogen binds first to carbon dioxide and then oxygen to form glucose, which is a basic sugar and an important source of energy. Some oxygen is left over from this process and is released back into the water, where it is either used up by bacteria and animals or released into the atmosphere at the water surface.

The glucose produced from photosynthesis is water soluble and, if stored in large quantities, will absorb water and enlarge the cells that contain it. Obviously, this is undesirable for plants, so the glucose is quickly converted into an insoluble starch compound and transported to various parts of the plant for storage, in most cases to the upper root area. Some plants can house vast amounts of starch in specially designed root structures. One of the most distinctive examples is the banana plant (*Nymphoides aquatica*), which produces numerous "banana-shaped" roots that store starch and other nutrients. Many plants store starch in tubers, rhizomes, and bulbs. The starch can be easily converted back into glucose and transported around the plant when needed.

Factors affecting photosynthesis

A plant has little control over the rate of photosynthesis that occurs within its cells. A number of environmental factors are responsible for the productivity of the photosynthetic cells and it is always the factor in least supply that limits the rate of photosynthesis. The aim in the aquarium is to remove the majority of constraints on photosynthesis to obtain the optimum level. Higher rates of photosynthesis will encourage faster growth, reproduction, and improved plant health. Light is the most obvious environmental factor, but temperature, carbon dioxide levels, and nutrient availability also affect the rate of photosynthesis.

Limiting factors on photosynthesis

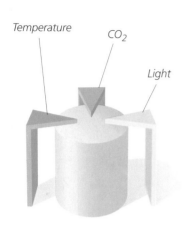

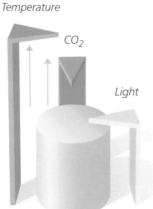

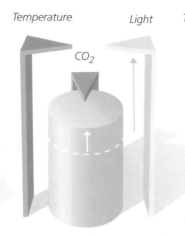

Assuming that the nutrient supply and other environmental conditions are correct, three factors affect the rate of photosynthesis: temperature, carbon dioxide (CO_2), and light.

If one factor is in short supply, photosynthesis will be restricted. Increasing the temperature and CO_2 content will not increase photosynthesis if the plants do not receive enough light.

In most aquariums, the CO_2 content of the water is the limiting factor. Even with the correct temperature and good lighting, plants will not grow well if they receive little CO_2.

Once CO_2 and lighting levels are sufficiently high, and the temperature is at an optimum level, the rate of photosynthesis will increase rapidly. Mostly, this will produce a healthier plant.

Light

Plants will only photosynthesize when suitable light is available to be trapped by the photosynthetic cells. At night, plants stop photosynthesizing and only start again in daylight. The intensity and duration of light are the factors that affect the rate of photosynthesis. In nature, most tropical plants experience about 12 hours of sunlight in a 24-hour period. The intensity of light varies throughout the day. Depending on the location of the plant and the shading, it is strongest in open areas around mid-day. In the aquarium, the same duration should be employed and in most cases, a bright light source is preferable. If the light is left on for a longer period, the photosynthetic period will also increase. This may bring its own problems; it is possible that plants will oversynthesize and become damaged by literally wearing themselves out.

Providing other factors are available in the right supply, the rate of photosynthesis is directly proportional to the intensity of light received by the plant until a light saturation point is reached. Slow-growing plants, which often grow in shaded areas in nature, may experience problems in strong light conditions. These plants will assimilate nutrients and carbon dioxide at a slower rate, so an increase in photosynthesis spurred on by bright light may cause nutrient deficiencies within the plant, even when large amounts of nutrients are available in the surrounding environment.

Temperature

Heat affects all the biological processes within an organism and, providing the change in temperature is within the tolerance of the organism, an increase in temperature generally causes an increase in metabolism. In plants, an increase of 18°F (10°C) will roughly double the rate of photosynthesis, assuming all other factors are favorable. However, if the surrounding environment becomes too warm, the plant will simply begin to die, and photosynthesis will stop. An increase in temperature affects not just photosynthesis, but the whole metabolism of a plant, so it also increases the plant's requirements for nutrients, carbon dioxide, and other elements. For this reason, simply increasing the temperature of an aquarium to aid plant photosynthesis and, therefore, plant growth, is unlikely to work. If the aquarium is set at a temperature based on the natural environment of the plants, then a lack of growth, or a need to increase growth rates, can be better explained or achieved by looking at the other limiting factors.

Carbon dioxide

Plants take up carbon dioxide from the surrounding water and substrate. If carbon dioxide is not available in sufficient quantities, many plants have developed ways of obtaining carbon-containing compounds and creating their own source of carbon dioxide. This occurs more in hardwater plants, including *Vallisneria* and *Egeria* species, which experience lower carbon dioxide levels in nature. In hard water, carbon dioxide is more likely to bind to minerals, creating carbonates. Many plants will take up these carbonates and break them down, allowing the carbon to become carbon dioxide.

Plants that regularly produce leaves above the surface have developed methods of utilizing carbon dioxide gas from atmospheric air, where the concentrations are much higher. Floating plants have constant access to the air, so it is far easier for them to obtain carbon dioxide from the surrounding air through the leaves, in the same way as terrestrial plants. Some stem plants also produce aerial leaves or stems above the surface. Air drawn down the center of the stem is used both to obtain carbon dioxide and to oxygenate root areas.

In most natural situations, it is a lack of sufficient carbon dioxide that limits photosynthesis and prevents strong growth in aquatic plants. In the

Below: These tropical lilies (Nymphaea sp.) *produce leaves above the surface to obtain carbon dioxide and sunlight with ease. They also provide cover for other aquatic creatures.*

aquarium, the aquarist has more control over carbon dioxide levels and can achieve a constant high level by using carbon dioxide fertilizer systems.

Nutrient availability

The photosynthetic pigments—usually chlorophyll—are produced by the plant within the cells. To do this, a number of nutrients are required, including magnesium (Mg), potassium (K), iron (Fe), and nitrogen (N). These nutrients, and others indirectly, are vital for the production and continual use of photosynthetic pigments and the cells containing them. A general lack of any of these nutrients can often be seen as a fading or change in leaf color, as the production of chlorophyll pigment is affected (see page 77).

Photosynthesis and leaf color

The color of an object that we perceive is produced by pigments that reflect certain wavelengths of light. A green pigment will absorb most of the light spectrum except for the green areas, which are reflected, making the object appear green (see page 56). The green

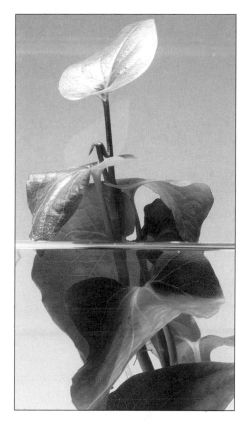

Above: This Saururus cernuus *plant is sending up leaves above the water surface, where they can absorb carbon dioxide directly from the air. The submerged leaves are larger and thinner than the aerial ones.*

photosynthetic pigment in most plants is chlorophyll and is contained in structures called chloroplasts within the plants' cells. Chlorophyll is produced in the greatest quantities in the parts of the plant that receive the most light, mainly in the leaves. The roots of plants receive virtually no light below the substrate, so do not contain chlorophyll and hence, do not appear green.

As we have seen earlier, plants have very little control over the rate of photosynthesis within their own cells and simply photosynthesize at the fastest rate possible, depending on environmental conditions. In bright conditions, a plant may receive more light than it needs to produce adequate

amounts of glucose. If this happens continually in the plant's habitat, it may develop another method of photosynthesizing at a slower rate. This often involves using a different photosynthetic pigment, which may be less efficient at breaking down water for photosynthesis. These secondary pigments are called carotenoids and vary in color from pale yellow to dark red.

Depending on the light conditions normally experienced by a plant, the leaves will vary in color and may appear in various shades of green, brown, orange, or red. Some plants will always keep the same color, while others may be able to vary their color depending on the light conditions. In the aquarium, looking at the leaf color of a plant can help to establish what kind of light is required by the plant. A plant that produces reddish leaves may be accustomed to bright light conditions in nature and will need the same conditions in the aquarium to photosynthesize properly. Sometimes, red plants first produce green leaves, which then change to red. If they stop turning red or revert back to green, this may indicate that the intensity of light in the aquarium is not sufficiently high. Alternatively, in very bright conditions, green plants may start to produce red leaves, but this should not be taken as an indication that the light is too bright.

Some plants, particularly within the cryptocoryne group, produce brown leaves. These plants are often found in shallow streams with overhanging vegetation and may have developed the use of photosynthetic pigments that are more efficient at using the green areas of the light spectrum. These may be more abundant in an environment shaded by other plants. Therefore, plants with brown leaves should do relatively well in shaded areas of the aquarium. In many cases, brown-leaved cryptocorynes will develop green leaves when kept in brightly lit areas of the aquarium. This color change occurs because of the change in light spectrum from the plant's natural environment. A green photosynthetic pigment such as chlorophyll may become more useful to the plant than its previous photosynthetic pigments.

Left: Alternanthera reineckii *has a distinctive red-brown leaf color. A red photosynthetic pigment is less efficient at utilizing light energy, a sign that this plant requires strong lighting.*

Below: Echinodorus *'Rubin' produces large, brownish leaves and may be able to utilize green light more efficiently than other plants. This is particularly useful in shaded areas.*

Above: The mottled green-and-red leaf of this Echinodorus *indicates that there are two separate photosynthetic pigments. In bright light, the less efficient red pigment helps to reduce the rate of photosynthesis, while in low light, the green pigment will spread and increase the efficiency of photosynthesis.*

How respiration works

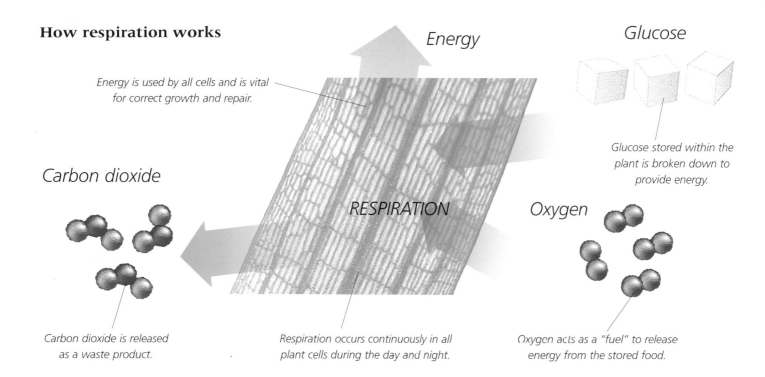

Energy

Energy is used by all cells and is vital for correct growth and repair.

Glucose

Glucose stored within the plant is broken down to provide energy.

Carbon dioxide

RESPIRATION

Oxygen

Carbon dioxide is released as a waste product.

Respiration occurs continuously in all plant cells during the day and night.

Oxygen acts as a "fuel" to release energy from the stored food.

Respiration and oxygen levels

The process of respiration occurs in all complex organisms and takes place in all plant cells. Respiration helps to break down food sources and release energy into the cells. During the process, oxygen is used up and carbon dioxide is released as a by-product. The chemical equation for the process of respiration is the exact reverse of photosynthesis, except that sunlight energy is not involved. Unlike photosynthesis, respiration is a continual process that does not stop at night. Thus, photosynthesis stores food "energy," whereas respiration releases energy.

It is important to be aware of respiration in plants, because in a heavily planted aquarium it has a significant effect on oxygen levels within the tank. In any 24-hour period, plants release more oxygen through photosynthesis than they use up during respiration. This is one reason why many fast-growing or "fast-photosynthesizing" plants are sold as "oxygenating" plants for ponds and aquariums. However, as well as the plants, fish and bacterial organisms also use up oxygen continually through respiration; in fact, bacteria are the biggest "consumers" of oxygen in the aquarium. In periods of darkness, a heavily planted aquarium can quickly use up oxygen until it is at such a low level that fish begin to suffer from oxygen deficiency. This problem is generally confined to heavily planted aquariums with little aeration or water movement, and can be remedied by increasing oxygenation during periods of darkness. Gentle aeration or strong surface movement provided by pumps and filters will usually allow enough oxygen to enter the aquarium at the water surface and prevent deficiencies. Plants do not generally appreciate a high oxygen level in the aquarium because it diminishes their ability to obtain nutrients. This means that constant aeration is not beneficial in planted aquariums and should be employed only at night, when oxygen deficiencies may occur. The aim is to balance the needs of the plants and the fish in a planted aquarium.

Plant anatomy

Although some plants lack a central stem, and plants such as mosses and ferns do not produce flowers, the anatomy of most plants can be split into four basic zones; the roots, stem, leaves, and flowers. All these parts play a vital role in the plant's basic functions, including growth, reproduction, nutrient collection, and storage.

Types of root Plants produce roots for three basic purposes: anchoring, nutrient collection, and nutrient storage. In most cases, roots do not contain green chlorophyll and normally lack pigments, appearing white in color. Terrestrial plant roots have a number of fine hairs for trapping moisture, but these are not present in aquatic plants, although they may develop on some bog plants when grown out of water. The roots of most aquatic plants are a combination of a number of central roots, up to 0.06 in (1.5 mm) in diameter, with many smaller roots trailing off. Within the roots there are many vascular

Above: *The fine, "hairlike" trailing roots of this floating plant have a greater surface area than most roots, which makes them ideal for obtaining large amounts of essential nutrients from the surrounding water.*

Anatomy of a plant

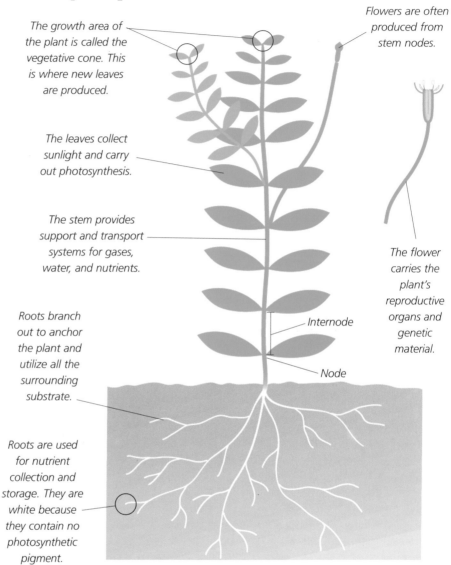

The growth area of the plant is called the vegetative cone. This is where new leaves are produced.

Flowers are often produced from stem nodes.

The leaves collect sunlight and carry out photosynthesis.

The stem provides support and transport systems for gases, water, and nutrients.

The flower carries the plant's reproductive organs and genetic material.

Roots branch out to anchor the plant and utilize all the surrounding substrate.

Internode

Node

Roots are used for nutrient collection and storage. They are white because they contain no photosynthetic pigment.

systems that transport water, nutrients, and gases to and from the root and the rest of the plant. Oxygen absorbed from the leaves or produced as a result of photosynthesis is readily transported down to the roots and released into the substrate. This prevents the roots from being damaged by stagnating substrates and acidic compounds (see page 47).

Large and/or "bulky" plants, such as larger *Echinodorus* sp., produce many long roots to provide good anchorage and a wide nutrient collection area. These long roots can quickly take over the aquarium substrate, which is relatively limited in size compared with the natural habitat. In the aquarium, trimming the roots is a method of controlling the eventual size of plants such as *Echinodorus*. Without a large rootstock, a plant will not reach its potential size and will remain conveniently small and compact.

In contrast, smaller plants from shallow or marshy areas have much shorter, thinner roots. In their natural habitats, the substrate is often very thin

and there is normally little water movement, so the plants do not need long roots for anchorage. The roots are thinner because the vascular systems are much smaller in shorter roots, since water, nutrients, and gases have less far to travel and because shallow substrates are much better oxygenated.

Some roots are adapted to live above the substrate and will attach themselves firmly to wood, rocks, and other solid objects. This gives the plant an advantage because it can grow in places

where other plants cannot anchor themselves. *Microsorium, Anubias,* and *Bolbitis* spp. all prefer to be planted on solid objects above the substrate. The roots of these plants will grow horizontally as well as vertically, as they "feel" for suitable places to attach themselves.

The trailing roots produced by floating plants below the surface are designed purely to absorb nutrients from the water. These roots are often long, thin, and almost feathery in appearance.

Root forms

Above: *In some roots, the upper part contains large amounts of nutrients in special storage organs.*

Above: *Many plants grow from bulbs or tubers, which contain large reserves of nutrients.*

Above: *Large plants produce longer and thicker roots for better anchorage and nutrient collection.*

Above: *Needing no anchorage, floating plants produce many branched, fine roots that help to assimilate nutrients.*

Above: *Some aquatic plants, such as ferns and* Anubias *species, produce roots from a rhizome that attaches to rocks and wood.*

Since they do not need to transport gases, their vascular systems are very simple, and because they do not anchor themselves they are hairlike in form. These numerous hairlike roots have a greater overall contact with the surrounding water, allowing floating plants to take up nutrients from the water more quickly than other plants.

The function of stems A stem is present in most aquatic plants and performs two basic functions: support

and transport. The stem's function is aided by supporting gas- or air-filled cells that provide buoyancy and help to keep the plant upright. Since the surrounding water provides much of a plant's support, aquatic stems are often much thinner and more flexible than terrestrial stems. Flexible stems allow the plant to move with the water, rather than try to hold steady against it, risking damage.

Like the roots, the stem contains vascular systems for transporting nutrients, water, and gases around the

plant. The stem area is called a stem axis and can vary considerably in size between different plants. In "stem" plants, the stem axis is elongated along the entire above-substrate area of the plant. This stem is divided into sections called internodes and at either end of these are nodes on which leaves are produced. The top part of a stem is called the vegetative cone, or point, and this is where new leaves are produced and grow. Some plants have a much shorter stem axis, sometimes less than a few inches, on which several leaves are produced in a spiral pattern. These plants appear to have no stem and are often called rosette plants.

In many plants, the base of the stem is adapted to form nutrient storage areas and appear as part of the root system. The rhizomes and tubers found on *Anubias, Echinodorus,* and *Aponogeton* species, among others, are typical examples of an extension of the stem used to store nutrients. Plants can draw

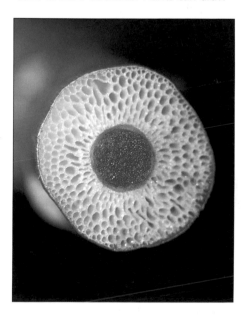

Above: *This cross section of a typical stem plant (Ammannia gracilis) clearly shows the internal structure. Here, there are air-filled cells to provide buoyancy and support and vascular cells for transporting nutrients.*

Right: These Echinodorus leaves are produced above the water surface, where there is less competition for light from other aquatic plants. In many plants, these aerial leaves are a different shape compared to submerged ones.

Left: Aquatic plants do not need a waxy cuticle layer to prevent drying out. This allows plants such as this Cabomba sp. to develop thinner and more complex leaf structures.

Below: Viewed from above, it is clear that the oval leaves of this cryptocoryne are arranged to be exposed to as much of the sky as possible, allowing each leaf to receive maximum light.

on these stores to survive harsh periods during the winter period and produce enough food to regrow when environmental conditions improve.

Leaves The leaves of a plant are essentially tools for collecting sunlight to use in the process of photosynthesis. Gas exchange and some collection of nutrients is also carried out by the leaves. The leaves of terrestrial plants have a thick, waxy outer layer called the cuticle, which protects the plant from drying out. In aquatic plants this layer is much thinner and liquid is able to pass through much more easily, which helps the plant to take up nutrients. Aquatic plants that produce aerial leaves often show two different leaf shapes below and above the water. This is due to the different environments and a change in the cuticle layer.

The variation in leaf shapes between aquatic plants is high and often relates to adaptations for survival in different environments. All leaves contain photosynthetic pigments and the

Plantlets can be separated and grown as new plants.

Above: These plantlets are produced in small groups on a thick stem runner and will become quite large before they separate and root as genetically identical versions of the parent plant.

Right: Flowers produced on the plantlets are raised above the main plant, where they are easily accessible to terrestrial pollen-transporting insects.

Left: In this Alternanthera reineckii 'Rosaefolia', small flowers are clearly visible developing in the leaf axils. These are borne on aerial shoots and are fertilized by insects.

concentration of these pigments is often higher toward the upper side of the leaf. This is why many leaves exhibit different colors or shades on each side.

Flowers Although not all aquatic plants are likely to produce flowers in the aquarium, the majority are flowering plants and will produce seeds and reproduce by flowering in nature. The flowers are usually produced above water, where they can be pollinated by insects, just as terrestrial plants are.

Some aquatic plants produce flowers beneath the water surface. In these instances, the seeds are capable of floating downstream and a few species do not produce flowers at all, preferring to reproduce by purely asexual means.

Cell structure

The vital life processes of plants, such as photosynthesis, respiration, nutrient transfer, and gas exchange, all take place

Plant cell structure

Typically, aquatic plant leaves are very thin, allowing light and gases to penetrate easily.

A single layer of small cells covered with a thin cuticle on both surfaces of the leaf.

Air spaces provide support and structure.

The conversion of CO_2 into glucose takes place in this nutrient-rich liquid.

Liquid vacuole used for storage and water transport.

Respiration occurs in these cell structures called mitochondria.

Cellulose cell walls made from strong polysaccharide matrix.

Inside each chloroplast, the green chlorophyll pigment is contained in plates that move toward the light like solar panels.

The nucleus is the "control center" for each cell.

within individual cells. All cells are made up of the same structural components and it is a variation in these that creates different cells for different purposes.

Adaptation to natural habitats

Aquatic plants occur in many shapes and sizes and are highly adapted to their individual natural habitats. Leaf shapes and colors are often related to lighting conditions, and the size of plants is also determined by environmental conditions. A small plant accustomed to low levels of light would not do well in deep, open water with plenty of light; conversely, a large plant that requires intense light would not do well in the shallow, shaded areas at the edge of a stream. By looking at the physical characteristics of plants, It is possible to determine what kind of conditions they experience in the wild and therefore what they will need in the aquarium. This is particularly important for setting up biotope tanks.

Lake plants

Freshwater lakes are found in many parts of the world and are usually fed or drained by at least one river. The plant species found in these lakes are, therefore, usually the same as those found in the accompanying rivers. However, whereas a river may have many different types of environment throughout its length, lakes are generally fairly uniform in the type of habitat they provide. This means that competition for certain areas is intense and usually a few plants dominate each area of the habitat in a particular lake. Also, due to the wide open space, light is usually easily available in most areas. These factors indicate that lake plants will be fast-growing, in order to compete for dominance, and able to take advantage of high light conditions. Typical examples of plants adapted to to lake environments are *Vallisneria* spp. and floating plants. The fast-growing, fast-

spreading vallisnerias are able to take advantage of the large substrate area of lakes, particularly in sandy areas, without requiring a deep substrate, while floating plants are able to take advantage of the large open water spaces. Minimal water movement ensures that they are not swept away.

Bog plants

Many aquatic plants are terrestrial plants found in damp areas that periodically flood. These plants must be able to survive throughout the year, both above and below the water surface. To do this, some plants have a growing period and a dormant period, which vary according to the environmental conditions. Depending on the plant, growth or dormancy may occur either when the plant is submerged or exposed. Some plants, such as many *Cryptocoryne* species, will produce flowers only when the water level begins to drop and then

PLANTS AS TOOLS AND PESTS

In many situations, plants are a vital tool used both by man and in nature for ecological purposes. Fast-growing plants are often used to remove wastes from water, allowing the cleanup of polluted waterways or to prevent toxic algal blooms from occurring in nutrient-rich areas. Aquarists use plants as a form of filtration, both in aquariums and ponds. Some special pond filters are designed to house a bed of aquatic or marginal plants that remove nutrients and toxic metals from the water, preventing algae and improving the water quality for the fish.

However, in the last few decades, the increase in the use of plants for commercial and ecological purposes and by aquarists has had its drawbacks. Any natural habitat that has not been significantly altered has a natural balance between all the plants,

animals, and organisms that inhabit it. Thousands of years of natural selection have ensured that the plants and animals that live there will exist happily alongside the other inhabitants. If a plant or animal from another place is introduced into that habitat, three things could happen. The first, and most likely, is that the new species will not survive and simply dies out within a few years or less. The second is that it may survive, reproduce, and sustain a level population alongside the existing species, although this is unlikely. The third possibility is that it may survive, reproduce, and increase its population. During this time, it will compete with native species for resources, and if it has a significant advantage, it may out-compete them and drive them out. The balance of nature in the area can be seriously disturbed in this way.

This can happen when commercially grown plants are introduced into local rivers, ponds, lakes, and waterways. The species that are introduced are called alien species and if they survive and spread, have the potential to kill off native species. This may have secondary effects, such as starving native animals of food sources, altering the composition of the substrate, blocking up waterways, and removing potential nesting or breeding sites.

An aquarium is an enclosed environment, and providing the chosen plants remain in it, there is no danger to local rivers and waterways. However, if plants are discarded in such locations, there is a great risk of introducing alien plants. The consequences of this can be ecologically catastrophic, so aquarists must behave responsibly. Any waste plants should be destroyed.

Left: *In the right conditions, one species of aquatic plant (here water hyacinth, Eichhornia crassipes) will spread and dominate a large stretch of water, allowing little else to grow. This can be advantageous or detrimental, depending on the effect on the environment.*

Below: *Many* Cryptocoryne spp. *grow in conditions that other plants do not favor. However, their slow-growing nature may mean that alien species could compete with them for light and nutrients.*

reproduce out of water. Bog plants usually have slightly thicker leaves, because their thicker cuticle helps to prevent the leaves from drying out when the water level drops. As we have seen, some plants produce differently shaped leaves, depending on whether they are submerged or out of water.

Fast-flowing streams

In small streams there is little room for plant growth, minimal substrate, high oxygenation, and few nutrients, but often plenty of light. These conditions are not ideal for aquatic plants and the growth of substantial, large-leaved plants is not usually possible. Carbon dioxide levels are usually low in such conditions, and the strong light is not as useful as you might expect, because photosynthesis is limited by carbon dioxide levels. Often, water movement is quite strong, making stemmed plants prone to damage. Therefore, smaller plants are often found in fast-flowing

Right: Cryptocoryne *species are ideally suited to the shallow depths of tropical streams. They flourish in specific environments where other plants would fail to grow.*

streams, since they do not require large amounts of substrate or nutrients for growth. Mosses and hairlike plants, such as *Eleocharis* sp., thrive in this environment, as do plants that root to wood and rocks, such as Java fern (*Microsorium* sp.).

River plants

Rivers have a wide range of habitats throughout their length, so classifying

plants as "adapted for river life" would be futile. Most aquatic plants come from various areas of rivers. *Echinodorus* sp. are often found growing above water in the middle of shallow rivers, or along the edges of deeper rivers. In these situations they can take advantage of the combination of nutrients from the riverbed, stronger lighting above water, and carbon dioxide from the atmosphere. Cryptocorynes and slow-growing plants

Light zones of a river

In a typical river or large stream, there are zones of light and water depth where different plants grow.

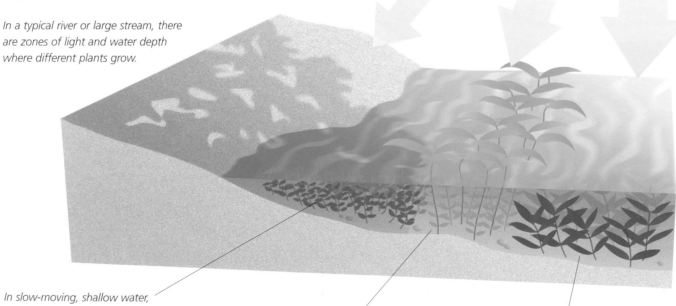

In slow-moving, shallow water, shaded by overhanging vegetation, plants are small and slow growing, needing little rooting depth and less light.

Once the water gets a little deeper, plants grow longer roots and thicker stems. They produce large aquatic and aerial leaves, which can use strong light and CO_2 from the surface.

Toward the center, the water is faster flowing and the light is bright. The plants here have flexible stems that bend with the flow, so aerial leaves are rarely produced.

are found near the edges, where they are often shaded by overhanging vegetation. Stem plants are also found toward the edges, but normally at a depth of at least 16–20 in (40–50 cm). Floating plants are not as common and are found only in the wider, open, and slow-moving sections.

Growth in nature and aquarium

The growth of plants is affected a great deal by their environment, and many plants appear quite different when grown in the aquarium compared to their wild counterparts. In the aquarium there is generally less available substrate, no seasonal variations, different light conditions, and variable water qualities. All these factors cause aquarium plants to grow slightly differently than they would in nature. In many cases, plants in the aquarium will not grow as large as in the wild. A notable example is the water lettuce (*Pistia stratiotes*). In the aquarium it produces compact leaves, normally up to about 2 in (5 cm) across. However, in its natural environment or in ponds, the leaves are much larger and fleshier, growing up to 6 in (15 cm) in diameter.

Left: Water lettuce (Pistia stratiotes) *will grow to significantly different sizes depending on its environment. In the aquarium, the leaves will grow up to 2 in (5 cm), whereas in an open stretch of water, they will grow more than three times bigger.*

Many aquatic plants are naturally bog plants with a submerged leaf form, and although they grow and reproduce perfectly well underwater, in their natural habitats they are usually found growing above water in marshy conditions or very shallow water. *Lobelia cardinalis* is often sold both as a pond marginal plant and an aquatic plant. In the aquarium it is a short plant (usually 6 in [15 cm], but up to 12 in [30 cm]), with fleshy leaves of a light green to purple-red color. When grown as a bog plant it reaches over 36 in (90 cm) in height and produces numerous red flowers set against beetroot-red leaves.

Below: The conditions that plants encounter in the aquarium are different from those found in nature. They respond by producing different leaf shapes, colors, and sizes to adapt to the aquarium environment. The results can be stunning, even though the display does not recreate the natural world.

Water quality and filtration

Pure water is made up from two hydrogen molecules and one oxygen molecule (H_2O). However, the water in which you house living aquatic organisms such as fish and plants is much more than a simple combination of molecules. Water can be described as hard or soft, alkaline or acid, and acts as a carrier for a wealth of minerals, nutrients, toxins, bacteria (both beneficial and harmful), and pollutants. Providing good water quality means ensuring that all these factors are at the correct level, so that the water in the aquarium is not only safe for fish and plants, but actively encourages their health and growth.

There are many different interactions between chemicals and minerals that alter the properties of water. To make things even more complicated, both plants and fish are found in many different habitats, each with their own water quality parameters. However, the basic principles of water quality and filtration are universal and apply to all aquarium environments. Other than the functions of nutrients, which are described on pages 66–77, all the important aspects of water quality and filtration in a planted aquarium are included in this chapter.

Filtration

In all aquariums, you can employ four types of filtration in one way or another: mechanical, biological, chemical, and sterilization. The function of filtration in the aquarium is to remove or neutralize substances that may be harmful, and to remove visible debris from the water. In nature, a combination of naturally occurring bacteria, organisms, and vegetation provide the waste disposal means to keep water quality stable and pollutants at a minimal level. In the aquarium, the ratio of plants and fish to the volume of water is far higher than in nature. This means that there is more waste to be removed than the natural processes can cope with. Artificial filtration is therefore essential if you are to maintain a healthy aquarium.

Mechanical filtration is the physical removal of matter from the water. In most cases, mechanical filtration simply removes visible debris and performs a purely aesthetic function. Generally speaking, mechanical filtration is achieved by passing water through a sponge, or series of sponges, to trap debris. The sponges can then be removed and cleaned. In the planted aquarium, mechanical filtration is important because it removes suspended debris that may otherwise collect in the

Below: These angelfish (Pterophyllum scalare) *from South American rivers enjoy the same warmth and soft water conditions as many popular aquarium plants.*

How reverse osmosis works

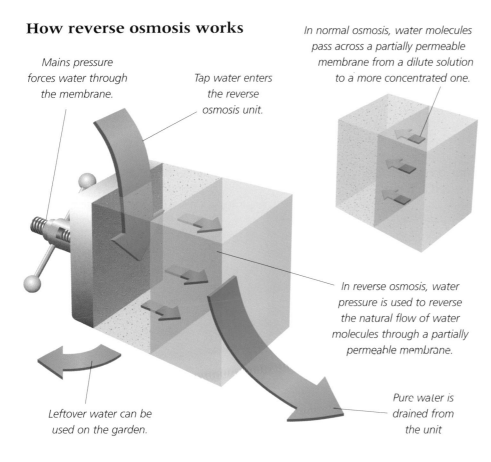

Mains pressure forces water through the membrane.

Tap water enters the reverse osmosis unit.

In normal osmosis, water molecules pass across a partially permeable membrane from a dilute solution to a more concentrated one.

In reverse osmosis, water pressure is used to reverse the natural flow of water molecules through a partially permeable membrane.

Leftover water can be used on the garden.

Pure water is drained from the unit

Above: *A commercial R.O. unit produces water with a pH of 6.5–7 and no hardness. Buffers, trace elements, and nutrients must be added to it before it is able to sustain plant and fish life in the aquarium.*

foliage of fine-leaved species. This prevents light from penetrating the chlorophyll cells, reducing their ability to photosynthesize. A buildup of organic debris in the aquarium may also encourage the growth of algae and increase the number of disease-causing bacteria in the aquarium.

Reverse osmosis (R.O.) water is also produced by a mechanical filtration unit, although in this case the sponge is replaced by an incredibly fine membrane. This removes almost all the contaminants (meaning everything other than water molecules – H_2O), leaving almost pure water. Reverse osmosis units are particularly useful when keeping softwater fish, which prefer slightly acidic water containing very few minerals. However, R.O. water is not suitable on its own for fish or plants

because it is deficient in some of the important elements of water that provide a stable and useful environment. R.O. water must be mixed either with normal tap water or a chemical "buffer" that introduces trace elements and carbonates to stabilise pH.

Water changes are another form of mechanical filtration as they constitute a physical method of removing substances.

Biological filtration is the most important type of filtration, especially for fish. It takes advantage of the natural process whereby living organisms (bacteria) remove or convert toxic substances (ammonia or ammonium) into less toxic substances. The filter medium has a very high surface area (meaning that under a microscope it would appear very porous rather than smooth) that is colonized by naturally

STERILIZATION

Sterilization as a form of filtration is normally employed in the marine aquarium, although there are situations when it can be useful in a freshwater aquarium. The process involves passing water through a pressurized unit containing an ultraviolet (UV) lamp. UV light at the right intensity is able to break down some algae cells and disease organisms, with obvious benefits for aquatic life. However, as with chemical filtration, it can also destroy useful elements. In general, because of the expense of UV sterilizers and their relatively limited use, they are not necessary in planted aquariums. Do not confuse UV sterilizers with UV clarifiers, which work on the same principle, but allow for a greater space between the water and the UV light, so that only algae cells are affected, not disease organisms.

occurring bacteria. As the aquarium water passes through the media, the bacteria remove ammonia by oxidation, creating nitrite (NO_2). The nitrite is then converted by other bacteria into less toxic nitrates (NO_3), which are released back into the aquarium. In some cases, anaerobic bacteria (meaning that they thrive in low-oxygen conditions) will obtain oxygen by converting nitrates into nitrogen gas (NO_3 to N_2), which then escapes through the water surface into the atmosphere.

Biological filtration is of greater importance to fish than it is to plants because plants readily use ammonium and nitrates as a source of nitrogen for their own needs. However, ammonia is dangerous to both plants and fish, so biological filtration is still required in a planted aquarium. The difference between ammonia and ammonium is discussed on page 73, but in aquariums where ammonium occurs in preference to ammonia, plants perform much of the function of a biological filter. This is one reason why living plants are a practical, not just aesthetic, addition to many aquariums.

Chemical filtration removes chemical substances from the water using a medium that binds chemical compounds to itself. This binding is called adsorption and a chemical filtration medium is described as an adsorptive medium. Most chemical media are indiscriminate and will adsorb a wide range of compounds, both good and bad. They remove not only toxins, such as heavy metals, nitrites, and nitrates, but also useful compounds, such as nutrients and many aquatic treatments. For this reason, chemical filtration is best employed as a temporary form of filtration. It can be very useful in the removal of disease or algal treatments, once these have done their job, to remove heavy metals such as copper, etc., and to filter rainwater or tap water before they are added to the aquarium.

The nitrogen cycle

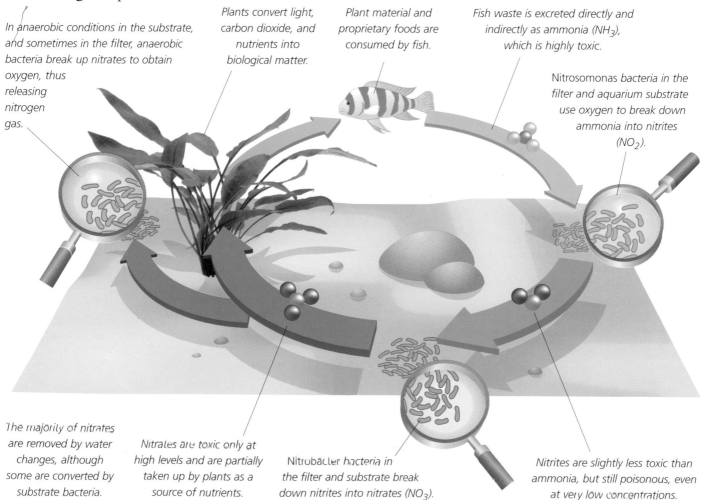

In anaerobic conditions in the substrate, and sometimes in the filter, anaerobic bacteria break up nitrates to obtain oxygen, thus releasing nitrogen gas.

Plants convert light, carbon dioxide, and nutrients into biological matter.

Plant material and proprietary foods are consumed by fish.

Fish waste is excreted directly and indirectly as ammonia (NH_3), which is highly toxic.

Nitrosomonas bacteria in the filter and aquarium substrate use oxygen to break down ammonia into nitrites (NO_2).

The majority of nitrates are removed by water changes, although some are converted by substrate bacteria.

Nitrates are toxic only at high levels and are partially taken up by plants as a source of nutrients.

Nitrobacter bacteria in the filter and substrate break down nitrites into nitrates (NO_3).

Nitrites are slightly less toxic than ammonia, but still poisonous, even at very low concentrations.

Chemical filtration media

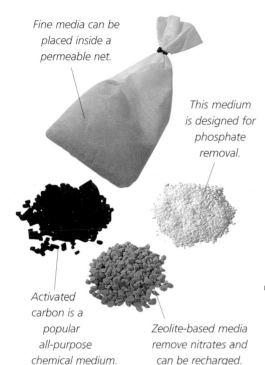

Fine media can be placed inside a permeable net.

This medium is designed for phosphate removal.

Activated carbon is a popular all-purpose chemical medium.

Zeolite-based media remove nitrates and can be recharged.

Types of filtration unit

Several types of filter are available for aquariums, although most work on the same basic principle, providing mainly mechanical and biological filtration. In most cases, water is drawn by a pump through a canister containing filtration media. Most filters are based on either internal or external designs. An internal filter is a compact unit that usually contains a sponge medium used for both mechanical and biological filtration. An external filter also uses sponge media, but because it is placed outside the aquarium it can be much larger without taking up space in the aquarium. The extra space available in the canister of an external filter allows you to use a wide range of media, which makes an external filter much more flexible and adaptable to the needs of the aquarium.

Because the bacteria that perform biological filtration require high amounts of oxygen, most filters have a high flow rate, allowing water to pass through the filter before the oxygen is used up. The water released from the filter outlet is lower in oxygen than when it entered the filter, although often, the surface agitation caused by the pump will quickly cause the aquarium water to become reoxygenated. Therefore, even though the bacteria in the filter are using up oxygen, filters will generally introduce sufficient oxygen into the aquarium. In some cases, this can cause problems for aquarium plants, because high oxygen levels make it difficult for them to assimilate nutrients. In a planted aquarium, it is sometimes best to use filters with lower flow rates, or undersized external filters to reduce the surface movement and keep oxygen levels low. Lowering the outlet of a filter will also help to reduce surface movement in the aquarium.

Aquarium filters

Below: *An internal power filter is ideal for the small aquarium. It consists of a sponge to provide mechanical and biological filtration and a pump to circulate water.*

This pump unit powers the filter. Clean the impeller periodically.

Filtered water returns to tank here.

Compartment for activated carbon to remove discoloration and pollutants.

Sponge traps particles and harbors beneficial bacteria.

Some internal power filters contain additional biological and chemical media in separate compartments.

Above: *An external power filter can sit beneath the tank. Place the return at the water surface, or lower down if you wish to reduce oxygen levels in a planted aquarium.*

Right: *Large external power filters house mechanical, biological, and chemical media. Water passes through the media and is returned to the tank via an outlet tube.*

Clean and dirty filter sponges

Relatively clean filter sponges provide an ideal surface for bacteria to colonize and are the basis of biological filtration.

Allowing one of the sponges to become clogged will encourage anaerobic bacteria to grow, which helps to reduce nitrates.

Below: Sponges should be cleaned only in water from the aquarium. Tap water contains chlorine, which may kill useful bacteria. Rinse sponges lightly; a slightly dirty sponge is more effective than a brand new one.

Anaerobic bacteria

If a filter with a relatively high flow rate is regularly cleaned and maintained, it will provide plenty of oxygen for the denitrifying bacteria within it. If the filter has a slower flow rate or becomes clogged, anaerobic conditions will appear in the filter and denitrifying bacteria will not be able to survive. In an anaerobic environment, different forms of bacteria will emerge that source oxygen from compounds such as nitrates. In this instance, the bacteria use up nitrates and release nitrogen gas, which escapes at the water surface.

If a filter is properly maintained, it is possible to sustain colonies of both aerobic and anaerobic bacteria that together will reduce ammonia, nitrite and nitrate levels in the aquarium. Although nitrates are used by plants as a source of nutrients, they require only about 1-2mg/l in nature; high levels (above 30mg/l) can be damaging to some plants. Fish can normally tolerate much higher levels of nitrates, so anaerobic filtration has minimal benefits to fish but can be an important method

of nitrate removal in planted aquariums. To encourage both aerobic and anaerobic bacteria in filters, allow part of the filter to clog, but keep the rest relatively clear. A simple way of doing this is to have a "clean" sponge and a "dirty" sponge in the filter. First, water passes through the clean sponge, where aerobic bacteria will reduce ammonia and nitrites and produce nitrates. Next it passes through the dirty sponge, where the nitrate is converted to nitrogen gas.

When you come to maintain the filter, either swap the sponges around (by cleaning the dirty sponge and leaving the clean one to become clogged) or wash the clean sponge, but only rinse the dirty one lightly. In larger external filters, you can use a number of sponges and swap them alternately.

Plants as filters

Aquatic plants also form part of the filtration process in well-planted aquariums. The uptake of metals and nitrogen compounds by plants and the release of oxygen has a significant effect on the overall water quality of the

aquarium. In some larger outdoor ponds, plants are actually used as part of the filtration process. In these cases, water from the pond is allowed to pass through or over a large bed of aquatic or bog plants. The plants reduce nitrate and/or ammonium levels and remove heavy metal compounds that may be damaging to fish and other animals. Because plants have little control over the amount of metals they assimilate, they are often used to remove toxic metals from water sources. In the aquarium, plants are especially useful in removing metals such as copper, which may be "left over" from aquatic treatments. If the function of plants and anaerobic bacteria are included in the nitrogen cycle, filtration in a planted aquarium becomes more complex and efficient. The dangerous compounds of metals, ammonia, nitrites, and nitrates are reduced to such low levels that you no longer need to carry out water changes so frequently. However, water changes are still important for other reasons, so they should never be entirely excluded from regular maintenance.

Water hardness

Water is often described as hard or soft, and these terms relate to the amount of dissolved salts and minerals present in the water. A high concentration of salts and minerals results in hard water, while a low concentration produces soft water. Usually, it is the calcium and magnesium salts that determine overall water hardness. In natural water supplies, hard water usually contains more nutrients than soft water, which is an advantage to aquatic plants. However, hard water generally contains less carbon dioxide and other nutrients in an available form, so plants that are not accustomed to hardwater conditions may not do very well in them. A preference for water hardness varies according to species, and in the aquarium it is quite common for aquarists to mix hard- and softwater species together. Providing you avoid extremes of water hardness, the majority of plants will do well in medium-soft water with additional carbon dioxide.

Water hardness is often linked with pH, and many of the elements that cause high water hardness also cause a high pH level. However, the two are only loosely connected and it is often possible to achieve high pH levels with soft water.

Acidity / alkalinity (pH)

Water is made up of positively charged hydrogen ions (H^+) and negatively charged hydroxyl ions (OH^-). The pH level is a measure of the ratio of these two ions in a body of water. Acidic water has more hydrogen ions, while alkaline water contains more hydroxyl ions. Neutral water contains an equal ratio. pH is therefore a measure of how alkaline or acidic the water is. Some fish, such as the Rift Lake cichlids, prefer alkaline, or high, pH conditions, while discus or dwarf cichlids prefer acid, or low, pH conditions. pH is measured on a scale of 1-14, with 7 being neutral. Anything below 7 is acidic and above 7 is alkaline. Aquarium fish generally live in

Below: Floating plants and fast-growing species, such as this Myriophyllum *sp., will take up nutrients and chemicals quicker than other plants, thus providing a useful service in maintaining water quality in the aquarium.*

How pH is measured

Water (H_2O) is made up of positively charged hydrogen ions (H^+) and negatively charged hydroxyl ions (OH^-). The pH level is a measure of the ratio of these two ions in a body of water. Acidic water has more hydrogen ions; alkaline water more hydroxyl ions. Neutral water has an equal number of both.

WATER MOLECULE

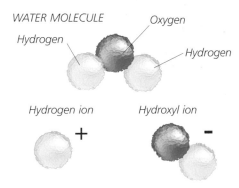

Hydrogen   Oxygen   Hydrogen

Hydrogen ion   Hydroxyl ion

+   −

The pH scale

The pH scale is logarithmic, meaning that each unit change in pH, say from 7 to 8, is a ten times change. A change of two units from 7 to 9 is a hundred times change, and from 7 to 10 reflects a thousand times change. This is why a sudden change in pH is very stressful and harmful to fish.

pH 9: 100 times more alkaline than pH 7.

pH 8: 10 times more alkaline that pH 7.

pH 7: neutral.

water with a pH of between 5 and 9; very few fish will survive happily in water with a pH level outside this range.

The pH level is closely linked to levels of carbon dioxide in the aquarium, because carbon dioxide produces carbonic acid, which is acidic and lowers pH. The pH in most aquariums will drop over time due to the acids produced by waste organic matter, respiration, and filtration processes. Regular removal of waste matter and regular water changes will reduce this effect. pH changes are damaging to fish and plants only if they happen suddenly. Because carbon dioxide and organic-rich substrates are used in planted aquariums, the water is more often slightly acidic than alkaline, although fluctuations occur within a 24-hour period due to the photosynthetic and respirational effects on carbon dioxide and oxygen concentrations in the water.

Buffering capacity

Buffering capacity describes the ability of a body of water to maintain a stable pH level, or more accurately, to withstand drops in pH levels. Water contains buffers, often in the form of carbonates, that reduce fluctuations in hydrogen ions, thereby reducing any severe drops in pH. Buffering capacity is closely linked to water hardness and the same substances apply for both parameters. Hard water is generally better buffered and has a higher alkalinity (pH) than soft water. The buffering capacity of water can be kept stable by regular water changes. It is vital that carbonate hardness is regularly measured in planted aquariums, as the use of CO_2 can reduce the aquarium's buffering capacity and/or hardness. If all the available carbonates are used up, a severe drop in pH can occur that will be harmful to any fish in the aquarium. Plants are also affected by changes in pH, but not as drastically as fish. Most aquarium plants are happy in water with a pH value between 6.0 and 7.5.

How buffering capacity works

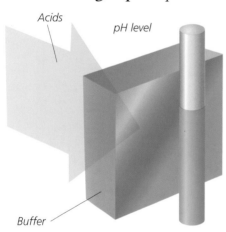

Acids
pH level
Buffer

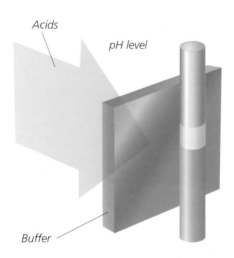

Acids
pH level
Buffer

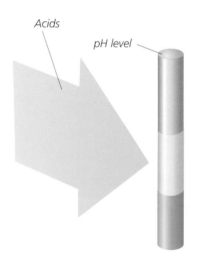

Acids
pH level

1 Regular water changes help to replenish carbonates, maintaining a good buffering capacity. In a well-buffered aquarium, the pH level will stay relatively constant.

2 A lack of water changes or using water with low hardness (such as R.O. water) without an artificial buffer reduces carbonate levels and pH fluctuations may occur.

3 With no carbonates and/or buffering capacity, any acids produced will lower the pH level. This can happen quickly, causing death to fish and damage to plants.

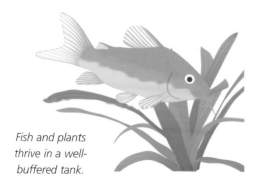

Fish and plants thrive in a well-buffered tank.

Minor pH fluctuations are not a problem.

Sudden drop in pH can be life threatening.

The day-night cycle in the aquarium

■ Oxygen   ■ Carbon dioxide

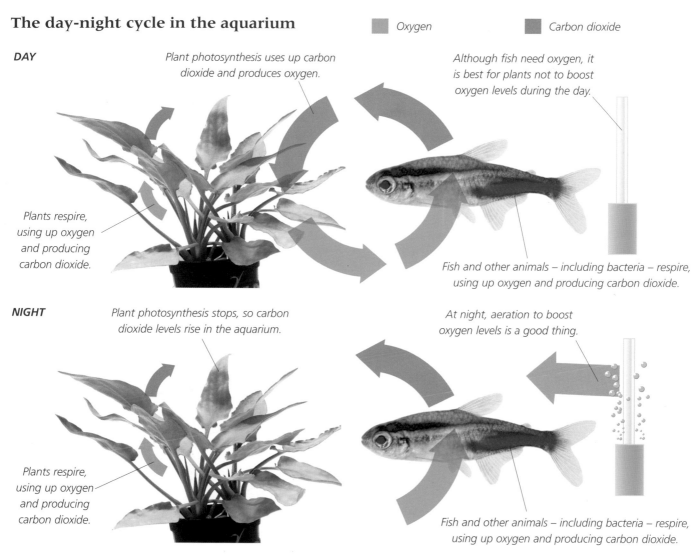

DAY

Plant photosynthesis uses up carbon dioxide and produces oxygen.

Although fish need oxygen, it is best for plants not to boost oxygen levels during the day.

Plants respire, using up oxygen and producing carbon dioxide.

Fish and other animals – including bacteria – respire, using up oxygen and producing carbon dioxide.

NIGHT

Plant photosynthesis stops, so carbon dioxide levels rise in the aquarium.

At night, aeration to boost oxygen levels is a good thing.

Plants respire, using up oxygen and producing carbon dioxide.

Fish and other animals – including bacteria – respire, using up oxygen and producing carbon dioxide.

Diurnal fluctuations

The combination of continual respiration and photosynthesis during daylight creates a fluctuation throughout the day that affects the oxygen and carbon dioxide levels in the surrounding water. Rising and falling oxygen and carbon dioxide levels have a direct effect on the pH and hardness of the water. These changes in water conditions are called diurnal fluctuations and occur in all natural waters. When there are plants in the aquarium, diurnal fluctuations are increased by the relatively high concentration of plants and small volume of water.

As plants start to receive light in the morning, they begin to photosynthesize and use up carbon dioxide while releasing oxygen. Although the opposite process is also being carried out through respiration, the process of photosynthesis is carried out much more quickly and with a greater quantity of gas exchange. As the plants photosynthesize, carbon dioxide levels in the water begin to drop and the amount of carbonic acid produced also falls. The release of oxygen will also bind organics and minerals, and combined with falling carbonic acids, this causes pH levels to rise (become more alkaline). Once

dissolved carbon dioxide is used up, plants begin to find other sources of carbon dioxide, mainly from bicarbonates. Bicarbonates form part of water hardness and as they are used up by plants, the surrounding water will become softer. These two processes create water with a high pH (alkaline) yet with a low hardness.

At night, plants cease to photosynthesize and stop producing oxygen, although they continue to respire. This has the effect of reducing oxygen levels and raising carbon dioxide levels in the water. The dissolved carbon dioxide will bind both with minerals such as calcium, creating bicarbonates that raise water hardness and buffering levels, and with organics, creating carbonic acid that will lower pH (more acidic). During a 24-hour period these processes have the effect of raising oxygen, hardness, and pH levels during the day, while lowering levels at night.

The same fluctuations occur in the aquarium, although if carbon dioxide is added artificially, the aquarist can control or reduce these fluctuations. Providing plants with an ample supply of carbon dioxide means that they will not need to use up bicarbonates, and fluctuations in water hardness are reduced. However,

pH fluctuations will still occur because of the difference in oxygen and carbon dioxide levels during the day and night. Some carbon dioxide systems can be linked to light units and/or timers so that carbon dioxide is only introduced when it is needed. This will help to reduce fluctuations in pH levels.

In most cases, both fish and plants are accustomed to these fluctuations in water quality, although you should regularly test pH and water hardness levels, both in the morning and at night, to ensure that any fluctuations are stable and not too extreme. Changes of more than 1° in pH may cause health

problems to some fish. Carbonate hardness should be tested, because a lack of bicarbonates will cause the aquarium buffering capacity to drop, which in turn creates larger fluctuations in pH levels. This is one reason why very soft water often causes problems when aquarium plants and fish are kept together.

Water testing
Ammonia, nitrite, nitrate, pH, and water hardness levels can all be tested using test kits that are easy to use and widely available. Nutrients, oxygen, and carbon dioxide levels are not as easy to test for

How pH changes over a 24-hour period

Test pH at the end of day/night to record highest/lowest readings.

DAY

NIGHT

Living organisms respire, producing CO_2. Plant photosynthesis uses up most of the CO_2, so carbonic acid cannot be produced at sufficient levels to keep pH low. Carbonates and minerals bind with any acids, removing their acidic effect and raising the pH level.

Plants stop photosynthesizing at night but continue to respire, as do fish and bacteria, producing CO_2. This creates a steady rise in CO_2 and carbonic acid is formed, causing the pH to drop throughout the night.

Using liquid test kits

Above: *Liquid test kits involve adding a specified number of drops of one or more reagents to a water sample. Hold the bottle vertically so that the drop sizes are equal and correctly measured. Compare the final color change to a printed chart.*

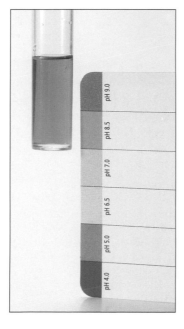

Above: *This broad range pH test shows a value of 8.5, reflecting alkaline water conditions. More specific high-range and low-range pH tests are available.*

Below: *This nitrite test shows a reading of 0.1mg/litre, which is low but could still pose a problem for fish in the aquarium. The ideal level is zero for animal life.*

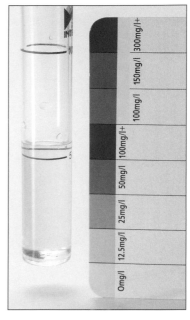

Above: *A nitrate reading of zero in a planted aquarium containing fish indicates that the filtration system is working well and that the plants are using up as food any nitrate produced in the nitrogen cycle – an ideal set of conditions.*

and some cannot be tested without incurring considerable expense. Most test kits are based on the principle of adding liquids or tablets to a sample of aquarium water. The sample will change color once the liquid or tablet reagent is added and the resulting color will relate to a specific measurement of the substance being tested for. "Dip-strip" tests are also available and these work in the same way, although in this instance, you dip the strip directly into the aquarium water. Chemically reactive "pads" change color depending on the levels of certain chemicals, and you simply compare the color changes to the chart. All these test kits will provide reliable results, where a degree of measurement either way from the actual concentration is acceptable.

More accurate and long-term water testing can be done using electronic monitoring systems. With an electronic meter, a probe is first calibrated (normally with a supplied calibration fluid) and then placed permanently in the aquarium. The probe is attached to an external monitoring device with an electronic display that continually shows the level of the substance being tested. The cost of electronic systems varies a great deal depending on the quality of the device and on the substance being tested. Although expensive, electronic monitoring systems can be useful in large display aquariums and provide a good method of continually checking water conditions.

Keeping a record of test results over time can be useful in determining trends such as steady rises in nitrates, which may indicate that more water changes are needed, or a steady drop in hardness, indicating that buffering

capacity is dropping and carbonates may need to be replenished. The ideal levels of the different water quality parameters can vary depending on certain factors and some are more dangerous than others. Clear water does not indicate a healthy aquarium; regular testing is the only way to ensure that an aquarium stays healthy.

Conditions for fish and plants

The water conditions of a planted aquarium should, of course, be designed to provide the best environment for plants to grow and thrive. However, in most cases, there will also be a number of fish in the aquarium and the water conditions must also be suitable for them if they are to survive in good health. The conditions required by plants and fish in the aquarium are slightly different and it is necessary to strike a balance between the two if you are to keep both successfully. In the wild, fish and plants survive in the same environment, which is normally ideal for the fish and plants in that area. To keep plants in the aquarium, it is not natural conditions that need to be created, but artificial ones. In nature, nutrients and carbon dioxide levels are minimal but constantly replenished and always available to plants. If you recreate these conditions in the aquarium, the nutrients and carbon dioxide would quickly run out and the plants would suffer. Furthermore, in the aquarium, plants from many different locations are kept together in the same space and the requirements of each plant must be met in abundance. To do this, the aquarium environment needs much higher nutrient and carbon dioxide levels and lower oxygen levels than would be found in nature. The problem is that low oxygen levels, high carbon dioxide levels, and diurnal fluctuations are damaging and stressful for many fish.

To keep fish and plants together in a heavily planted aquarium there are two options. The first is only to keep fish that can withstand such conditions – namely small catfish, anabantoids, or fish from acidic areas. The second option is to try to minimize fluctuations and ensure a constant oxygen level. This can be done using timed carbon dioxide releases, so that carbon dioxide is added only during daylight hours. In aquariums where oxygen levels may drop heavily at night, introduce additional aeration at this time, for example by using an air pump controlled by a timer.

Sourcing water

Creating the right water conditions can be tricky or easy, depending on the source of the aquarium water. In most cases, this will be tap water, which varies a great deal according to geographic location. It is vital to test tap water to find out what qualities it may possess. It is particularly important to test tap water for both pH and hardness. Although the two are often related, some water companies add substances to the water

Testing carbonate hardness (KH)

1 Add the KH reagent to a 5 ml sample of water and gently swirl the tube to mix it up. Count the numbers of reagent drops added.

2 Initially, the sample turns blue. This will change as more reagent is added to the sample.

3 Continue adding drops of reagent until the sample turns a stable yellow color. Each drop added since the beginning of the test represents 1°dH.

Below: Some aquarium fish will live happily in conditions ideal for plants; other fish may need some help from the fishkeeper to ensure that they have a balanced environment. This pearl gourami (Trichogaster leeri) *will thrive in a wide range of water conditions and in a densely planted tank, particularly (as here) with feathery leaved plants.*

Creating soft water

For soft water, mix reverse osmosis or filtered rainwater with dechlorinated tap water. Add a pH buffer to retain stability.

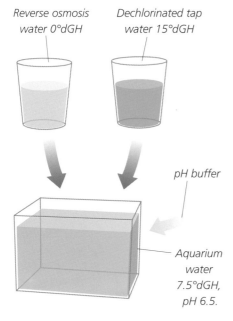

Reverse osmosis water 0°dGH

Dechlorinated tap water 15°dGH

pH buffer

Aquarium water 7.5°dGH, pH 6.5.

Creating hard water

Use calcium-based substrates and rockwork with dechlorinated tap water. Also use calcium-based trace element additives.

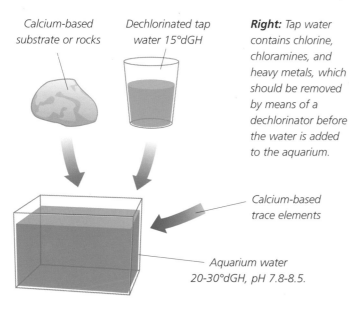

Calcium-based substrate or rocks

Dechlorinated tap water 15°dGH

Calcium-based trace elements

Aquarium water 20-30°dGH, pH 7.8-8.5.

that may alter one or the other but not both. Tap water also contains heavy metals, chlorine, and, in many cases, chloramine, which releases chlorine over time. Remove these substances before you use the water by adding a simple water conditioner. Then leave the water to warm up a little before using it for water changes, as this will help to minimize temperature shocks to both fish and plants.

To reduce metals and pollutants, and to soften water, tap water can be mixed with rainwater or reverse osmosis water. Rainwater collected in water casks should always be prefiltered through a chemical medium such as carbon to remove any dangerous substances. In most cases, collected rainwater is safe to use directly in the aquarium, but it can easily become contaminated by atmospheric pollutants or from objects collected in household gutters.

Altering water quality

In a stable aquarium environment and with a suitable source of water, altering various aspects of water quality should not be a regular requirement. Over time however, buffering capacity and hardness will drop and pollutants such as nitrates may rise. In most cases, plants will remove pollutants, and water changes will replenish carbonates, keeping hardness and buffering capacity at suitable levels. Occasionally, the levels of pollutants such as ammonia and nitrite may rise quickly as a result of unexpected (and often unnoticed) fish deaths, and these will require immediate attention. If a filter is not working for more than a few hours, the same thing can happen. In these cases, the best approach is to carry out a number of small water changes and cut back on fish feeding levels for a short period.

Altering the levels of hardness and pH is a little more difficult and should be carried out before the water is added to the aquarium. Raising hardness and pH is relatively easy and can be done by adding proprietary chemical treatments or certain rocks and substrates. Lowering pH and hardness is more difficult, as it involves removing substances from the water rather than adding them. One of the best methods is to dilute the tank water with R.O. water (see page 27). Another way is to use chemical treatments, but apply these with care, as sudden changes can be damaging to both fish and plants.

Right: *Tap water contains chlorine, chloramines, and heavy metals, which should be removed by means of a dechlorinator before the water is added to the aquarium.*

The right substrate

In the rivers and streams in which many aquatic plants grow, the substrates vary depending on the environmental and geological conditions of the river system and the local area. Aquatic plants are often found in sandy, muddy, or gravel beds. An important point to bear in mind is that in virtually all natural areas the substrate is usually warmer than the surrounding environment. This happens because the heat from the sun is absorbed and retained by the substrate. The difference may be less than one degree but it is enough to create convection currents between the substrate and the water. These currents slowly and continually move water down through the substrate (where it warms

Below: The roots of these plants will extend deep into the heavy substrate at the bottom of this temperate pond, holding the plants in position and collecting vital nutrients.

up slightly) and back up into the main water body as it cools. As water passes through the substrate it takes nutrients with it, giving the roots access to a continual supply of nutrients.

In many streams and rivers, there are certain areas where plants grow together in groups, while just a short distance away there are no plants at all. This happens because natural springs occur along the river or stream system and water from other areas enters through the ground. Most of these springs are hidden from view and may carry only a trickle of water, but the water is rich in organic and mineral nutrients, which the plants quickly absorb through their roots.

The dense muddy substrate found in many places provides an ideal anchoring medium that holds plants firmly in position. In natural conditions, the roots may grow far wider and deeper than

they possibly could in the aquarium. When keeping some larger plants, such as many of the larger *Echinodorus* species, take into account the fact that their roots will quickly spread and literally "take over" the aquarium substrate if allowed to do so.

Substrates in the aquarium

In an average aquarium, the substrate is likely to be a fairly straightforward affair, usually a simple covering of pea gravel. Plants use the substrate not only as a place to root, but also as a source of nutrients and, in some cases, a medium through which to reproduce. The root systems of aquatic plants vary between species, but all are highly evolved to work effectively in a given natural environment. Most of these environments are nothing like those found in an aquarium with a simple pea gravel substrate. Difficulties encountered

Nutrient flow in nature

The substrate acts as a "nutrient sink," trapping nutrients where plant roots can easily obtain them. The nutrients are moved by gentle convection currents.

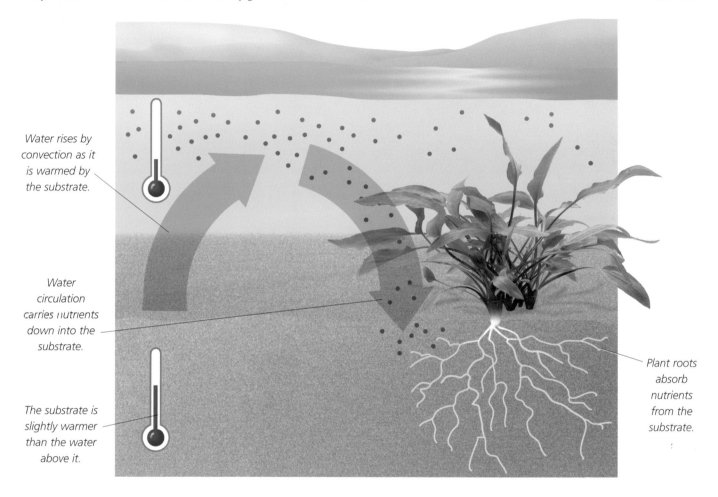

Heat from the sun warms the substrate.

Water rises by convection as it is warmed by the substrate.

Water circulation carries nutrients down into the substrate.

The substrate is slightly warmer than the water above it.

Plant roots absorb nutrients from the substrate.

when keeping aquatic plants can often be attributed to the lack of a good, useful substrate. Clean, inert gravel creates a fairly biologically inactive substrate. Because the water flows easily through such a medium, it removes nutrients, cools the plant roots, and creates an oxygen-rich area, all of which are undesirable and hinder the development of aquatic plant roots.

So which substrates are best? This is not an easy question to answer. Some plants do not need any specialized substrates, while a few need no substrate at all! However, for the most

part, a mixture of substrates will create an environment suitable for all the plants in the aquarium. The points to consider are: the size and shape of the particles, the depth of the substrate layer, and its mineral and organic content.

Size and shape

If the particle size of the substrate is wrong, it may cause problems for aquatic plants. A substrate made up of particles that are too large will allow water to pass through easily, removing nutrients. Furthermore, debris will collect in the gaps between the particles, which

may muddy the water. Large-grade substrates also cause problems for the growth of long roots and should be used only as a thin top layer.

If the substrate is too fine it may compact, halting the movement of oxygen and nutrients, and causing damage to the root structure.

A suitable aquarium substrate should have a particle size of about 0.04–0.12 in (1–3 mm) and be rounded in shape; sharp substrate particles can damage roots. The only exception is sand, which can be used as a thin bottom layer to support heating cables (see page 44).

Substrate depth

Substrate depth does vary a little, depending on which species of plant you are keeping. Plants that produce long roots, such as *Echinodorus* species and some cryptocorynes, will need a substrate deep enough for the roots to penetrate. If the substrate is too shallow, the roots of these plants will become dense and tangled. In this situation, the plant cannot obtain nutrients and the roots will become starved of oxygen.

Generally speaking, foreground plants do not produce long roots, so it is possible to slope the substrate upward toward the back of the aquarium. This also makes the aquarium appear deeper than it is. A good substrate depth is 2.4–4 in (6–10 cm).

Mineral content

Plants require minerals in small amounts, but it is difficult to provide these through the substrate, although some nutrient-rich substrates do contain the essential minerals that aquatic plants require. In general, the quantities of minerals required by plants are usually readily available in tap water. However, if the source water for your aquarium is relatively soft it may be lacking in these minerals, in which case you can use liquid fertilizers.

More importantly, a substrate should not contain harmful minerals, most notably, compounds with a high calcium content. Limestone and coral-based substrates, often available for marine aquariums, are high in calcium and should never be used in a freshwater planted aquarium. Substrates such as these will increase the alkalinity and pH of the water, making it harder for plants to obtain nutrients and CO_2.

Organic content

The organic content of a substrate includes organic nutrients, as well as waste matter from the aquarium (mainly from fish). A substrate without any organic matter is simply an "anchor" for the plants and of little other use. You can add organic matter by using a nutrient-rich substrate, which can either be mixed with the main substrate or arranged as a layer between two substrates. Soil and peat have a very high organic content, so use them with care to avoid overloading the aquarium with organic matter.

Choosing substrates

Several different substrates are available for the aquarium, and making the right choices can be a little tricky. It is possible to have a reasonably good planting substrate using just one medium,

Below: Not all plants need a deep substrate. This Java fern is happy above or below water, but prefers to root on rock or wood. Although unusual, this preference gives the plant an advantage over other species that could not survive in locations such as this.

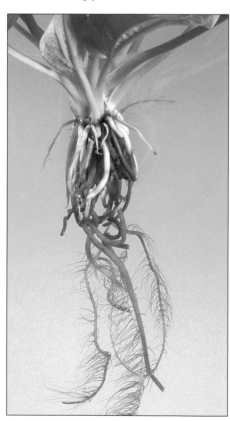

Above: This Echinodorus *has two distinct root areas: the thicker upper portion is used for nutrient storage, while the thinner lower roots with their numerous fine "secondary" roots are used for nutrient collection.*

Right: *Sand makes an interesting and attractive substrate for an aquarium display, but it will require regular maintenance to prevent compaction and stagnation.*

SUBSTRATES AND THEIR USES

Type of substrate	Base substrate	Main rooting substrate	Top substrate	Nutrient content
Pea gravel	Not suitable	Small-grade pea gravel can be used as a main substrate.	Ideal top-level substrate.	None
Quartz gravel	Small grades can be used with a heating cable.	Ideal as a main substrate.	Looks good as a top layer, but due to the small grade, mulm will collect more readily. Not normally a major problem.	None
Sand	Ideal for use with a heating cable.	Not suitable due to compaction.	Not suitable	None
Laterite/clay substrates	Not suitable	Not suitable	Not suitable	High
Nutrient-rich substrates	Not suitable	Some nutrient-rich substrates are designed to be used in large quantities as a main substrate. If the grade size is greater than 0.16 in (4 mm), mix it with a smaller lime-free substrate.	Not suitable	High
Soil-based substrates	Suitable	Suitable if covered by a 1 in (2.5 cm) layer of gravel.	Not suitable	High, may be lacking hardwater nutrients.

although combining a number of substrates will usually produce much better results. When mixing substrates, bear in mind that each one should have a place and a function. Assessing substrates on the basis of their usefulness for a specific purpose will make it easier to choose the right ones.

Base substrate A base substrate is necessary only when a heating cable is present. To be effective, the heat from the cable must be well distributed through the surrounding substrate and this is easy to achieve using a very fine substrate with a particle size of about 0.04 in (1 mm). Sand is ideal for this purpose, but use just enough to cover the heating cable.

Main rooting substrate The main body of substrate is used principally as a rooting medium, but also for the uptake of nutrients. This substrate should be compact enough to prevent excess water movement and oxygenation, but loose enough so that it does not become stagnant and produce toxins. A grade of 0.08–0.12 in (2–3 mm) is suitable and the substrate can be mixed with nutrient-rich additives. More than one main substrate can be used.

Nutrient-rich substrate This substrate should provide the plants with a constant and long-lasting supply of a range of nutrients. Depending on the concentration of nutrients present, use either a wafer-thin layer or a layer 0.4–1.6 in (1–4 cm) deep. Nutrient-rich substrates are usually highly compact and soil-like, so "sandwich" them between other substrates to prevent muddying of the water. Some nutrient-rich substrates can be mixed with the main rooting substrate.

Top level substrate This will be the most visible substrate and need only be a thin layer placed on top of other substrates. It need not provide any function for the plants and may be used purely for aesthetic purposes.

Types of substrate
Here we look at commonly available aquarium substrates and their suitability.

Pea gravel The most common form of aquarium gravel is called pea gravel, due to its smooth, rounded appearance. Pea gravel is available in a number of different grades, although only the smaller grades should be used as a main substrate. Although pea gravel is generally inert, it does contain some rock types that may affect the hardness of the water. Aquatic plants will not benefit much from pea gravel, except as a rooting substrate.

Quartz gravel Quartz is a completely inert substrate and ideal as a main rooting medium and/or top layer for the planted aquarium. Quartz gravel is often sold

Aquarium substrates

Silver sand is made up of very fine grains. Its compact nature makes it an ideal medium for heat transfer and a good supportive medium. When using a heating cable, sand is the best medium to cover the base of the aquarium.

Laterite-based substrates are ideal as a long-term source of nutrients. Laterite can be mixed in with the main substrate or used toward the lower half of the substrate, where plant roots are most effective at obtaining nutrients.

and labeled as lime-free substrate and usually available in grades of 0.04–0.12 in (1–3 mm). In smaller aquariums, or tanks with few plants or simple designs, quartz gravel is the best option for a sole substrate. It makes a better alternative to pea gravel due to its inert nature and smaller grade size, which provides a better support for plant roots.

Sand Fine-grade sand can cause problems if used as the sole substrate in an aquarium. Over time it will compact, preventing water movement and causing anaerobic conditions, which result in stagnation and the release of toxins. Stirring the sand gently and regularly will prevent this problem, although most plants do not appreciate constant disturbance. However, due to its small size, sand is very effective at distributing heat in a localized area, such as around a heating cable. If the sand layer is not too deep (about 1.6 in/4 cm), convection currents from a heating cable will ensure

a small amount of water movement through the substrate, allowing useful anaerobic conditions to develop without stagnation. When using sand, be sure to choose a completely inert form. Many commercial sands contain traces of lime or calcareous materials, although most of the products sold by aquatic retailers are safe. Silver sand is commonly available and suitable for the aquarium.

Laterite/clay substrates Clay-based substrates, often called laterite, are usually available as a substrate additive, reflecting the fact that only a small amount is needed. These substrate additives are usually very fine, sometimes even powdery, and reddish colored. They release a number of nutrients, including iron, over a long period. Clay-based substrates are best used as a layer toward the bottom third of the substrate or mixed in with the lower half of the main substrate. This is where the fine roots absorb the nutrients.

Nutrient-rich substrates Certain planting substrates are specifically designed for aquarium plants. Most of these substrates are laterite-based but contain additional organic and mineral materials that release a number of nutrients over long periods of time. Special planting substrates are available as additives and as main substrates. Use additives in small quantities, either as a thin layer or mixed with the main substrate.

Soil-based substrate Generally speaking, beginners should avoid using soil in the aquarium, as results can vary wildly. However, more experienced aquarists find that soil can be one of the best long-term planting substrates. It contains large amounts of carbon and iron, both readily used by aquatic plants, as well as a number of other nutrients that are slowly released or retained by the soil. If you do decide to use soil, a 1–1.5 in (2.5–3.75 cm) layer of soil used as a

Lime-free substrates are made up of inert quartz granules and will not affect water quality in any way. This medium is ideal for supporting roots and should be used as a main substrate.

Pea gravel is the most commonly available aquarium substrate, although it is best used as a top layer in planted aquariums. Smaller grades can be used as a good supportive rooting medium.

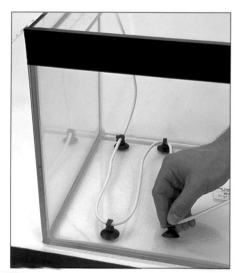

Soil can make an excellent planting medium, but use it with care.

base layer and main substrate, topped with 1 in (2.5 cm) of fine gravel, will suit most aquariums. The safest strategy is to use only sterilized potting mixture – not garden soil – to prevent contamination.

Due to the breakdown of organic matter within the soil, low levels of CO_2 are constantly released. In many planted aquariums with a soil substrate, additional CO_2 fertilization is not needed and neither are additional substrates or iron fertilization.

During the first few weeks of soil use, the aquarium may experience a high release of nutrients and organic matter.

Although plants should be able to cope with this, it can occasionally cause problems or produce dangerous conditions for fish. For this reason it is a good idea to wait a few weeks before introducing any fish, and to filter the water using carbon or carry out regular water changes.

Although potting mixture can become an excellent planting medium, and using even small amounts of nutrient-rich substrates may be more expensive, it could be argued that specifically designed substrates are a safer and more predictable option than soil substrates.

Other substrates

In addition to these common substrates there are some other, less-often used substrates available for aquariums and aquarium plants. Many "brand-name"

substrates are variations or combinations of nutrient-rich and inert substrates. Ready-made mixes are fine for aquarium plants and offer an easier alternative for beginner aquarists.

Peat is often promoted as a partial substrate for aquatic plants. Much like a combination of soil and nutrient-rich substrates, peat is very high in organic matter and provides plants with a wealth of nutrients. However, it tends to release some nutrients quickly, which can encourage algae, so it may not be suitable for long-term use.

Large-grade and sharp substrates are not particularly suitable, nor are colored substrates as they have a smooth surface that hinders the growth of useful bacteria.

Substrate heating

As we have seen, the substrate is slightly warmer than the main body of water in natural rivers and streams. The currents produced as a result of the temperature differences help to move nutrients

Substrate heating

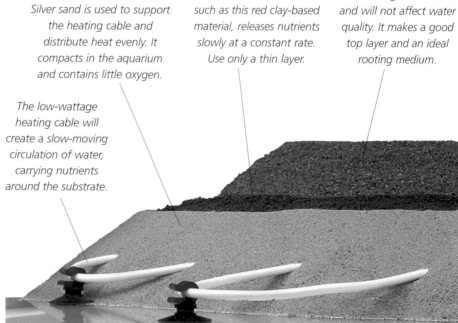

Silver sand is used to support the heating cable and distribute heat evenly. It compacts in the aquarium and contains little oxygen.

A nutrient-rich substrate, such as this red clay-based material, releases nutrients slowly at a constant rate. Use only a thin layer.

Lime-free gravel is inert and will not affect water quality. It makes a good top layer and an ideal rooting medium.

The low-wattage heating cable will create a slow-moving circulation of water, carrying nutrients around the substrate.

Above: *A heating cable can be fixed onto the base of the aquarium with suction cups. Depending on the cable power, leave a gap of about 2–4 in (5–10 cm) between the loops.*

Right: *The shy horse-face loach (Acanthopsis choirorhynchus) will spend hours either hiding or scavenging on the substrate for food particles. This feeding activity will help to keep the substrate free of accumulated debris.*

around the roots of the plants. Similar currents can be created in the aquarium using a substrate heating cable. Placed at the base of the substrate, it produces a very gentle heat that raises the temperature of the surrounding substrate. This heat rises through the water in the substrate to the surface and cooler water is drawn down through the substrate so the circulation begins again. The substrate around the heating cable should be fairly dense so that the heat is distributed quickly and the cable is supported and held firmly in place. A very fine substrate such as sand is ideal for this purpose.

A heating cable does not need a thermostat and can be left on continuously. The heat output and power consumption are very low, so the overall aquarium temperature should not be significantly affected. Substrate heating is not a vital part of a good planting substrate, but where thin layers of nutrient-rich substrates are used, the currents produced by a heating cable will significantly improve the distribution of the nutrients.

Maintaining the substrate

A good substrate will require little maintenance and is often best left undisturbed for the majority of the aquarium's life. Once an aquarium is well established and if the fish and plants are healthy, it is a major disruption to alter the substrate. It is therefore important to choose the correct substrate right from the start.

Over time, organic waste and debris will collect in the substrate, making it denser and creating anaerobic conditions (see page 47). In a well-planted aquarium, the majority of organic debris will be broken down by bacteria and the resulting nutrients are taken up by plant roots, which in return release small amounts of oxygen into the substrate and help to prevent stagnation. So the substrate in a well-planted aquarium may actually last longer than a substrate without the benefit of dense planting. However, a buildup of organic debris in

Above: *Thoroughly washing gravel substrates is vital to remove dust and debris that will cloud the water. Soil and nutrient-rich substrates do not need to be washed.*

Left: *In open areas, cleaning the gravel (here with a siphon device) can remove large amounts of debris. In a well-planted tank, you need only clean the top layer in this way.*

the uppermost layer may not be broken down very quickly and plant roots are not present in sufficient quantities in this area to keep the substrate oxygenated. Regular gentle stirring or siphoning of the top layer will help to remove debris and keep the substrate clean and healthy. Only the top layer should be regularly disturbed; the deeper substrate contains the dense plant roots that will not appreciate the disruption.

If the main substrate, or substrates, are very fine – about 0.08 in (2 mm) – they will compact over time, reducing the water flow. This in turn allows toxic gases (produced by the breakdown of organics) to build up. These gases will

damage plant roots, so that they are unable to release oxygen and stagnant areas of substrate are created. But a certain amount of anaerobic substrate is not necessarily a bad thing (see the panel opposite). Where fine-grade substrate is used, check the density every few months by pushing a finger down through the substrate. This should be possible with only a little resistance. If it becomes difficult, gently disturb and loosen the deeper substrate.

The nutrient-containing elements of a substrate will diminish over time and will need to be replaced. Most nutrient-rich substrates will last for about three years before they begin to run out and

Above: Larger-grade aquarium substrates allow water to pass easily between the grains, preventing stagnation, although too much water movement in the substrate can be detrimental to good plant growth.

become ineffective. However, this does vary depending on a number of factors, such as the quantity and type of plants, additional fertilization, the quantity and waste from fish, water conditions, etc. When the substrate needs replacing, the plants will need to be removed and replanted. This process will be damaging for some of the plants and you should take great care, closely following the guidelines for replanting (see page 55).

ANAEROBIC CONDITIONS – GOOD OR BAD?

A substrate rich in organic material (waste matter and nutrient-rich substrates) will naturally contain large numbers of bacteria that break down these organics into usable nutrients. The majority of these bacteria quickly use up oxygen, with the result that the substrate becomes anaerobic. In anaerobic conditions, different types of bacteria form, which do not need to use large quantities of oxygen or can create their own oxygen. These anaerobic bacteria can release toxic gases, most notably hydrogen sulphide, which can cause plant roots to rot, damage fish health, and encourage algae to flourish.

However, anaerobic conditions also allow nutrients to become more readily available to plants by preventing the binding of nutrients with oxygen molecules. As the bacteria use up the nitrates, nitrogen is released, which is also an important plant nutrient.

A mixture of aerobic and anaerobic substrate zones can provide the benefits of both conditions. As long as the substrate is not too fine and compact and/or substrate heating is employed, the combination of a slow-moving current and the release of oxygen by plant roots should prevent the majority of the substrate from becoming anaerobic. Anaerobic patches will then appear in denser areas of substrate without plant roots. Because these patches are small, they will not produce large amounts of toxic gases yet still allow nutrients to be produced and available to the plants. So a low-oxygen substrate is often best, where anaerobic conditions are allowed to develop in some places but not in others.

Aerobic and anaerobic substrate conditions

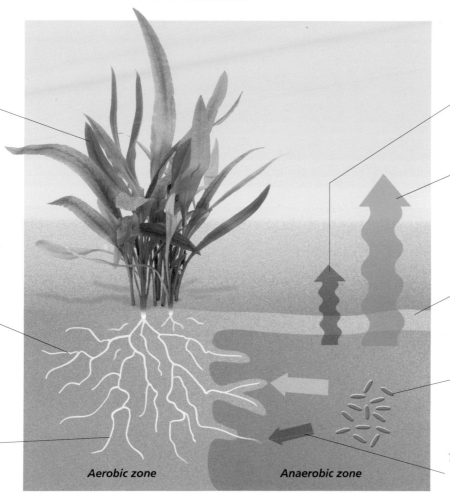

Oxygen is taken in (as well as produced during photosynthesis) by the plant's leaves and transported down to the root system.

Plants will extend their roots into both aerobic and anaerobic substrate.

Oxygen released by plant roots keeps the substrate around the root aerobic.

Hydrogen sulphide produced by bacterial breakdown of organic material.

Nitrogen gas released by the action of denitrifying bacteria, which obtain oxygen from nitrites and nitrates.

At the surface, the substrate is aerobic, due to close contact with the oxygen-containing aquarium water.

Bacteria in the anaerobic area break down nutrient bonds, allowing nutrients to be easily assimilated by plants.

Toxic substances, such as hydrogen sulphide, can damage plant roots.

Aerobic zone

Anaerobic zone

Choosing and planting

Finding a reliable source of healthy plants is vital, especially when you introduce the first plants into the aquarium. Only a small selection of the large variety of aquarium plants may be available from one dealer, so to obtain all the species you require, you may need to locate several suppliers. Choosing different plants and estimating the quantities required takes careful thought and planning. The overall display should be the result of a buildup of plants that gradually become established. They need not all be introduced at the same time; indeed, there are advantages to taking a staggered approach (see page 50).

Identifying healthy specimens is relatively easy and also important, as healthy plants are better able to survive transportation, establish more quickly, and live longer once established.

Unhealthy plants take far longer to start growing, and if they are in particularly poor condition, may never establish and simply die within a matter of weeks. Once you have selected and bought healthy plants, you must plant them properly and in

Above: *Finding a good source of healthy plants is vital. The plants in this aquatic outlet are kept under strong lighting and well presented. The tanks are kept clean and tidy.*

Left: *The dealer will pack the plants in plastic bags with plenty of air to provide cushioning and prevent damage. The bags are tied to retain moisture, although the plants do not need to be submerged in water.*

Right: *You can buy aquarium plants by mail order. They should arrive as here, with the plants in plastic sleeves and slotted into a tray to keep them separate and stable. Newspaper laid over the top of the outer plastic bag helps to insulate them from temperature variations.*

Choosing a healthy plant

GOOD PLANT

Look for fully formed leaves, with no holes or weak stems.

Lack of photosynthetic pigment is caused by low nutrient availability.

BAD PLANT

Here, roots are growing through the pot, along with a few small plantlets and fully formed leaves. This shows vigorous growth and general good health.

These roots are not in perfect condition, but given the right environment and providing the roots are intact, even plants in this condition may start to grow new, healthy leaves.

Bent and broken leaves, along with small holes, are an indication that the leaves on this plant will not last long before they begin to rot.

the correct places to ensure that problems do not develop as they grow and spread.

Even in well-equipped and well-tended planted tanks there are always some plants that do better than others, and a few that simply never "take" to the aquarium. Bearing this in mind, it is always worth introducing a number of different species to see which ones do better than others. Then you can simply remove and replace the ones that do not thrive with more suitable alternatives.

Identifying healthy plants

Keeping an eye out for a few simple clues should enable you to choose the best specimens. As a general rule, new growth is a good sign of a healthy plant.

Leaves The appearance of plant leaves varies a great deal between species, but generally speaking, leaves should not have any holes, yellow or brown patches, or transparent areas. If they are in a weak condition, many stem plants lose their lower leaves, so check to see if any of these are missing. Nevertheless, if such a plant has good root growth, you

can still plant it, leave it to establish for a period of time, and then take top cuttings to replace the original plant.

Yellow patches on leaves, particularly toward the edges, indicate a lack of iron or other nutrients. Plants in this condition will recover, but the damaged leaves usually die before being replaced by new growth. Yellowing of the leaves is particularly common in *Echinodorus* species. Brown patches or holes indicate overall poor health, but if only one or two leaves are affected, the rest of the plant may be healthy and you can simply remove the damaged leaves. Remember that some plants, such as many *Cryptocoryne* species, have naturally brown leaves.

Leaves that appear transparent and thin in places may be showing signs of physical damage and affected areas are likely to die, often taking the rest of the leaf with them. *Vallisneria* species are particularly prone to this problem. This kind of damage often occurs during

transport and handling, although it may take a few days to show up.

Roots Good root growth is vital for the overall health of plants, although many plants can survive with little or no root growth by taking nutrients directly from the water through their leaves. These plants are often sold in bunches rather than pots, and close inspection will usually reveal that they are top cuttings and not fully formed plants. Most plants sold in this way are relatively hardy and adaptable and should grow new roots as soon as they are planted in a suitable substrate. Potted plants should have good root growth, which can often be seen emerging from the pot. The roots need not be long, but should be white and free from obvious damage.

Selecting plants

Depending on the parameters of the aquarium you are planting, there are several factors to consider when aiming for a varied mixture of plants. Choose plants on the basis of their aesthetic appeal, practicality, and compatibility.

Growth rates Plants can be described as fast- or slow-growing, but a more important consideration is the time they take to become established. Fast-growing plants, such as *Cabomba, Ambulia,* or *Egeria,* will establish and grow quickly. They soon begin to use nutrients in large amounts, which may cause problems for other plants that need a "settling in" period before they start to grow. The faster-growing plants may use up nutrients in the water before the slower-growing ones have become established, making it even more difficult for them to get started. You should therefore introduce the slow-establishing plants (including many foreground and harder-to-keep species) before fast-growing and fast-establishing species, or give them additional help in the form of substrate fertilizer tablets.

Planting areas Choose a good mixture of foreground, midground, and background plants, plus floating plants if you wish. Many background plants are sold well before they reach their potential height, so picking plants on the basis of their size at the point of sale will not ensure a mix of plant heights when the aquarium is established. Midground plants should be species that can sustain regular trimming without suffering any long-term damage.

Leaf shape and color Selecting plants with different leaf shapes, sizes, and colors will create a varied, interesting, and contrasting display. A good approach is to restrict the choice of foreground plants to just a few species, but to include a number of different midground and background plants. Remember that different leaf shapes and colors require different conditions in the aquarium. For example, red-leaved plants should be placed in areas where they can receive the most light, while fine- and feathery-leaved plants prefer areas of moderate, but not strong water

flow, so that they do not trap too much debris between their leaves.

Environmental conditions The plants you choose should all be able to thrive in the conditions provided by your aquarium. This means they should share the same requirements with regard to temperature, light, and water hardness. Careful research is vital when choosing

plants, so make a list of all the suitable species that could be included and identify alternatives for each if your first choice is not available.

Transporting plants

Most aquatic plants are fairly hardy and will transport well if packaged correctly. If you are moving a few plants, simply place them in small plastic bags (such as

---

PLANTING AREAS WITHIN THE AQUARIUM

When you choose plants for your aquarium, you will need to bear in mind their eventual size and where they will look best in the finished display. This is a selection of plants that will suit the main planting areas of background, midground, and foreground in the aquarium. A much more extensive list appears on pages 100–101.

Background planting

Bacopa caroliniana
Cabomba caroliniana
Crinum thaianum
Echinodorus major
Egeria densa
Limnophila aquatica
Ludwigia palustris
Myriophyllum hippuroides
Rotala macrandra
Vallisneria americana

Midground planting

Alternanthera reineckii
Anubias barteri
Bacopa monnieri
Cardamine lyrata
Didiplis diandra
Heteranthera zosterifolia
Hydrocotyle leucocephala
Hydrocotyle verticillata
Lysimachia nummularia
Microsorium pteropus

Alternanthera reineckii

Vallisneria americana

Cryptocoryne willisii 'Lucens'

Foreground planting

Anubias barteri var. *nana*
Cryptocoryne willisii
Echinodorus tenellus
Eleocharis parvula
Lilaeopsis novae-zelandiae
Marsilea hirsuta
Micranthemum umbrosum
Sagittaria pusilla
Samolus valerandi
Vesicularia dubyana

Separating plant stems

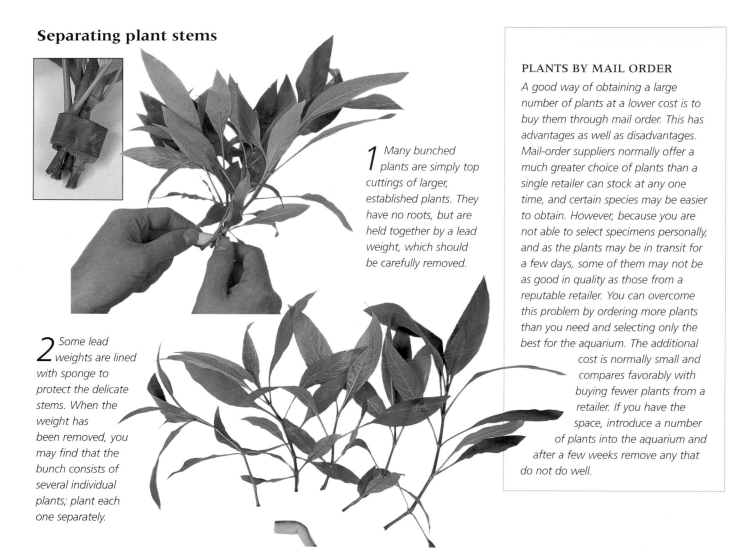

1 Many bunched plants are simply top cuttings of larger, established plants. They have no roots, but are held together by a lead weight, which should be carefully removed.

2 Some lead weights are lined with sponge to protect the delicate stems. When the weight has been removed, you may find that the bunch consists of several individual plants; plant each one separately.

those used for transporting fish). The bags should be filled with air and tightly sealed. As long as some moisture is retained in the bags, the plants will not dry out. Filling the bags with air provides cushioning, which helps to prevent damage by crushing during transport. If you are dealing with large numbers of plants, wrap them in layers of damp newspaper and transport them in a sealed container or polystyrene box. Most plants can recover following 24 hours or more in transit. The changes in light, temperature, and water conditions will be damaging, although the effects may not become evident for a number of days. In a new environment that

provides good lighting, nutrients, and available CO_2, the majority of new plants will quickly become established and begin to grow.

Before planting

There are a few points to bear in mind before you put any plants into the aquarium. To begin with, the substrate and decor (rocks, wood, etc.) should already be in place, as well as the filtration, lighting, and heating equipment. Secondly, although most plants should be snail-free, you should examine the leaves and stems thoroughly for both snails and snail eggs. It is possible to "dip" plants in a

proprietary treatment to kill any snails and/or their eggs (see pages 92–93).

Make sure the roots are healthy (see page 49) and remove any damaged leaves and/or stems, as these are unlikely to recover. Removing the leaves should encourage new growth.

Planting methods vary according to the type of plant and its root structure, but a good planting technique should always aim to minimize damage and encourage new and uninhibited growth.

Planting bunched plants

Plants sold as bunches are usually held together at the base by a lead strip, which you should carefully remove before planting. The bunch usually consists of two or three plants and these should be separated and planted individually. If there is a long root growth on the plants, trim it down to about 0.8–1.2 in (2–3 cm) using sharp scissors. This will minimize any damage to the roots during planting and encourage the plant to produce new roots that will grow downward, anchoring the plant in a natural fashion. Stem plants, which are often sold as cuttings, may have no roots present. In this case, remove the lower pair of leaves and plant the stem at least 1 in (2.5 cm) into the substrate. The plant will produce roots from the nodes where the lower leaves were removed, so make sure that these are also just beneath the substrate.

Potted plants

Plants supplied in pots are likely to have a much more developed root structure and may establish more quickly. Most potted plants are rooted in an inert medium called rock wool, which can be left on the plant or removed. However, in either case, you should remove the pot before planting. Leaving it in place may restrict or alter root growth, and seeing the pot rims above the substrate is not aesthetically pleasing. If there is a large amount of root growth, cut it back as described for bunched plants to minimize damage during planting. Place the plants in the substrate in much the same way as you would a terrestrial plant. First create a dip in the substrate, place the plant into it, cover it with more substrate, and apply a little pressure to ensure that it is firmly in place. Close up any gaps around the plant roots.

Planting vallisneria

Vallisneria creates height at the back of the aquarium. The straplike leaves are quite tough and will not be damaged by the gentle flow from a filter. Before planting, check each plant and remove any brown leaves.

Remove the lead weight. Do not be tempted to plant the slim plants in one clump.

Left: Removing the lead weight from this vallisneria produces five individual plants, each with healthy roots. Plant them separately, leaving space between them to allow for growth.

Right: Gently hold the plant near the base and, using a finger of the same hand, make a hole in the substrate. Slide the plant into the hole, just deep enough to prevent it from coming loose.

Preparing and planting ludwigia

Ludwigia palustris, *an attractive and versatile aquarium plant.*

1 Ludwigia palustris is usually sold as cuttings embedded in rock wool with a little root growth. The plant, with rock wool, should slide easily out of the pot.

2 Carefully unravel the rock wool. There may be as many as three separate pieces of rock wool, each containing two or three individual plants.

3 If there are developed roots embedded in the rock wool, leave the plants grouped in the wool. For the best effect in the aquarium, place the separate groups close to one another.

4 Supporting the plant lightly, use your fingers to create a dip in the substrate and hold it open. Try to disturb the substrate as little as possible.

5 Place the roots, embedded in rock wool, into the substrate. Push the plant down until the top of the rock wool is just below the surface.

6 Use the remaining substrate to cover the surface of the roots and compact around the base, just as you would with a terrestrial plant.

7 Place the same plants close together. Here they are 1–2 in (2.5–5 cm) apart. Alternatively, leave room so the tips of leaves on separate plants just touch.

Attaching Java fern to bogwood

Some aquatic plants, including Java fern (below), prefer to be planted on objects such as wood and porous rocks, rather than in the substrate. Many of these "object-rooting" species will also grow, at least partially, out of water and can be raised to the upper reaches of the aquarium and allowed to grow through the water surface.

1 Removing the rock wool from Java fern can be tricky, as the roots are often dense and tangled. However, with a little care, any plant damage can be limited.

Try not to keep the plant out of water for too long.

Always choose specimens with healthy leaves, as they grow away more quickly.

3 Set the plant on the wood in a natural position. Tie the root firmly but gently to the bogwood with black thread, which will be hardly noticeable and soon covered by new roots.

2 To minimize damage and encourage regrowth, trim any excess root with sharp scissors, leaving 0.4–0.8 in (1–2 cm). Take care not to cut or damage the rhizome (the main root).

If there is room, add other plants, such as dwarf anubias and Java moss.

Nonsubstrate rooting plants

A few common aquatic plants are better suited for planting on porous rocks and/or wood rather than in the substrate. Typical examples include *Anubias, Microsorium, Vesicularia,* and *Bolbitis* species. They are often sold as potted plants, so take them out of their containers and carefully remove any rock wool. Trim the roots to about 0.4 in (1 cm), but make sure you do not cut into the main root, or rhizome, from which the leaves and stems are produced. Tie the rhizome firmly in a few places to a suitable rock, piece of wood or other item, using black thread. The thread will slowly degrade as the plant roots onto its support.

Allowing space for growth

When putting in the first aquatic plants, leave space between them for growth and propagation. Most stem plants should be planted at least 2–4 in (5–10 cm) apart to allow room for the leaves to grow without blocking out light to the foliage of their neighbors. This will also give you space to plant top cuttings at some future date if you wish.

Many foreground plants reproduce by means of runners. Allowing existing plants to grow and spread naturally often creates a more realistic effect than filling the foreground area with new plants. Plants that develop from runners in the aquarium are often healthier and better looking than the parent plant, so allowing them plenty of space to grow will result in an enhanced display when the aquarium is fully established.

Using nutrient tablets

Plants use nutrients in the greatest quantity when they are established and growing, not when they are first introduced into the aquarium. However, producing new roots and leaves uses up a large amount of energy, so lighting and CO_2 fertilization are particularly important for plants during

their first few weeks in the aquarium. Liquid fertilization is not vital during the first week or two and should be avoided to prevent encouraging algae to form. Nutrient-rich capsules or tablets placed in the substrate are ideal for encouraging root growth in new plants, particularly species that are harder to keep or do not adapt easily to living in aquarium conditions. These tablets can be placed directly beneath new specimens when they are planted, giving them an immediate source of nutrients just beneath the roots, which will soon grow around the tablet.

Right: *Place fertilizer tablets under or close to the roots of individual plants. This new addition to the tank will soon be able to absorb the nutrients.*

Below: *Move large plants, such as some* Echinodorus *spp., with care. First remove any very large leaves and trim the roots. This prevents damage to the roots and means that the plant will not require large amounts of nutrients when it is replanted.*

Moving established plants

The procedure for moving and replanting an established plant is much the same as for planting a new one. The only difference is that the root growth is much more widespread. The roots should still be trimmed, but only to about 1.6–2.4 in (4–6 cm), and older or damaged leaves should be removed. If the plant has a number of large leaves (as is often the case in larger *Echinodorus* species), remove the biggest ones before replanting. This reduces the plant's nutrient requirement and encourages new leaf growth.

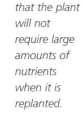

Lighting the aquarium

As we have seen, plants use light to photosynthesize – a vital process that allows a plant to create its own energy (food) reserves (see pages 12–16). Without sufficient light, photosynthesis will be impaired and plant health will diminish. Providing a suitable light source, combined with good environmental conditions, will ensure that plants are able to photosynthesize at an optimum rate and remain healthy. In most aquariums, a single fluorescent tube is the norm, but unfortunately, this fails to meet the light requirements of many plants. Correct lighting in general is an area where many aquarium plants suffer. To provide the correct light source for aquarium plants it is important to understand how plants use light in nature and what qualities light possesses.

The ingredients of light

Visible light forms a small part of the electromagnetic spectrum, which includes radio waves, microwaves, and X rays. White light is made up from a number of different wavelengths, each corresponding to a specific color. This can be seen in the colors of a rainbow, which are created by water droplets breaking up sunlight into its separate wavelengths and, hence, colors. Wavelengths of light are usually measured in nanometers (nm) – billionths of a meter. The light that the human eye can see ranges between 380 and 700 nm and is called the visible spectrum. At the "short" end of the visible spectrum is ultraviolet (UV) light with a wavelength of between 300 and 350 nm and at the "long" end is infrared light (700–750 nm). Different light sources produce different light spectrums depending on the strongest wavelengths emitted. For example, a light that appears blue produces more light at the lower (400–500 nm) end of the spectrum, while a light that appears red produces more light at the higher (650–700 nm) end of the spectrum.

The colors of the physical objects we see around us are generated by the color of the light reflected off them; all

Right: Bright lighting is essential for many plants, although only a small portion of the overall light is used for photosynthesis. The blue and red zones of the spectrum are the most beneficial.

How plants use light

Sunlight peaks in the blue area of the spectrum. This short-wave light is used by both plants and algae.

Green light is reflected by the majority of plants.

Aquatic plants' photosynthetic ability is most sensitive to red light between 650 and 680 nm.

Light in the infrared area (700–750 nm) cannot be used by plants,

nm   400   500   600   700

the other colors of the spectrum are absorbed. This is why the sea appears blue – because blue light is energetic and less readily absorbed by water.

Plants use only some of the light they receive, concentrating on specific areas of the spectrum and using only certain wavelengths, usually those that are most readily available. As light passes through water, its intensity decreases but some areas of the spectrum pass through water more easily. Shorter wavelengths of light are more "energetic" than longer wavelengths and it is the more energetic light that is able to pass through water more quickly. Less energetic light passes through water slowly and is quickly absorbed, so it is not much use to plants submerged at a significant depth. High-energy light with shorter wavelengths (blue and ultraviolet light) is not as quickly absorbed, so plants are more likely to receive greater quantities of blue light than red.

The photosynthetic pigment chlorophyll, used by the majority of plants for photosynthesis, "traps" mostly blue and red light, although it is most efficient at trapping red light at around 650–675 nm. Blue light is used just as much as red light simply because it is far more available, is stronger in natural sunlight, and passes through water more easily. In the aquarium, artificial light should peak, ideally, in the red area of the spectrum although this can produce an undesirable appearance. Artificial light with a strong blue and red spectrum is often much more appealing to our eyes and will still provide the plants with suitable light. It is worth remembering that strong blue light will also promote algal growth, so aim for a balance of red and blue light.

On reflection...

The color of a plant's leaves provide an important clue to its lighting requirements. Most plants are various shades of green, but many also produce

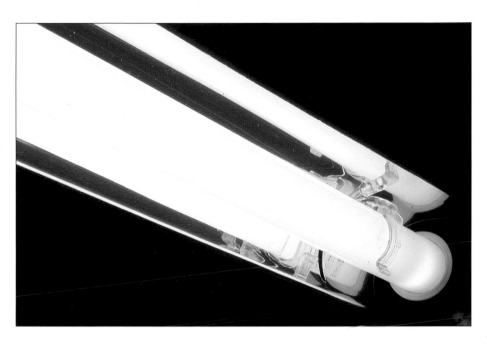

Above: *Fluorescent tubes emit light in all directions. Using a reflector can redirect light into the tank and significantly improve light intensity. These reflectors are made of mirror-finish flexible plastic or polished aluminum.*

Below: *Incorrect lighting is one factor that can influence the growth of algae in the aquarium. Varying the intensity and duration of the tank illumination can help to resolve the common problems caused by algae.*

brown or red leaves. Because we understand the light spectrum, we know the natural intensities of sunlight and which wavelengths (colors) pass through water more easily. We also know that the color of an object is generated by the light reflected from it (i.e., not absorbed). Therefore, we can work out which wavelengths are used by plants and the efficiency of photosynthesis within them based on the color of the leaves.

Light green leaves Because white light is made up of many different colors, a lighter color indicates that less light is absorbed across the entire spectrum (i.e., more is reflected). A plant with light green leaves is therefore likely to be less efficient at photosynthesis and lacking in the photosynthetic pigment, chlorophyll. Light green plants are likely to require bright light to compensate for a lack of chlorophyll in their tissues.

Dark green leaves Dark green leaves are a sign that the plant absorbs less green light compared with light from other areas of the spectrum. This indicates an abundance of chlorophyll (because more green light is reflected). An increase in the amount of chlorophyll in the leaves allows the plant to take maximum advantage of a given light source. Dark green plants are adapted to grow in low-light conditions and will not require bright lighting. When dark green plants produce new leaves, these are often much lighter in color, because the large amounts of chlorophyll present in mature leaves have not yet developed.

Red leaves The red part of the spectrum is usually the area where plants are most photosynthetically sensitive, although in red-leaved plants this light is reflected and not absorbed. The change in color is due to the fact that the plant is using a less efficient carotenoid pigment to trap light energy than the usual "green" chlorophyll pigment. To compensate for the lack of available red light the plant must receive greater quantities of blue and green light and thus requires brighter lighting in the aquarium. Some plants can change the pigment used for photosynthesis depending on light conditions. In this case, red-leaved plants will turn green if the lighting is not adequate, and some green-leaved plants will produce red leaves toward the top of the plant (i.e., closer to the light source) or in overall bright lighting.

Light in nature

Aquatic plants are found in virtually all freshwater habitats, the majority of which are river systems. A typical river has many different stages and the light that plants receive depends on their location within the river system. Near the source of the river, the surrounding environment is often open and lacking in vegetation, so sunlight is available at full intensity all day long. The same occurs much further down the river where it often travels through open plains. Many tropical rivers, however, flow through areas of dense vegetation and a significant amount of sunlight is blocked by overhanging trees and bushes. Aquatic plants are generally found near the riverbanks of medium-sized to large rivers where the water is shallower and the plants can obtain light more easily.

Below: A contrasting mixture of leaf colors can look very attractive in a planted aquarium, although the lighting must be tailored to the needs of the different plants.

Stop

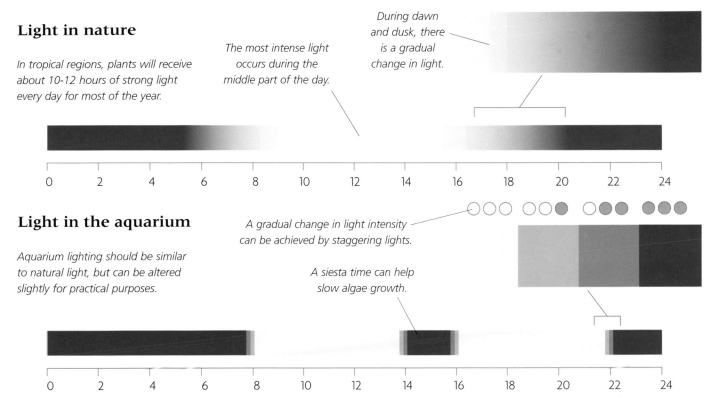

Light in nature

In tropical regions, plants will receive about 10-12 hours of strong light every day for most of the year.

The most intense light occurs during the middle part of the day.

During dawn and dusk, there is a gradual change in light.

Light in the aquarium

A gradual change in light intensity can be achieved by staggering lights.

Aquarium lighting should be similar to natural light, but can be altered slightly for practical purposes.

A siesta time can help slow algae growth.

The location of plants in nature affects the amount of light they require in the aquarium. Plants that are accustomed to open environments will require strong lighting for longer periods, while plants found in the shade of vegetation will require a less intense light source. In nature, a number of plants, such as *Echinodorus* spp., also produce leaves above the water surface, where both light and CO_2 are more easily available. The advantage of producing aerial leaves is that faster-growing plants are able to photosynthesise more quickly and utilize CO_2 more readily. Aerial leaves also provide vital shading for less vigorous submerged plants.

Light duration
Most tropical regions receive roughly 12 hours of daylight, with 10 hours of strong light and 10 hours of complete darkness and this daylength varies little throughout the year. It is important to make sure that plants in the aquarium receive a similar amount of light on a regular basis. The best way to achieve this is to use a timer that automatically switches on the aquarium lights for 10–14 hours a day. In aquariums with more than one light, say, a number of fluorescent tubes, you can adopt a "staggered" approach, with each light being turned on (or off) in a sequence, five to ten minutes apart. This will benefit both the fish and the plants by reducing the shock of a sudden change in light intensity. It is also important that aquarium plants receive periods of complete darkness. During this time, plants stop photosynthesizing but continue to respire, so a dark period can be considered a period of "rest" for the plants' biological functions.

Creating a siesta period
Plants are able to regulate the rate of photosynthesis relatively easily, and quickly respond to changes in light conditions. In other words, they do not take long to warm up and start photosynthesizing once there is sufficient light. However, algae are not as biologically advanced as plants and need a long and relatively uninterrupted period of light to function properly. It is possible to combat algae in the aquarium by controlling the intensity and period of lighting in the aquarium and creating a "siesta" period. This is a period of darkness that interrupts the normal day/night light cycle in the aquarium. If the aquarium receives 5–6 hours of lighting followed by 2–3 hours of darkness and then another 5–6 hours of light, the plants will be relatively unaffected and receive enough light throughout the day, but algae growth rates will be significantly reduced and may even start to die back.

Reducing light loss
In most cases, maximizing the amount of light plants receive in the aquarium has a beneficial effect. There are several reasons why a significant amount of light is lost between the light source and

MEASURING LIGHT INTENSITY

The intensity of a light source reaching any surface is measured in units of lux. Natural bright sunlight produces about 70,000–80,000 lux, although much of this is lost by the time it reaches aquatic plants. The lux requirement of aquarium plants varies between roughly 300 and 6,000 lux, depending on the species. Plants such as Anubias and Cryptocoryne spp., which are often found in shaded streams, require less light than plants found on or above the water surface and in open, shallow areas, such as dwarf Echinodorus and Myriophyllum. Lux can be measured by a photographic luxmeter, although measuring lux readings in the aquarium to ensure correct light intensity is unnecessary. It is much better to start by looking at the output of various light sources.

Output of light

The output from a light source is measured in lumens. (Lux is a measure of lumens per square meter.) If the optimum output of light is achieved, taking into account losses of light, it should be possible to ensure that the plants receive the correct amount of illumination. As a rough guide, a standard, rectangular, planted aquarium will require around 30–50 lumens per liter of water.

Light efficiency

The efficiency of a light source can be measured by the amount of lumens produced per watt. An artificial light source uses electricity (watts) and converts it into light and heat. A fluorescent tube never gets very hot, and can be touched when in use. This is because most of the electricity used is converted into light, making a fluorescent tube very efficient. On the other hand, a 60-watt household incandescent tube will get much hotter and produce less light than one 60-watt fluorescent tube (or two 30-watt tubes). However, this does not mean that the most efficient light source is always the best one. For larger and deeper aquariums, a number of fluorescent tubes may be needed to produce enough output (lumens). Each of these fluorescent tubes requires costly starter units and space above the aquarium. Before long, the cost and practicality of fluorescent tubes may become unwarranted and you should consider alternative light sources.

Although less efficient than fluorescent lamps, because they produce more heat and less light per watt, mercury-vapor or metal-halide lamps (halogen) lamps are a good choice. Their much higher wattage ensures a higher light output and higher light intensity. Initially these lamps may seem expensive, but compared to the equivalent light output of fluorescent tubes, they are actually considerably cheaper.

Useful definitions

Lumen: Unit of luminous energy, historically the light from one candle.
Lux: Unit of illumination representing one lumen falling on one square meter.
Watt: Unit of electrical power.

Left: Plants that are highly adapted to different light conditions can nevertheless live in the same areas in nature. This tropical lily requires strong light, while the plants shaded beneath it need only moderate light.

the surface of plant leaves. Suspended debris in the aquarium water can cut down the amount of light reaching the plants quite considerably, but is easily removed using a fine floss medium in the filter. Cover glasses and condensation trays can screen out up to 30% of the light output from a given source. Plastic condensation trays are particularly bad in this respect because they quickly discolor and are difficult to clean. If possible, use glass covers and clean them on a weekly basis to reduce any significant loss of light. The light from fluorescent tubes is given off in all directions and much is lost as it is absorbed by the aquarium hood or released through the aquarium glass. Using specially designed reflectors, you can angle the light so that it is only directed into the water and not outward. Reflectors can increase the effectiveness of fluorescent tubes by up to 40%.

Choosing lighting

What we can conclude from looking at different types of light is that the best type of light depends on the function it is required to perform. Household incandescent lights are inefficient and produce a lot of heat, but are very cheap and ideal for domestic use. Fluorescent tubes are very efficient and relatively cheap if used in small numbers, and ideal for smaller planted aquariums. The less efficient, but higher output/intensity lamps are ideal for larger planted tanks. Remember that it is often better to provide too much light rather than too little, although far too much light will be damaging. When choosing the correct lighting for a particular system, the four main factors to consider are:

1. Efficiency (output in relation to power consumption)
2. Output/Intensity
3. Initial cost
4. Light spectrum

Fluorescent lighting

Fluorescent tubes emit light by electrically charging a gas contained within the tube. The light produced by the gas is mostly in the invisible areas of the spectrum, but the fluorescent coating on the inside of the tube converts this into visible light. By altering the chemical coating on the inside of the tube, the spectrum of light emitted can be changed, so fluorescent tubes can be designed for specific purposes and to emit specific colors. Fluorescent tubes designed for aquarium plant growth often produce a red-yellow or red-violet-blue color, which, although ideal for plants, may give the aquarium a slightly garish look. To remedy this, full-spectrum tubes can be added to balance the color output.

Fluorescent tubes are the most widely used method of lighting aquariums,

How light is lost in the aquarium

Light from a fluorescent tube is emitted in all directions.

Reflectors help to redirect light into the aquarium.

Condensation trays must be kept clean to reduce light absorption.

As light passes through the water, its spectrum is altered and intensity is reduced as it is absorbed and converted into heat energy.

Some light is refracted and/or reflected from the water surface.

Particles in the water will soak up a large amount of light.

Some light is lost through the aquarium glass.

Large-leaved and tall plants take up light in the upper areas of the aquarium and reduce the light reaching smaller and/or lower plants.

Plants toward the bottom of the aquarium receive only a small proportion of the emitted light.

mainly because they are very efficient, use little electricity, and are relatively cheap when used in small numbers. Most fluorescent tubes will last up to two years before they start to flicker and eventually become useless. However, their light output drops considerably within the first year of use, so the tubes become less effective and useful for plants unless they are changed at least once a year. Fluorescent tubes are by far the best lighting solution for smaller or shallow tanks, but for deeper or larger tanks or for plants that require intense lighting, there are other alternatives.

Although light is measured in lumens and lux (see page 60), fluorescent tubes vary in the intensity and output of light depending on the chemical coating used inside the tube and are rarely labeled in lumens or lux. Fluorescent tubes can be adequately rated for most purposes by the wattage of the light tube rather than its output of light. In aquariums that are 15 in (38 cm) deep or less, use 1.5–2 watts of light for every 4 liters (about 1 gallon) of aquarium water.

Metal-halide lamps

Metal-halide, or halogen, lamps provide intense, high-output light via a tungsten filament. They are ideally suited to deeper aquariums, with a water depth of 24 in (60 cm) or more. Suspended at least 12 in (30 cm) above the aquarium to allow ample ventilation, a single unit will illuminate approximately 2 ft^2 (1,800 cm^2) of surface area. (An aquarium 24 in/60 cm long and 12 in/30 cm wide.) Halogen lights are usually available in 150-watt or 250-watt versions; a 150-watt light should provide a suitable output for most aquariums. (250-watt versions are better suited to marine invertebrate aquariums, where demand for light from corals is higher.) You may need more than one lamp for aquariums longer than 42 in (107 cm). Halogen lights are initially the most costly method of lighting, but provide the best output for demanding aquarium plants.

Mercury vapor lamps

Like halogen lamps, mercury vapor lamps are suspended above the aquarium and provide a high-intensity light that is able to penetrate deeper water than fluorescent tubes. For aquariums with a depth of 18–24 in (45–60 cm), mercury vapor lamps

Left: *Metal-halide lamps are widely used for marine aquariums, where their spectral output suits marine algae and corals. A lighting canopy with metal-halide lamps and fluorescent tubes will produce a balanced light output for healthy plant growth. The intensity provided by this sort of lighting setup is ideal for deeper planted aquariums.*

Right: *The spectral output of a metal-halide lamp shows useful peaks in the blue and yellow areas. The large volume of the curve reflects the high light intensity these lamps produce.*

nm   400   500   600   700

CHANGES IN INTENSITY

Plants adapt to a given light source relatively quickly, but a sudden and prolonged significant change in light intensity can be harmful and sometimes deadly. High-intensity lights, such as mercury vapor or metal-halide lamps, may produce too much light for many plants. If the light source is too bright, plants are able to create protective pigments that reduce any harmful effects. However, if a sensitive plant (notably floating species) is transferred from an aquarium with single fluorescent tubes to an aquarium with high-intensity lamps, the plant may not have sufficient time to produce enough protective pigments and will suffer, often dying back quickly.

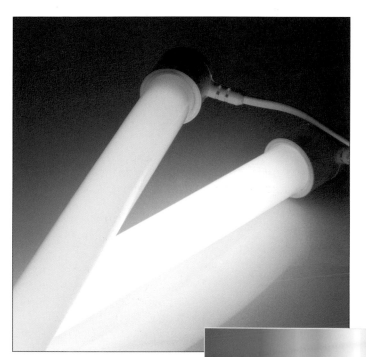

Left: *Fluorescent tubes are available in different color spectrums for different purposes. Using a combination of tubes in a planted aquarium can create good light for plant growth, as well as creating a pleasing color balance for the human eye.*

Right: *The spectral output of a white triphosphor fluorescent tube peaks at 400 and 600 nm, ideal for photosynthesis, and at 500 nm, which creates a more balanced light appearance.*

nm   400   500   600   700

Above: *Although mercury vapor lamps do not produce an ideal spectrum for aquarium plants, their high output easily compensates for this. Mercury vapor lamps also produce an aesthetically attractive light.*

provide the most cost-effective and practical solution, as they are cheaper than halogen lamps and provide a much higher output than fluorescent tubes. Common mercury vapor lamps use between 60 and 125 watts, which makes them relatively low-cost to run. If they are within your budget, halogen lamps will provide the best source of light, but mercury vapor lamps are an excellent low-cost alternative.

Other light sources
As well as fluorescent, halogen, and mercury vapor lamps, there are other, less commonly used sources. Sodium lamps and blended spotlamps are two reasonably good sources of light. Sodium lamps are efficient and long-lived although they do lack suitable blue light and may need to be combined with

an additional light source. Blended spotlamps are a combination of mercury and tungsten and provide a very well-balanced output at low cost.

Unsuitable lights include any light that does not provide suitable red or blue light and/or provides too low an output. A typical example is the household incandescent (tungsten) bulb, which, although peaking in the red spectrum, is highly inefficient and provides little available light for aquarium plants.

Natural sunlight
At first glance, using natural light to illuminate aquarium plants seems an ideal solution; it is far brighter than fluorescent tubes, has a suitable spectrum, and is cost-free. However, there are disadvantages and generally speaking, you should avoid direct

sunlight unless you have plenty of experience and/or are willing to experiment a little. Providing the aquarium is in a place where it can receive sunlight for the majority of the day, all year round, it is possible to create a healthy, well-planted aquarium where fast plant growth will prevent algae from forming. However, this balance is difficult to achieve, and in most cases the plants will either receive too little or too much light. In addition, light levels may vary wildly throughout the year in northern and southern climates or an incorrect balance may cause algal blooms. Sunlight does have advantages in aquariums where light is blocked from overhead, for example from floating plants. In this instance, sunlight through a window will provide lower-growing plants with additional light.

Lighting levels for aquarium plants

BRIGHT TO VERY BRIGHT

These plants require a high-intensity light for a large proportion of daylight hours. In most cases, fluorescent tubes will not provide sufficient light to promote good growth. Use metal-halide or mercury vapor lamps.

Above: *Red plants, such as this* Myriophyllum tuberculatum, *thrive in very bright light.*

Alternanthera reineckii
Ammannia gracilis
Bacopa monnieri
Blyxa echinosperma
Blyxa japonica
Cabomba aquatica
Cabomba piauhyensis
Cryptocoryne parva
Didiplis diandra
Echinodorus macrophyllus
Eichhornia azurea
Eichhornia crassipes
Eleocharis parvula
Eusteralis stellata
Fontinalis antipyretica
Glossostigma elatinoides
Heteranthera zosterifolia
Hydrocotyle sibthorpioides
Hydrocotyle verticillata
Hygrophila corymbosa 'Crispa'
Hygrophila corymbosa 'Strigosa'
Hygrophila difformis
Hygrophila guianensis
Hygrophila stricta
Lilaeopsis novae-zelandiae

Limnophila aquatica
Limnophila indica
Limnophila sessiliflora
Ludwigia brevipes
Ludwigia glandulosa
Ludwigia palustris any variety
Lysimachia nummularia
Micranthemum umbrosum
Myriophyllum aquaticum
Myriophyllum hippuroides
Myriophyllum scabratum
Myriophyllum tuberculatum
Nesaea crassicaulis
Nymphaea lotus var. rubra
Nymphaea stellata
Nymphoides aquatica
Potamogeton crispus
Potamogeton gayii
Rotala macrandra
Rotala wallichii
Shinnersia rivularis
Trapa natans

BRIGHT

Metal-halide or mercury vapor lamps are still the ideal choice for these plants although in aquariums less than 18 in (45 cm) deep, two or three fluorescent tubes (with reflectors) may be sufficient. If the plants are densely grouped together, use metal-halide or mercury vapor lamps; if they are not and there is plenty of open space, then fluorescent tubes will be adequate.

Alternanthera reineckii
Anubias gracilis
Aponogeton boivinianus
Aponogeton crispus
Aponogeton ulvaceus
Aponogeton undulatus
Bacopa caroliniana

Bacopa monnieri
Bacopa rotundifolia
Barclaya longifolia
Bolbitis heudelotii
Cabomba caroliniana
Cardamine lyrata
Ceratophyllum submersum
Ceratopteris cornuta
Crassula helmsii
Crinum natans
Crinum thaianum
Cryptocoryne albida
Cryptocoryne balansae
Cryptocoryne beckettii
Cryptocoryne ciliata
Cryptocoryne moehlmannii
Cryptocoryne siamensis
Cryptocoryne undulata
Cryptocoryne wendtii
Cryptocoryne willisii
Echinodorus amazonicus
Echinodorus bleheri
Echinodorus bolivianus
Echinodorus grandiflorus
Echinodorus horemanii
Echinodorus major

Below: Echinodorus osiris *is typical of its group in needing bright light.*

Above: *The elegant strands of* Ceratophyllum demersum *need only moderate tank lighting.*

Echinodorus opacus
Echinodorus osiris
Echinodorus parviflorus
Echinodorus quadricostatus var. *xinguensis*
Echinodorus tenellus
Echinodorus uruguayensis
Eichhornia crassipes
Eleocharis acicularis
Eleocharis vivipara
Elodea canadensis
Gymnocoronis spilanthoides
Hemianthus callitrichoides
Hemianthus micranthemoides
Hydrocotyle leucocephala
Hygrophila corymbosa
Hygrophila corymbosa 'Glabra'
Hygrophila corymbosa 'Gracilis'
Hygrophila polysperma
Lagarosiphon major
Lemna trisulca
Limnobium laevigatum
Lobelia cardinalis
Ludwigia helminthorrhiza
Ludwigia repens
Marsilea hirsuta
Najas indica
Nuphar japonica
Nymphaea lotus
Pistia stratiotes
Potamogeton mascarensis
Riccia fluitans
Rotala rotundifolia

Sagittaria platyphylla
Sagittaria pusilla
Sagittaria subulata
Salvinia auriculata
Salvinia minima
Salvinia natans
Salvinia oblongifolia
Samolus valerandi
Saururus cernuus
Vallisneria americana
Vallisneria asiatica var. *biwaensis*
Vallisneria gigantea
Vallisneria tortifolia

MODERATE

These plants can be kept with two or three fluorescent tubes and are relatively hardy species. Although some will survive and grow under only one or two tubes (with reflectors), they will not grow at an optimum rate and may not show their full health. Most of the plants in this group will do better with brighter light, but they do not require it.

Anubias
   angustifolia 'Afzelii'
Anubias gracilis
Azolla caroliniana
Azolla filiculoides

Ceratophyllum demersum
Crinum thaianum
Cryptocoryne balansae
Cryptocoryne cordata
Cryptocoryne pontederiifolia
Echinodorus cordifolius
Echinodorus macrophyllus
Egeria densa
Vallisneria spiralis

UNDEMANDING OR SHADED

The plants in this group are ideal for aquariums with just one or two fluorescent tubes. Some will live happily in a wide range of lighting conditions, others prefer to be in shaded areas or away from bright light.

Anubias barteri var. *barteri*
Anubias barteri var. *nana*
Anubias congensis
Anubias lanceolata
Aponogeton elongatus
Aponogeton madagascariensis
Cryptocoryne affinis
Cryptocoryne lutea
Cryptocoryne walkeri
Lemna minor
Microsorium pteropus
Spathiphyllum wallisii
Vesicularia dubyana

Microsorium pteropus is a tough aquarium plant that will appreciate a shady spot.

Feeding aquarium plants

Plants require a number of organic and mineral nutrients in order to maintain steady growth and good general health. Most of these nutrients are required only in tiny amounts but without them, vital biological functions cannot be carried out properly. Nutrients can be considered as a plant's "diet"; without a proper diet, health problems arise and the plant will become "ill." The number of nutrients that any given plant requires is extensive and can be provided in a number of ways. Looking at the function of various nutrients, their availability in the aquarium and assessing their importance is a good way of devising a "shopping list" for suitable sources of fertilization.

Macro- and micronutrients
Plant nutrients are often described as macro- or micronutrients, depending on the quantities of a particular nutrient required by a plant. Macronutrients are required in the greatest quantities; these include calcium, carbon, hydrogen, magnesium, nitrogen, oxygen, phosphorus, sulphur, and potassium. Micronutrients are required only in very small quantities and are often described as trace elements. Micronutrients include boron, copper, manganese, molybdenum, chlorine, nickel, iron, and zinc. Both macro- and micronutrients are equally vital to the overall health of aquatic plants.

Providing macronutrients
Many macronutrients are readily available in the aquarium; for example, oxygen and hydrogen are normally always present in more than sufficient quantities, while calcium and nitrogen are usually present. Calcium is only found at low levels in very soft water, and nitrogen can be absorbed by plants in the form of nitrates and ammonium, which are normally present as a result of biological filtration or from fish/organic waste. Therefore, the only macronutrients that the aquarist normally needs to supply are carbon, magnesium, phosphorus, sulphur, and potassium.

Micronutrients
Although required in far lower quantities, micronutrients are equally important to plant health. Whereas macronutrients are usually used for structural components, such as cells, proteins, and fats, micronutrients are used for cellular functions and the activation of vital enzymes. Micronutrients can be considered as important for the correct "management and control" of plant biology. These "trace elements" can be found in many liquid fertilizers, as well as in most tap water sources, although they are often used up quickly in aquariums both by plants as nutrients and through binding to organic molecules.

Tapwater
Although tap water is a good source of many micronutrients, its qualities vary a

Left: *Many* Echinodorus *species require high amounts of iron. Pale leaves are a major indication of a lack of iron, although a lack of other nutrients may also be to blame.*

OTHER NUTRIENTS
When you come to select suitable nutrient mixes, bear in mind that some fertilizers include other micronutrients that are not essential for aquatic plants and need not be added to the aquarium. Some terrestrial plants may require these nutrients for functions that are not present in aquatic plants, such as nitrogen fixation (obtaining nitrogen from the atmosphere). These nutrients include sodium, silicon, iodine, and cobalt. Aquatic plants do not need these nutrients.

great deal depending on location. Tap water sources vary in hardness, acidity, and metal toxicity and should be checked before use in a planted aquarium. Hard water generally provides more nutrients, and regular small water changes will keep these nutrients at suitable levels for most aquatic plants. The use of tap water should depend on the preferences of the plants in the aquarium and whether they are softwater or hardwater species. In either case, it is usually best to use tap water (rather than reverse-osmosis or rainwater) at least partially as a source of nutrients in a planted aquarium.

Hardwater and softwater plants

Depending on where individual plant species occur in nature, they are adapted to the quantities of nutrients in that area. The major factor that affects the quantity of nutrients is water hardness, which, in tap water, should not be confused with pH and acidity/alkalinity. Aquatic plants from hardwater areas require more calcium, magnesium, and potassium than softwater plants, because these elements are present in higher quantities in hard water. On the other hand, softwater plants are well adapted to cope in water with low levels of these nutrients and do not need so much. Some nutrients, including many of the micronutrients, are less available in hard water because they are more likely to form metal oxides and become unavailable as nutrients. In this case, hardwater plants in the aquarium will require less of these nutrients because they are better adapted to maximize their uptake of them.

Generally speaking, the majority of aquarium plants come from softwater areas, so most aquarists will try to recreate softwater conditions when keeping aquatic plants to ensure that they are able to obtain all the nutrients they require. However, softwater plants can be kept in hard water, providing you

Chelated nutrients

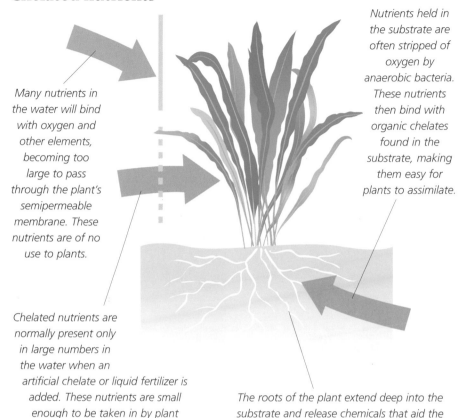

Many nutrients in the water will bind with oxygen and other elements, becoming too large to pass through the plant's semipermeable membrane. These nutrients are of no use to plants.

Chelated nutrients are normally present only in large numbers in the water when an artificial chelate or liquid fertilizer is added. These nutrients are small enough to be taken in by plant leaves above the substrate.

Nutrients held in the substrate are often stripped of oxygen by anaerobic bacteria. These nutrients then bind with organic chelates found in the substrate, making them easy for plants to assimilate.

The roots of the plant extend deep into the substrate and release chemicals that aid the assimilation of nutrients.

continually add carbon dioxide (CO_2), which is the only nutrient that may be in short supply for softwater plants. It is more difficult to keep hardwater plants in soft water than the other way around, so if you have a mixture of hard and softwater species, it is best to augment a moderately hardwater source with CO_2. In this mixed environment, the majority of plants should do well.

Sources of nutrients

In the aquarium, nutrients can be supplied to plants from a number of sources. Because plants take up nutrients both through their leaves and the roots, nutrients should be made available in the substrate and the water. Micronutrients, or trace elements, are only needed in small amounts and are often present in most tap water supplies.

However, some may quickly bond with other elements, making larger molecules that are unavailable to plants. They may also need to be supplied in quantity in the substrate or additionally through liquid fertilizers.

The major difference between liquid and substrate fertilization is that liquid fertilizers may need to be replaced weekly or every two weeks, whereas substrate fertilizers are normally present for longer periods. The substrate in the aquarium acts as a "storage" facility for some nutrients. The lack of high oxygen levels and water movement in a compact substrate will prevent nutrients from being moved around, oxidated, bonded with carbonates, or otherwise made unavailable to plants. In addition, the high amount of organic matter in most substrates will allow natural chelates to

Above: *Many fish foods are high in nutrient content, and once the food has been broken down, these nutrients are available for plants to use. Many of the nutrients in fish food are likely to have originated in plant matter.*

Right: *Small fish digest food quickly, excreting a large majority of the food's "useful" elements. Both fish and plants benefit from the fact that plants use fish waste as a source of fertilization.*

bond with nutrients (see page 67), allowing a large quantity of nutrients to be present, while a slow release reduces the amount of available nutrients. Substrate fertilization can be achieved through the use of proprietary substrate mixes or localized tablet fertilizers.

Fish food

All higher organisms are made up from the same basic elements. It therefore follows that fish food, which is manufactured mainly from living organisms (usually fish in the case of dry foods, such as flake, tablet, or pellet foods) contains almost all the nutrients required by plants as well as fish. Most of these elements are excreted by the fish and then become available to plants as nutrients. Many fish foods are particularly high in phosphate and potassium, and in a well-fed aquarium, may provide enough of these nutrients

for most plants. Never be tempted to overfeed, however, as leftover, rotting food will create a number of problems in the aquarium.

Nutrient-rich substrates

Ready-made, nutrient-rich additives are widely available and usually designed as a main substrate, or to be mixed with a small-grade inert substrate. These substrates are high in many of the nutrients required by plants and not commonly available through other sources (tap water, natural processes, etc.). In an established aquarium, most of these nutrients are released slowly over long periods of time, making nutrient-rich substrates an ideal long-term fertilizing solution. Most nutrient-rich substrates will begin to run out of nutrients after only two to three years. However, if you carry out regular small water changes and allow some organic

waste to build up in the substrate, it will naturally become a "sink" for trapping and slowly releasing nutrients indefinitely. Regular small water changes and liquid iron fertilization should be enough to continually recharge an established substrate incorporating a nutrient-rich additive.

Soil-based substrates

Although you must exercise caution when using soil-based substrates (see page 43), it is nevertheless true that soil contains a large quantity of many nutrients—far more than are produced through other fertilization methods. Apart from carbon, chlorine, hydrogen, nickel, and oxygen, soil will provide every other nutrient required by aquatic plants for a number of years. Because hydrogen, chlorine, nickel, and oxygen can be readily obtained from the water, it is possible to use just soil and CO_2 as a complete fertilizing solution. During the first 6–12 months of soil use in the aquarium, carbon is also produced as CO_2 in sufficient quantities to make additional CO_2 fertilization unwarranted.

Liquid fertilizers

Several "off-the-shelf" liquid fertilizers are available for aquatic plants, but they should be used with caution because over-fertilization can cause problems with algae and metal toxicity. Generally speaking, you get what you pay for when you buy liquid fertilizers; some of the more specialized products are far more valuable and contain the correct quantities of the required nutrients without oversupplying or lacking some elements.

Liquid fertilizers can be particularly useful in supplying chelated iron to the aquarium. Although iron is a micro-nutrient and needed only in small quantities, it is often unavailable in the aquarium unless it is provided in a chelated form that will slowly release a usable form of iron over long periods.

Many of the nutrients in liquid fertilizers will become unusable after a short period, usually through binding with other elements or through oxidation. For this reason it is important to dose the aquarium on a regular basis, normally weekly or every two weeks.

Tablet fertilizers

Tablet fertilizers provide a localized supply of nutrients. They are concentrated forms of nutrient-rich substrate additives and particularly high in iron. Some faster-growing plants use vast amounts of iron, and supplying a concentrated source at the roots will help to prevent iron deficiency problems. Deficiencies in other plants, which may not be able to compete for available iron as quickly, will also be reduced or prevented. Do not use tablets as a "whole-aquarium" solution to universal fertilization or iron fertilization, but only to provide an additional source of nutrients for individual plants. Tablets are not required, even locally, when soil-based substrates are used.

Above: *Liquid fertilization is a useful method of short-term fertilization, although correct dosage is important. Pour the measured dose into the water. Adding too much often causes more problems than adding too little.*

Right: *A thin layer of nutrient-rich substrate at the level of the lower half of the roots will provide a valuable long-term source of nutrients for all the rooted plants in the aquarium display.*

Carbon dioxide fertilization

In most planted aquariums, CO_2 fertilization is essential for good plant health and is often the limiting factor in overall growth. Without adequate levels of CO_2, plants cannot photosynthesize effectively and therefore cannot produce the energy needed to perform basic physiological functions. There are several ways of introducing CO_2 into the aquarium. It is created naturally through fish and plant respiration, but mostly by bacteria as they break down organic matter. Many soil-based and established substrates will continually release CO_2, which can be used by aquatic plants. However, the quantities produced by these processes are minimal and would not be enough for heavily planted tanks. This is why additional fertilization is essential. Furthermore, the air/water exchange in an aquarium continually releases a large quantity of CO_2 into the atmosphere that must be replaced.

Because CO_2 is a gas, it is not possible to introduce it into the aquarium through conventional means, such as by way of liquid or substrate fertilizers. Various devices designed to introduce CO_2 into the aquarium are available for hobbyists and these include those using tablets that slowly release CO_2, slow-release chemical reactors, and pressurized CO_2 cylinders that can be adjusted and set by timers. All these systems introduce CO_2 gas directly into the aquarium water. The aim is to keep the gas in contact with the water long enough for it to be available for plants to absorb.

Simple methods of CO_2 fertilization

Tablets and powders that produce CO_2 when added to water provide the working principle for a range of simple CO_2 fertilization techniques.

A chemical reaction is activated inside this disposable container, which releases CO_2 over a month at a steady rate.

CO_2 collects under the "bell" and is absorbed into the water.

Above: *In this chemical-based system, a reaction between two compounds in a plastic container gradually releases CO_2, which is absorbed by the water. These aquarium carbonators are effective but inexpensive and simple to install in the tank.*

Slow-release CO_2 tablets

Slow-release CO_2 and potassium tablets

Slow-release CO_2 and manganese tablets

This powder is used to start the reaction inside the unit.

These tablets slowly dissolve, producing CO_2. Replace them when fully dissolved.

How CO$_2$ cylinder fertilization works

The aquarium lights provide an energy source for photosynthesis.

This valve closes when the lights are off, preventing the release of CO$_2$ gas.

Cylinder systems can be connected to a light timer so that gas is only released when the lights are switched on. Plants have no use for CO$_2$ at night and an excess at night can harm the aquarium.

The cylinder contains compressed CO$_2$ gas, which is released at a controlled rate via a regulator. The two dials indicate the release rate and the pressure of the gas in the cylinder, which reflects the amount of gas remaining.

The bubble counter allows tiny CO$_2$ bubbles to travel slowly upward, allowing maximum time for the gas to diffuse into the water.

Right: Cylinders containing compressed CO$_2$ are ideal for larger aquariums and long-term CO$_2$ fertilization. The gas produced is sent to a bubble counter, where it is kept in contact with the water for an extended time.

Connectors and valves are standard fit and suitable for all systems.

Right: Carbon dioxide gas enters at the bottom of this diffuser, or bubble counter. After a running-in period of about 48 hours, the bubbles stabilize and become smaller as they rise and release CO$_2$ gas into the water.

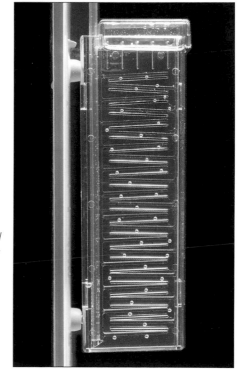

Macronutrients

These nutrients are used in the greatest quantity by aquarium plants and are vital to many plant functions. Without them, plants would be unable to grow, repair, or maintain healthy tissue.

Calcium

Calcium is a vital element used by plants in the formation of cell wall structure and to maintain cell permeability. It may also activate some enzymes. Although calcium is present in sufficient quantities in most water supplies, it may be deficient if only rainwater or reverse osmosis water is used in the aquarium. Many gravel-based substrates (other than quartz substrates) contain some calcium and this, combined with at least a partial use of tap water, should provide sufficient quantities of calcium for the majority of plants. In most cases, calcium should not be added artificially to the aquarium, as an excess will limit the availability of other nutrients and raise water hardness. However, many plants from naturally hardwater areas will require higher levels of calcium. Due to the fact that it is readily available in their natural environment, these "hardwater" plants are not evolved to collect calcium efficiently in low-level conditions.

Calcium is essential for basic plant structure and particularly important for plants from hardwater areas. This Crinum natans will thrive in medium water hardness levels.

Hydrogen

Hydrogen is used as water (H_2O), mainly as a structural component to fill cells, provide support, and as a means of transporting properties throughout the plant. Clearly, hydrogen as H_2O is easily available in the aquarium and there is no need to add more.

Carbon

Carbon is used by all living organisms as a basic structural "building block" and makes up 40-50% of a plant's dry biological mass. In terms of quantity, carbon is by far the most important nutrient. Plants obtain carbon from carbon dioxide (CO_2), which is broken down into oxygen (O_2) and carbon through the process of photosynthesis. Although plants need oxygen as well as carbon, the amount of oxygen required compared to carbon is minute, so the majority of oxygen is expelled as gas bubbles from the leaves.

CO_2 is a gas, so the amount present in a body of water is affected by the air/water exchange. If a body of water is highly agitated at the surface, then the air/water gas exchange is increased and the level of CO_2 in the water will rise or drop, depending on the level of CO_2 in the immediate atmosphere. For plants to obtain enough CO_2 from the water, the level of CO_2 needs to be much higher than normal atmospheric levels allow. This means that it must be introduced into the water from an internal source (i.e., not from the surrounding air). In nature and in the aquarium, CO_2 is introduced into the water as a result of the breakdown of organic waste by bacteria and by plant and animal respiration.

Plants can acquire the CO_2 they need by a number of methods, including direct uptake from the substrate through the roots, direct uptake from the water through leaves, "recycling" of respired CO_2, and through the breakdown of bicarbonates in the water. Although the concentration of CO_2 is highest in the substrate (due to the large amount of organic matter) it does not diffuse readily and therefore is not always available in large quantities in the immediate vicinity of the plant roots. The easiest way for plants to obtain CO_2 is directly from the surrounding water and through the leaves. In some aquariums, CO_2 levels are sufficient for good plant growth, although in most cases growth is limited by the amount of CO_2 present. Usually, it is necessary to introduce additional CO_2 to maximize photosynthesis and hence the amount of carbon available to the plants. There are several methods of introducing CO_2 to the water and these are discussed on pages 70–71.

Nitrogenous wastes produced by fish are a major source of nitrogen compounds in the aquarium. Plants absorbing these can help to keep the water safe for animal life.

Magnesium

Magnesium is a vital macronutrient for all plants with a part to play in numerous important functions, and an important ingredient in chlorophyll. Magnesium is also used to activate enzymes that form vital fats, oils, and starch. Magnesium is a "hardwater" nutrient and often found in levels proportionate to calcium levels. However, levels of magnesium in tap water vary a great deal depending on local conditions, so it is difficult to know whether additional fertilization is needed. Water authorities can often provide readings of quantities in the local tap water and test kits are available to measure levels of magnesium. The ideal level of magnesium in a planted aquarium should be about 5–25 mg/liter, although many plants live outside this range in nature. In general, there is usually sufficient magnesium in tap water in hardwater areas. Using a nutrient-rich substrate additive or soil-like substrate should provide a constant release of magnesium into the water. Alternatively, you can use liquid fertilizers, which are especially recommended for softwater aquariums. Many liquid fertilizers contain magnesium sulphate (better known as Epsom salts), which is ideal, as it provides both magnesium and sulphur. Bear in mind that an excess of magnesium in the water will inhibit the uptake of other nutrients, particularly potassium. In fact, potassium deficiency is often due to an excess of magnesium.

Tap water from hardwater areas has high levels of mineral salts and is a good source of magnesium and calcium.

Nitrogen

Nitrogen is one of the major nutrients required by all plants, both aquatic and terrestrial, for strong growth and good health. It is used mainly in the production of proteins and nucleic acids and makes up about 1-2% of a plant's dry weight. Plants do not take up nitrogen in its "raw" gas state (N_2) but can obtain it in a number of forms, including ammonia (NH_3), ammonium (NH_4^+), nitrite (NO_2^-) and nitrate (NO_3^-). Most plants take up nitrogen in the form of ammonium and nitrates, and although the preference varies according to species, ammonium is mainly preferred to nitrates. The main reason for this is that plants use ammonium to synthesize proteins, and if nitrogen is absorbed as nitrates, the plant must expend energy converting the nitrates back into ammonium. In the aquarium, ammonium is produced by fish in waste matter and as a result of the decomposition of organic materials. It is normally converted first into nitrites and then into nitrates by the bacteria in a biological filter. Many plants will take up ammonium before the filter bacteria are able to convert it, although the two are both in competition for the ammonium. However, do not be tempted to reduce the biological filtration with the aim of increasing the amount of ammonium available to plants. In soft, acidic water, ammonium is not dangerous to fish but in hard water with a pH above 7, ammonium is converted into ammonia, which is highly toxic to both fish and plants, making biological filtration even more important in hardwater aquariums.

Plants rely heavily on nitrates rather than ammonium as a source of nitrogen in hardwater aquariums. Although plants will often use nitrates only in quantity once the ammonium source is depleted, bear in mind that nitrates are a much safer source of nitrogen where fish are concerned, especially in harder water. Many liquid fertilizers contain nitrates as a nutrient ingredient, but it is important to keep a check on nitrate levels within the aquarium. In most cases, plants can obtain enough nitrogen from natural levels of nitrates produced as an end result of the biological filtration of aquarium waste (mainly from fish and, indirectly, fish food). Nitrate is easy to test for in the aquarium and many simple test kits are available for this purpose. Ideally, nitrate levels should be kept below 25 mg/liter. Many tropical aquarium fish can cope with levels higher than this, but in natural conditions plants rarely experience levels above 2 mg/liter, and levels above 30 mg/liter may be harmful.

Macronutrients

Oxygen

Oxygen is taken up by plants in its gaseous form (O_2), as water (H_2O) and as carbon dioxide (CO_2). Oxygen is a vital structural component of cells and used during photosynthesis, although it is also a waste product of photosynthesis. Plants obtain the majority of their oxygen through their roots and from respiration. (It is also released from the roots.) Aquatic plants have large internal "channels" that make up a high proportion of their structure. These are used for transporting oxygen around the plant, most notably to the roots. Once oxygen is transported to, and released by, the roots, it combines with carbon and/or organic elements within the substrate, creating CO_2, which is taken up for photosynthesis. Releasing oxygen around the roots also helps to prevent localized anaerobic conditions, which can damage roots.

Despite this high usage and waste of oxygen, plants do not do well in high-oxygen conditions and require only a small dissolved oxygen (D.O.) content. This is because when dissolved oxygen levels are high, a number of nutrients, especially iron (Fe), bind with oxygen and become too large to be assimilated by plants. High oxygen levels prevent plants from obtaining other vital nutrients in sufficient quantities. During the day, plants photosynthesize and produce waste oxygen, so there are never oxygen-deficiency problems at this time. The only time when oxygen becomes low is at night, when plants do not photosynthesize but continue to use up oxygen through respiration. In a heavily planted aquarium with little water movement or a large number of floating plants, the air/water gas exchange is reduced and oxygen levels may drop severely. However, levels rarely drop too low for plants, although they may drop below the levels needed by fish. In most cases, it is not necessary to provide oxygen and/or aeration in planted aquariums.

Adding oxygen through aeration is not normally needed in a planted tank.

Phosphorus is mainly absorbed through the roots, here of Crinum thaianum

Phosphorus

Phosphorus plays a vital role in energy transfer and is an important "ingredient" of genetic compounds and enzymes. Healthy root development and flower formation also depend on phosphorus availability within the plant. Phosphorus is taken up by plants through the roots in the form of phosphate (PO_4^-), which is present in the substrate at much higher levels than in the water. This is because phosphate will react with metal oxides – notably iron oxide – more frequently in open water, creating insoluble forms, such as iron phosphate, that cannot be used by plants. In open water, there is greater movement and mixing, hence the increased likelihood of contact between phosphates and metal oxides. This contact does not occur as often in the substrate, where phosphate remains in a usable form. In some cases, CO_2 produced by the roots during respiration can break down the bonds within insoluble phosphate compounds and allow phosphates to become available for plant uptake.

Phosphate is often present in fish food, so levels are rarely deficient in the aquarium. In an average aquarium phosphate levels are frequently 1–3 mg/liter, while in natural conditions levels are normally only about 0.005–0.02 mg/liter. Low phosphate levels are not normally a concern, but high levels can encourage algae to bloom. To grow strongly, algae require phosphate levels above 0.03 mg/liter; since these levels are usually exceeded in the aquarium, algae blooms are often the result. Under normal conditions, most phosphate is "locked away" in the substrate and unavailable to algae. There should be no need to add phosphate to a planted aquarium, although it may be present in some nutrient-rich and soil-based substrates.

Potassium

Potassium is a very important plant nutrient that should not be ignored in a planted aquarium. It is a key component of a plant's biological systems and used in protein synthesis, the opening and closing of stomata (pores), seed development, root production, disease resistance, and photosynthesis. A potassium deficiency creates an overall weakness in a plant's development and appearance and also impedes photosynthesis.

Plants absorb potassium as an ion (K^+) from the water, rather than from the substrate, despite the fact that both in nature and in the aquarium, most potassium leaches from the soil or substrate. We do not entirely understand why this should be so, but allowing potassium to remain in the substrate may increase the availability of ammonium to plant roots. As tap water contains very small quantities of potassium, it is important to introduce it artificially to the aquarium, either by means of a liquid fertilizer or, more commonly, as one of the ingredients contained in nutrient-rich or soil-based substrates. Potash and/or granite dust are often mixed with nutrient-rich substrates to provide potassium.

Floating plants, such as this *Salvinia natans*, are ideally placed to receive light and nutrients.

Sulphur

Sulphur is used in the production of amino acids, proteins, and chlorophyll, and is normally present in adequate quantities in tap water. Plants absorb sulphur in the form of sulphate (SO_4^{2-}), and many aquatic soil-based substrates contain sulphate in quantities that are quite adequate for most plants. Some fertilizers also contain forms of sulphate. Rainwater also contains relatively high levels of sulphate, but these levels vary considerably. One of the main reasons why you should be cautious about using rainwater in the aquarium is the high level of sulphur that can be present during the first few minutes of rainfall. Sulphur in its raw form is a dangerous chemical and should not be introduced into the aquarium in large quantities.

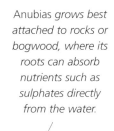

Anubias *grows best attached to rocks or bogwood, where its roots can absorb nutrients such as sulphates directly from the water.*

Micronutrients

These nutrients are required only in extremely small quantities and are often described as "trace elements." They play important roles in the biochemical processes that sustain life and are vital for good plant health.

Boron

Boron is absorbed by plants in the form of borate (BO_3^{3-}) and is required for cellular membrane function, root growth, carbohydrate transport, metabolic regulation, and flower production. Aquatic fertilizers often contain boron in the form of borate or borax (sodium borate) and it is also present in most tap water sources. Normally, boron deficiency is unlikely to occur in the aquarium and the nutrient is not considered a vital additional source of fertilization.

Iron

Iron is an important micronutrient used in respiration, enzyme production, and chlorophyll synthesis. Plants will absorb iron both through their roots and leaves. As a nutrient, iron is most useful to plants in the ion form Fe^{2+}, although in the presence of oxygen it converts into Fe^{3+}, which is difficult for plants to assimilate. This problem can be overcome by using chelates or chelated iron. (Chelates are dissolved organic substances that bind to metals and prevent them from forming larger molecules through oxidation.) The most common chelate used in fertilizers is EDTA, which is often used to supply chelated iron (FeEDTA). Fe^{2+} is then slowly released by the chelated iron and becomes available to plants.

Although iron – or, more precisely, chelated iron – is heavily promoted as a vital plant fertilizer, there is a plentiful supply in soil-based or nutrient-rich substrates. Iron and natural organic chelates, combined with a low-oxygen substrate, ensure that iron is always present in an available form. Most aquatic fertilizers contain iron and chelates and should always be used in aquariums without soil-based substrates.

Chlorine

Chlorine is absorbed by plants in the form of chloride (Cl^-) ions and is used for osmosis, ionic balance, and also in photosynthesis. Chloride is normally present in sufficient quantities in tap water (even after the use of dechlorinators), so should not present any nutritional problems for plants.

Nickel

Aquatic plants use nickel as an ion (Ni^{2+}) in extremely tiny amounts in the production of the enzyme urease (which breaks down the nitrogenous compound urea into ammonia). It is normally present in tap water and soil or in nutrient-based substrates. Nickel deficiencies or excesses should not occur under the vast majority of aquarium conditions.

Tiny quantities of micronutrients are needed by aquarium plants, such as this Echinodorus 'Rubin' narrow leaves.

Copper

Plants absorb copper as an ion (Cu^{2+}), both from the water and the substrate, although humic acids and organics in the substrate often bind with copper and other metals, making them unavailable for plant uptake. Copper is a key part of enzymes that facilitate respiration, but is only needed in tiny amounts by plants. Additional fertilization with copper is not required. Indeed, in most cases, tap water contains far more copper than plants require, but since they have little or no control over how much they absorb, they simply take up whatever is available. If they absorb too much, the result is metal toxicity, typically resulting in brown spots and tissue breakup. Copper is occasionally used in treatments to control parasites or algae, so use these with care.

The maximum safe level of copper in water is much higher for humans: 1.3 ppm (parts per million, equivalent to mg/liter) than for fish: 0.02 ppm. For this reason, plants offer themselves as a vital resource for reducing copper concentrations in the aquarium, which may be at dangerous levels for fish if the water is sourced from tap water. Plants are sometimes used exclusively for the purpose of removing copper and other dangerous metals.

Manganese

Manganese is absorbed as an ion (Mn^{2+}) through the roots and leaves of aquatic plants. It activates enzymes used in chlorophyll production and photosynthesis. Plants require relatively low levels of manganese, but it is still an important micronutrient. In most cases, manganese is present in tap water in sufficient quantities, but fertilizing with a liquid fertilizer will ensure that plants do not suffer a manganese deficiency.

Aquarium fish (here Apistogramma agassizi) are very sensitive to copper in the water, which plants can help to reduce.

Molybdenum

Molybdenum is an important nutrient for aquatic plants. It is a component of an enzyme used by plants to reduce nitrates (NO_3^-) into ammonium (NH_4^+) for protein synthesis, and is especially important in hardwater conditions, where little or no ammonium is available as a source of nitrogen. Plants absorb molybdenum in the form of molybdate (MoO_4^{2-}). This is available in tap water, but additional fertilization with substrate, tablet, or liquids will ensure sufficient levels in the aquarium.

Zinc

Zinc, an important nutrient for overall plant health, is a component of many enzymes and is involved in chlorophyll formation. Zinc is taken up in its nutrient form (Zn^{2+}) through the leaves and roots. At high concentrations it is toxic to both fish and plants, although sensible use of liquid fertilizers should ensure that these do not occur. Traces of zinc at levels high enough for aquatic plants are present in tap water, liquid fertilizers, and nutrient-rich substrates.

NUTRIENT DEFICIENCIES AND EXCESSES

An excess or deficiency of one or more nutrients can cause problems to both fish and plants in the aquarium. Because plants have no control over the amounts of some of the nutrients they absorb (such as copper) excesses can cause fundamental problems within individual cells that in turn affect the entire plant. Providing a correct balance of nutrients without supplying too much or too little of any particular nutrient is very difficult. The levels of most nutrients cannot be easily determined and the only way to judge whether there is a nutrient problem is to observe the health of the plants. Deficiencies can be spotted in many ways, mainly in the form of slow or deformed growth, alterations in the color of leaves, or a breakdown of cell structure. They may only affect some plants due to differences in individual nutrient requirements.

Sometimes, a deficiency of one nutrient can be caused by an excess of another. In this instance, the nutrient present in excess "competes" with the second nutrient, preventing it from being absorbed by the plant and causing a deficiency.

A good indicator of whether a particular problem is caused by an excess or a deficiency of a nutrient can be seen in the difference in symptoms between slow-growing and faster-growing plants. If there is an excess of a certain nutrient, faster-growing plants may not be affected because they can essentially 'dilute' the nutrient through fast production of new leaves. Slow-growing plants have no choice but to increase their buildup of the nutrient until signs of excess begin to show. The same process works in reverse; faster-growing plants will show signs of nutrient deficiencies before slow-growing plants, which have higher reserves.

Plants will generally take up more nutrients than they need and simply store them in the cell tissue for later use. Problems occur when the storage capacity of a plant is exceeded and the nutrient buildup becomes toxic, affecting the function of cells. For example, a buildup of iron manifests itself in the form of brown spots on the leaves. These are literally deposits of iron that have collected in one area. Over time, further deposits prevent the cells in that area from functioning properly and the affected area dies back.

Many nutrient problems take the form of yellowing of the leaf tissue – chlorosis – caused by a lack of chlorophyll. Chlorosis occurs when a plant is unable to produce normal amounts of chlorophyll due to a lack of nutrients. Since chlorophyll is used for photosynthesis, a lack of it prevents this vital process and affects every aspect of a plant's health. Many nutrients are used in the production and correct functioning of chlorophyll, so chlorosis can be used as a general indicator of nutrient problems in the aquarium.

The yellow areas on this leaf may be signs of poisoning or a deficiency of iron.

Propagating aquarium plants

In a healthy aquarium environment, many common aquarium plants will propagate themselves without any intervention from the fishkeeper. Other plants, often those with central stems, can be propagated by a number of artificial methods. Propagation is a good way of increasing the number of plants in the aquarium, as well as replacing old or tattered ones.

Sexual propagation

In the wild, many aquatic plants reproduce sexually, much like terrestrial plants, by producing flowers and seeds, or spores. When a flower is pollinated with the pollen from another plant of the same species, a viable seed is produced with the potential to grow into a new plant. The combination of genetic information from the two parent plants will produce a genetically different plant. Sexual propagation requires two or more plants to produce flowers above the water surface, and although this does occur in the aquarium if the environmental conditions are favorable, it is difficult to control. First you must encourage the plants to produce the strong aerial stems on which the flowers will be borne, so provide a well-ventilated area above the aquarium and below the light unit. Most plants that can produce aerial flowers will eventually do so, although this does depend on the water level, which may have to be lowered for some species. Most stem plants and lilies will produce flowers in the aquarium under the right conditions.

Once the flowers are produced they must be pollinated. In nature, insects are responsible for the transfer of pollen, both in aquatic and terrestrial plants, but to carry out the process artificially, transfer pollen from the stamen (male) to the stigmas (female) using a fine artist's brush. In some cases pollen can be used to fertilize the same plant from which the pollen was taken, thus creating seeds with an identical genetic makeup.

If pollination is successful and seeds are produced, plant them up immediately, as often they do not last long before starting to germinate. In many cases, it is better to plant the seeds in damp soil, rather than submerged in water, and grow them out of water until the seedlings are about 4 in (10 cm) tall. Then you can transfer them to aquarium conditions.

Right: The flowers of some aquarium plants are quite stunning in design. Spathiphyllum wallisii produces blooms that are robust and well able to withstand environmental pressures, both above and below the water.

Above: The flowers of this Bacopa monnieri are produced above water and will be fertilized by insects, much like terrestrial plants. This plant can also be propagated by cuttings and side shoots.

Propagating aquarium plants from seeds

The seeds of most aquatic plants are quite delicate and need not be planted deep in the substrate. Simply sprinkle them onto damp soil.

As the seeds begin to sprout, add a little water, so that the leaves are just covered. Some aquatic plants can be grown from seed above water, but they may not acclimatize quickly to the aquarium.

As the new plants grow, raise the water level so that the leaves remain covered. Once the seedlings have at least four or five leaves and are about 4 in (10 cm) high, they can be moved into the aquarium.

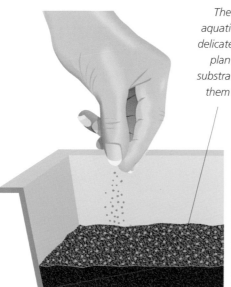
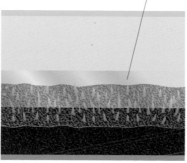
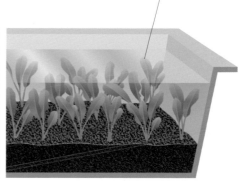

Above: *Barclaya longifolia (the orchid lily) can be propagated only by seed. At this stage, the seeds are ready to be removed and sown in damp substrate. Most should sprout and produce new plants, which can eventually be moved into an aquarium.*

Asexual propagation

The majority of aquatic plants propagate themselves asexually, both in nature and in the aquarium. In asexual reproduction, the parent plant produces "daughter" plants that are genetically identical. Although asexual reproduction occurs frequently in healthy, mature plants, you can encourage the process and ensure the survival of new plants.

Natural aquarium propagation

Aquarium plants reproduce naturally by means of runners, offsets, and adventitious plantlets.

Runners Runners are horizontal branches produced at the base of the plant that develop daughter plants (called slips) at the ends. The rootlike runners normally grow just above, or sometimes just below, the surface of the substrate and may continue to extend, producing slips along the runner at intervals of about 2.4–6 in (6–15 cm). The new slips obtain the majority of their nutrients from the parent plant and

quickly produce roots and new leaves, eventually anchoring in the substrate and becoming completely formed adult plants. The runners between the parent and new adult plants may break down or stay attached and continue to grow new slips. Each new slip produces a new segment so that a chained runner develops, rather than a long, single one.

To remove a daughter plant, cut and shorten the runner and trim the roots on the new plant before replanting it. The new plant should be at least a quarter of the size of the adult plant before it is removed. Detaching daughter plants may prevent the runner from continuing to produce new slips. A good method of selecting new plants is to allow the runner to produce several slips and then remove and replant the healthiest and/or fastest-growing ones.

Many floating plants also produce new plants on runners, although these should be left attached until the runner breaks down naturally. This will happen when the new plant is sufficiently well developed to survive on its own.

Common species of aquarium plants that propagate by runners include *Cryptocoryne, Echinodorus, Sagittaria, Vallisneria,* and some floating species.

Offsets Offsets are produced in a similar way to runners, but are formed much closer to the parent plant. Many plants that grow in clumps reproduce in this way. Some *Cryptocoryne* and *Echinodorus* species produce offsets, creating the appearance of a larger individual plant. Offsets can be gently removed from the main plant and replanted elsewhere in the aquarium once the roots have been trimmed. Separating offsets normally requires removing the whole plant from the tank first, so do not carry out this procedure too often, otherwise the parent plant

may sustain lasting damage. When moving established plants, be sure to remove the entire rootstock from the substrate. Any root left in the substrate will rot and could prevent plants from rooting in that area or adversely affect the health of nearby roots.

Adventitious plantlets Small plantlets that form on various parts of an adult plant are described as adventitious plantlets. Depending on the species, these may form on the leaves, stem nodes or on shoots. Small leaves are produced first, followed by roots, and the new plant remains attached to the parent plant until the area of attachment dies back and the new plant is released. Once a plantlet has a few leaves and at least 1.2–1.6 in (3–4 cm) of root growth,

Above: Water lettuce (Pistia stratiotes) produces new plants on runners. Eventually, the runner will begin to die and break apart, leaving a fully formed plant that will later produce its own daughter plants.

Propagating from a runner

These daughter plants of Echinodorus sp. are ready to be planted in the substrate.

The mother plant may produce more than one runner at a time.

Above: Many plants produce several daughter plants from one runner, so to obtain a larger number of plants, do not remove the runner until it has produced at least five or six plants.

1 Once the mother plant has produced a number of daughter plants with at least two or three leaves each, you can cut the runner with a pair of sharp scissors.

2 Separate the individual plants, or slips, leaving a small length of runner on either side. Handle them carefully, holding them by the leaf and not by the stem.

3 Put each new plant into the substrate, as described on page 53, leaving a gap of at least 2 in (5 cm) between the plants to allow for future growth.

it can be carefully removed from the parent plant and replanted. It is often best to leave the new plantlet to grow as much as possible before doing this.

Common species to propagate by plantlets include *Echinodorus, Microsorium, Aponogeton,* and *Bolbitis.*

Artificial aquarium propagation

Aquarium plants can also be propagated artificially by means of cuttings, and by dividing rhizomes and rootstocks.

Cuttings All plants with a central stem supporting a number of leaves can be propagated by cuttings. Most stem plants sold either as bunches or potted up are simply top cuttings from established plants. Cuttings can be taken from both the top and middle stem sections, as well as from side shoots. However, the top section of a stem plant includes the growing point and a top cutting is likely to establish more quickly than a cutting taken from other areas of the plant.

A normal stem will have a number of nodes (points at which leaves are produced) and these will also form roots if a cutting is taken. Using sharp scissors, take a cutting just above a node, with at least four or five nodes below it. The bottom set of nodes on the cutting will be the area where new roots develop. Carefully remove the leaves on these nodes and plant the stem cutting in the substrate so that the stripped lower nodes are just covered by the substrate. The cutting will start to produce roots and once firmly anchored in the substrate, should start to grow and produce new leaves. The plant that "supplied" the cutting should also continue to grow and may produce side shoots from the point where the cutting was taken. Since taking cuttings from parent plants or regular pruning encourages the production of side shoots, it can also be used as a method of creating a bushier plant.

Propagating from adventitious plantlets

Right: *New plantlets with well-developed roots are clearly visible at the tip of this Java fern leaf. You can either separate and replant these or leave them to develop and drop off naturally. Several plantlets may be produced from the same leaf before the leaf dies back.*

1 *The plantlets underneath this leaf are well developed, while the mother leaf is beginning to die back to allow the plantlets to drop off. This makes them easier to remove by hand and plant out separately.*

2 *The new plantlet is now large enough to be replanted. Simply pull it from the main leaf. As the mother leaf is beginning to fall apart, remove it from the main plant and discard it. Otherwise, it will simply rot away.*

Left: *One leaf may produce several plantlets in close proximity. When removing plantlets, check to see how many individual plants there are. Even quite small plantlets can be carefully separated and replanted.*

Rhizomes A rhizome is a modified stem that resembles a thick root at the base of the plant. It is often used as a storage organ, as well as for the production of new shoots. To get to it, you will need to remove the whole plant from the substrate, taking care not to damage the roots. To produce new plants, cut the rhizome with a sharp knife and divide it, ensuring that each division has at least one good shoot. If the original plant or any cuttings or divisions have a large amount of rootstock, trim this to about 1 in (2.5 cm) in length before replanting. Trimming the old roots will reduce the amount of damage caused by replanting and ensures that fresh, new roots develop quickly. Plants that root on rock and wood, such as *Microsorium* or *Anubias* species, can be propagated in this way. Using cotton, tie the new divisions either to porous rock or to suitable pieces of bogwood until they have become firmly anchored.

Division Plants that grow in clumps will either produce offsets or carry on producing leaves from the main rootstock. If a plant is large enough, you can divide the main root, creating two or more separate plants. Depending on the condition of the rootstock, either pull the plant apart gently or cut it with a sharp knife. Plant the divisions separately and they should develop into healthy new plants.

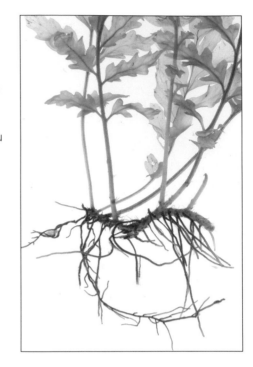

Right: The rhizome of this African fern (Bolbitis heudelotii) is clearly visible. A new shoot to the right of the rhizome indicates that this is the growing end and the best area from which to take a cutting.

Propagating from cuttings

Virtually all stem plants can be propagated by cuttings, taken from both the top and middle stem areas. Taking cuttings is also a good way of thickening up plants, as side shoots are often produced from the main plant as a result of cutting.

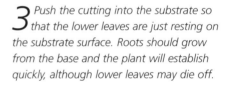

3 Push the cutting into the substrate so that the lower leaves are just resting on the substrate surface. Roots should grow from the base and the plant will establish quickly, although lower leaves may die off.

1 To take a top cutting, snip off a length of stem with several leaves or nodes. Cut between the nodes with sharp scissors. For the best results, take cuttings from the fastest-growing and/or healthiest stem.

2 Strip away the leaves from one or two nodes at the base of the cutting to allow the plant to root more quickly. Roots will form from the stripped node. Make sure it is beneath the substrate when planting.

Dividing cryptocoryne

Cryptocorynes are good examples of plants that produce many offsets directly next to the parent plant.

1 Start by removing the main plant from the substrate. Carry out this procedure with care to avoid any damage to the plant's roots.

2 Separate the leaves to establish the natural divisions within the plant. If the roots are relatively untangled, the plant can be separated by hand.

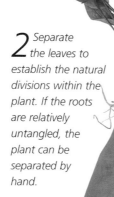

3 Once the plant has been divided, either by hand or using a sharp knife, trim the roots and replant the two separate sections into the aquarium.

Dividing Java fern

Because Java fern is grown above the substrate, the rhizome is easy to see and division is relatively simple.

Right: *This Java fern can be left to spread across the wood or divided into two, with one half replanted elsewhere in the aquarium.*

Below: *A good specimen can be divided into a number of plants. As they already have established roots, they should begin to grow almost immediately.*

Trim the trailing roots before replanting.

Left: *Cut the rhizome with a sharp pair of scissors. Each division should have at least two or three well-developed leaves, as well as a good root system.*

Maintaining a planted aquarium

Just like any other aquarium, a planted aquarium needs regular maintenance to keep the environment and the fish and plants within it healthy and active. Thankfully, a well-planted aquarium will virtually look after itself, as healthy plants will act in part as water purifiers, keeping the water conditions good for both fish and other plants. Because of this, most of the maintenance in a planted aquarium is concentrated on the plants themselves, which need constant trimming, separating and tidying up. If maintenance is carried out continually, but in small amounts, a mature planted aquarium will need only minimal attention, allowing you more time to spend appreciating the display.

The substrate

In many aquariums, it is necessary to clean the substrate regularly and remove the debris using a gravel cleaner. Removing organic debris helps to prevent decomposition, which releases ammonia and nitrites, and also combats bacterial diseases and algae. However, in a heavily planted aquarium, the organic debris produced from fish, fish food, and plant waste is often beneficial in the production and storage of nutrients within the substrate. As organics build up in the substrate, they act as "storage" components for nutrients, helping to replace those that may be lost over time from the initially nutrient-rich substrates. Gentle water movement from substrate heaters, and oxygen produced around the roots of aquatic plants prevent the substrate from becoming anaerobic.

Although it is true to say that a good substrate will look after itself for the most part, it will require a little maintenance and should not be left alone completely. First, you should remove any organic debris resting on the surface of the substrate. This "surface debris" does not help to store nutrients, but will promote bacterial problems in bottom-dwelling fish and may also clog fine-leaved plants, preventing light from reaching the leaves. Gently stirring the water above the substrate will cause the debris to rise higher into the water, where it can be taken up by filters. In an aquarium with a great deal of surface debris, this should be done at least three times a week, preferably more. Alternatively, surface debris can be siphoned away, but take care not to damage any plants in the process.

Despite the oxygen production from plant roots, and water flow through the substrate from heater cables, it is inevitable that anaerobic patches will occur. In most cases, small areas of anaerobic substrate are not harmful, and in some cases even beneficial (see page 47). However, a buildup of anaerobic substrate is harmful to the roots of aquatic plants, mostly through the production of toxic hydrogen sulphide, which will kill plant roots and other organisms. To avoid this problem, gently disturb the substrate every month or so simply by moving your fingers slowly through it, loosening the whole of the substrate, and creating gaps in it.

Over long periods of time, all substrates will lose their ability to hold one or more vital nutrients. This nutrient depletion can be countered by increasing other forms of fertilization, such as liquid fertilizers. Nevertheless, there usually comes a point when it is best to replace the entire substrate in the aquarium. This process is highly disruptive and it is vital to handle all the plants with great care. Remove each one individually and trim all the roots before replanting them in the new substrate.

Siphon gravel cleaners

Squeezing this bulb will start the siphonic water flow.

Some cleaners have taps in the pipe, allowing the siphon to be turned off and on again with ease.

Left: Various gravel cleaners are available, although all work on the same basic principle of gravity suction, removing the lighter wastes while leaving the substrate relatively intact.

Different-size gravel cleaners are available for different tank sizes.

Normally, you can replace the substrate and replant the plants right away, so simply store the plants in water from the aquarium while you replace the substrate. If the new substrate is to contain soil-like media, such as nutrient-rich substrates, you may need to strip the aquarium completely and add the substrate while the aquarium is empty. In this case, house the plants and fish in a separate aquarium with the water and filter from the original tank. Once the new substrate is in place, return the fish, plants, filter, and mature water to the original aquarium. A normal substrate, high in organics, will need to be replaced after about three years of use.

Equipment

Any pumps or filters in a planted aquarium will need the same maintenance as those in any other type of aquarium to keep them functioning correctly. Clean out internal filters and the media in them at least twice a month. External filters should be cleaned at least once a month. Always clean any

Below: *Sponge filters do not need thorough cleaning. Simply rinse them in water from the tank. Tap water contains chlorine, which may damage the useful bacteria in the sponge.*

ROUTINE MAINTENANCE IN THE AQUARIUM

Daily
- *Check for any missing livestock and examine the health of all the fish. Look for red marks on the body and gills, excess mucus, gasping or unusual behavior.*
- *Check the water temperature.*
- *Check that filters and lights are working.*

Twice weekly
- *Gently disturb any fine-leaved plants, such as cabomba, and dense foreground species, such as hairgrass, to remove any trapped detritus, which can hinder photosynthesis.*

Weekly
- *Test the water for nitrites (NO_2), nitrates (NO_3), pH and hardness.*
- *Remove dead leaves and other plant matter.*
- *Siphon out or remove any mulm from the top layer of substrate and replace the water removed during this process with new, dechlorinated water. This will also constitute a small water change, replacing minerals and helping to lower nitrates and phosphates.*
- *Replenish liquid fertilizers after water changes according to the maker's instructions.*
- *Using an algae magnet, pad, or scraper, clean the inside front and side glass, even if little algae is present. This prevents a build-up of algae that can be hard to remove.*
- *If you have a condensation cover, wipe it clean to avoid a reduction in light penetration to the plants.*

Every two weeks
- *Thoroughly clean half the sponge in the internal filter, using water from the aquarium. Then tip this water away.*

Monthly
- *Switch off external filters and clean the media in water from the aquarium. Then tip the water away.*
- *Replace any filter floss in an external filter.*

Every three months
- *Check the substrate for compaction and gently loosen it with your fingers.*
- *Remove and clean any impellers and impeller housings in pumps and filters.*

Every 6-12 months
- *If fluorescent tubes are the main source of lighting, replace them even if they are still working. After 10–12 months they will have lost much of their intensity.*
- *Replace filter sponges. Over time, the bacterial capacity of sponges will diminish and they need to be replaced. If sponges are the main biological medium, then replace half at a time, leaving a month in-between. This will reduce the loss of beneficial filter bacteria.*

When needed
- *Replenish liquid or tablet fertilizers according to the maker's instructions.*
- *Check and replenish any CO_2 supply systems that may be in use in the aquarium.*
- *Trim any tall stem plants, so that they do not grow across the surface and block out light to other plants. Replant the cuttings if you wish.*
- *If tall-stemmed plants are looking thin near the base, remove them, cut off the upper halves and replant.*
- *If the leaves of plants such as large Echinodorus sp. have grown too big, remove the outermost leaves and trim the roots slightly. The plant will respond by producing fresh, smaller leaves.*
- *Old plant leaves may become tattered or covered in algae. Remove them to prevent the spread of algae and to allow new leaves to grow.*
- *Over time, some plants will age and begin to look less healthy. They stop growing and become tattered. If this happens, remove and replace them. Be sure to take out the entire rootstock, as any pieces left over may rot and pollute the substrate.*

Above: *Chemical filter media, such as activated carbon, can be used to remove color and toxins from the water. Use them with care, as they can remove nutrients and treatments at the same time.*

Left: *Tannins released from wood can discolor the water. Although not harmful, this can look unsightly. Regular, but limited, use of chemical media should effectively remove such discoloration.*

filtration media in water from the aquarium; never use tap water, which may contain enough chlorine to kill beneficial bacteria. To ensure that any pumps remain in working order for as long as possible, be sure to clean both the impeller and the impeller housing. This can normally be done with a specially designed brush or pipe cleaner.

If the light in the aquarium is provided by fluorescent tubes, be sure to replace these every 12 months, even if they still appear to be working properly. The intensity of light from a fluorescent tube diminishes quickly and although a year-old tube may seem to be functioning correctly, its output will be less than half that of a new tube.

Any condensation trays or cover-glasses should be cleaned every week to prevent the buildup of deposits, as these will also significantly reduce the amount of light reaching the plants.

Water quality

It is important to check the levels of ammonia, nitrites, nitrates, pH, and hardness in the aquarium on a regular basis. If possible, carry out these tests every week and keep a record of each

one and the date it was performed. It is also possible to test for the presence of certain nutrients, but this needs to be done only when plants show signs of a deficiency or excess of nutrients. Keeping a record of test results is a good way of checking any trends in the aquarium, such as rises in nitrates or softening of the water over time. In most cases, regular water changes, using at least half tap water, will keep the aquarium water in good condition. The frequency of water changes depends on the individual requirements of the aquarium. For most planted aquariums, a small (10–15%) water change every week or two should be sufficient. Remember that water changes do not only reduce toxins, but also replenish nutrients, so even if the water quality seems good, you should still carry out water changes.

Tap water often contains high levels of chlorine, which will need to be removed before the water is added to the aquarium. There are many proprietary dechlorinators available for aquariums, but use these with care in a planted aquarium. Many water conditioners contain properties that remove metals

from tap water. Normally this is beneficial for both plants and fish, but many metals are also nutrients vital to plant health. Using metal-removing dechlorinators to condition water will not only remove useful nutrients from the new water, but also nutrients already present in the aquarium. There are various ways of preventing this. First, if you use dechlorinators, stick to the simple products and avoid those with "added benefits," such as metal removal, aloe vera and "conditioners." Second, remember that water can be naturally dechlorinated by aeration over a 24-hour period, without any need for chemical dechlorinators. This method is often preferable to using dechlorinators. Special "prefilter" units are also available that remove chlorine from tap water, but these are expensive and often unjustified.

Over time, water in a planted aquarium may appear to turn a slightly tea-yellow color. This happens as humic acids are released from organic material, particularly bogwood, and is sometimes unsightly, although the water is perfectly healthy. The coloration has no effect on plants or fish and is not a sign of poor water conditions. However, if you wish, you can remove the coloration using absorptive chemical media such as activated carbon. These types of filtration media should be used only for short periods, as they will also remove many useful nutrients (as well as medications) from the water.

The occasional use of chemical media in the planted aquarium may be valuable not just for removing water discoloration, but also to eliminate build-ups of unwanted metals and other chemicals. When using chemical media, do not carry out additional fertilization (other than CO_2 fertilization), as the introduced nutrients will simply be taken out by the chemical media.

Fertilizing

Establishing a good regime for introducing nutrients into the aquarium is vital for the continued health and growth of plants. The type and quantity of fertilization depends to a great extent on the dynamics of the individual aquarium. An aquarium with nutrient-rich or soil-based substrates may need only regular water changes with tap water and carbon dioxide fertilization to maintain sufficient nutrient levels. On the other hand, an aquarium with an inert substrate and few additional substrate fertilizers will need regular dosing with a liquid fertilizer, in conjunction with carbon dioxide fertilization. If an aquarium is deficient in only a few nutrients, such as iron and potassium, it may be necessary to add specific fertilizers regularly. Whatever the circumstances, it is important that any fertilizer regimes are maintained on a consistent basis to ensure good plant health in the display aquarium.

Keeping plants tidy

In a healthy planted aquarium with good lighting and balanced nutrients, the plants should grow and propagate at a relatively fast rate. If left unchecked, an attractive display can quickly become a tangled mess of vegetation. To keep plants looking their best, they will need to be regularly trimmed and/or older leaves must be removed to allow healthy, new ones to grow in their place.

Stem plants will often continue to grow until they reach the surface, at which point they either grow horizontally across the water or produce aerial leaves above it. Unless you want to encourage this growth habit, you should regularly trim the top portion of stem plants. When trimming plants, it is often better to take off a significant amount – say 4–6 in (10–15 cm) – every other week, rather than small amounts two or three times a week, which could eventually damage the plants. Taking off a larger portion also allows you to replant the cutting as a separate plant if you wish. In any case, since the stem plant will eventually become worn out from continual growth and trimming back, you should use at least some of these top cuttings to replace the original plant.

Plants that produce leaves from the base, rather than on stems, can also be trimmed to prevent the leaves from growing too large. Older leaves (normally the larger ones) can be carefully separated from the base and discarded, allowing new leaves to form in their place. Applied over a period of time, this method of trimming can be used to influence the eventual size of the plant. For example, if older leaves are regularly removed before they reach their full size, the plant will remain small and compact. However, if the plant is allowed to grow large leaves initially, it will continue to produce larger and taller leaves in succession, and the plant will eventually attain a substantial size.

As leaves age, they often become covered in algae or may begin to die off at the edges, sometimes developing dark

Below: Stem plants that reach the water surface can be trimmed with sharp scissors. Remove larger portions as needed, rather than regularly cutting small trimmings.

patches or even holes. At this point they should be removed from the aquarium, because not only do they become unsightly, but they are often less useful to the plant than the new leaves that would grow in their place.

Plants do not have an unlimited lifespan; there comes a point when individual plants simply stop producing new leaves and will need to be replaced. When taking out old plants, it is very important to remove as much of the root as possible. Any root left in the substrate will rot and may create anaerobic conditions.

Plant diseases and poisoning

Plants are as susceptible to disease as any other complex living organism, but luckily, plant diseases in the aquarium are very rare except in one case: cryptocoryne rot. Cryptocoryne rot is a disease that affects mostly the cryptocoryne family of plants. Its cause is not entirely understood, but it is often triggered by changes in environmental conditions. The symptoms include holes or perforated patches in the leaves, followed by a complete degradation of the leaf tissue, sometimes resulting in the death of the plant. If aquarium conditions are good in terms of water quality and nutrients, most plants recover once they become established.

Like fish and other living organisms, plants can be adversely affected by a number of chemicals, and poisoning can easily occur in plants. The symptoms of poisoning often show as a random degeneration of leaf tissue, holes, or generally ill or weak-looking plants. Sometimes the symptoms are very similar to those produced as a result of nutrient deficiencies, although in cases of poisoning, the symptoms appear much more quickly. Poisoning can occur as a result of using chemical treatments in the aquarium. Disease treatments and algae treatments, as well as snail-killers all contain strong chemicals, so always

check that a particular treatment is safe to use with plants, particularly in the case of algae treatments.

Allelopathy

Allelopathy describes the production of chemicals by an organism that adversely affect another organism and/or advantageously affect itself. In the case of plants, these chemicals (called allelochemicals) are often readily produced to inhibit the growth of other plants or algae, or to prevent animals from eating the plant. Plants depend heavily on allelochemicals because they are unable to defend themselves in a mobile way (i.e., they cannot run, move, or fight in the traditional sense). In nature, although these chemicals may be produced in abundance, they are often diluted in effect where a single plant is concerned. Only when a particular species is grouped over a wide area can a noticeable effect be seen. However, in the enclosed environment of the aquarium, allelochemicals can quickly

build up, with various effects on some plant species. For example, it is not unusual for an aquarist to have problems keeping certain species of plant, even though the lighting, temperature, and water quality are at ideal levels, and there is an abundant supply of nutrients. Often, the reason for this common occurrence is that another plant in the aquarium is producing particular allelochemicals that inhibit or prevent the growth of the problem plant.

The allelochemicals produced by some aquatic plants have a particularly adverse effect on floating plant species and algae. This is one of the main reasons why a well-planted aquarium may not show signs of algae blooms, despite high nutrient levels and strong lighting. Although some information is available

Below: There are many reasons why algae may bloom in the aquarium. Normally, a change in the aquarium environment will help to remedy algae blooms. Take action before the algae swamp the aquarium.

relating to specific plants and the allelochemicals they produce, little is known about the process of allelopathy, so it is impossible to produce a list of compatible plant species. In most cases, it is a combination of chemicals, rather than a single allelochemical, that has an adverse effect on plant species. In any case, it is worth being aware of the process when keeping aquatic plants, because it can sometimes explain an inability to keep one species of plant, while others thrive.

Algae

Many forms of algae grow in the aquarium environment and an algal bloom can quickly swamp plants, competing for light and nutrients, until the plants are choked to death. Not only do algae inhibit plant growth, but they also look unsightly and can release dangerous toxins into the water, affecting both plant and fish health. It is impossible to eradicate algae completely, because wherever there is water, light and a minimal supply of nutrients, algae will grow. However, it is possible to keep algae to a minimum, and a little algae growth on rocks and wood may even add to the appeal of a display, as well as providing a source of food for some fish.

In most cases, a well-maintained planted aquarium experiences fewer problems with algae than an unplanted aquarium, despite the additional nutrients. Algal blooms occur in the aquarium only when certain conditions become ideal for algal growth. Fortunately, you can take steps to prevent those conditions from occurring.

Countless types of algae may be present in the aquarium environment, but most are variations on a few groups of common algae. The causes and remedies vary for each type, as does the severity of algal blooming. In many cases, an excess of organic materials and poor water quality or excess nutrients are the main causes of algal growth. An

excess of soluble iron is often a key factor in blooms of "green" algae, such as single-celled or filamentous algae. Some of these algae will suddenly bloom in the aquarium, while others grow slowly but continually.

Single-celled algae As the name suggests, these algae develop as single cells that do not join together or form larger organisms. In the right conditions, these waterborne algal cells can quickly multiply, creating "green water" in the aquarium. Since the individual cells are

Above: *Cleaning the aquarium glass every week, even when it appears clean, can help to prevent the formation of red and other algae. Use an algae pad designed for the aquarium and keep it solely for that purpose.*

too small to be trapped by conventional mechanical filtration, increased filtration, which is often the first obvious course of action, will not work. Although mostly seen in ponds, single-celled algae blooms can occur in the aquarium and the cause is usually a combination of bright, direct sunlight and a high level of dissolved organic matter. In ponds, UV (ultraviolet) clarifiers are used as part of the filtration system to kill single-celled algae. Although UV light units are available for aquariums, they are not recommended for planted systems because the process can break down some nutrients. The best course of action is to reduce or block any natural sunlight reaching the aquarium and try to reduce the amount of dissolved organic matter. A reduction in the amount of fish feeding and liquid fertilizer dosing, combined with a siphoning or gravel cleaning of the uppermost layer of substrate, should achieve a significant reduction in dissolved organics. If no improvement is seen within a week, a chemical solution may be required.

There are several algae treatments available specifically for single-celled algae. These are often labeled as "green water" treatments. Most of them work by binding the individual algal cells together into larger clumps (a process known as "flocculation"), which can then be taken up by a mechanical filter or siphoned away from the substrate during routine maintenance.

Filamentous algae This is one of the most common aquarium algae and occurs in a number of forms, variously described as thread algae, hair algae, or blanketweed. The algae is produced as long, fibrous, hairlike threads that grow from any surface, usually toward the top of the aquarium and often on the aquarium glass and in areas of water movement. If the conditions are right, this algae will bloom quickly and cover plants and decor, causing many problems within the aquarium. Again, strong light or sunlight, combined with an excess of organic material, may cause this algae to grow. An excess of nutrients or slow plant growth also encourage filamentous algae, among other types, to bloom. Physically remove as much of the algae as possible and gravel clean the top layer of substrate to reduce organics. A temporary reduction in lighting may also help to eradicate the algae. Chemical treatments are available, but use them with caution, as many are harmful to plant life.

Blue-green algae The causes of blue-green algae are not entirely understood, although most occurrences are associated with high nutrient levels, poor water quality, and a lack of water changes. The velvety-looking algae appears as a thin, blue-green blanket across the substrate and/or decor and plant leaves. It is slimy to the touch and breaks up relatively easily. Often, the algae has a distinctive smell, which emanates from the aquarium surface. The algae is toxic as a food source, so algae-eating fish will not go near it. Treatment is not easy; only the most potent algae treatments will have any effect. The algae can be easily siphoned away, but may quickly regrow. A top-layer gravel cleaning and water changes may help to prevent regrowth.

Brown algae Brown algae is the most common type of algae found in aquariums and depending on various parameters, it may grow continually or never at all. The brown-colored algae is not fibrous and forms a covering on any solid objects, most notably, the aquarium glass. Providing any surfaces that show the algae are regularly cleaned, it very rarely causes any problems. Brown algae on the glass can be simply wiped off with a suitable cleaning pad. If there is

Left: Filamentous algae occur in a number of forms. In this case the algae is relatively short, but has spread rapidly to cover the leaves of smaller plants.

Below: Several liquid algae killers are available, but their effectiveness varies and the algae may return after treatments.

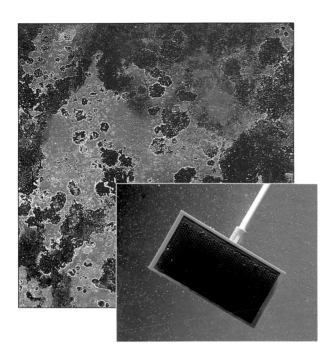

Right: *Brush algae is slow-growing but difficult to treat and/or prevent. Although it is not harmful, it should be removed to prevent excess growth, which may result in an unsightly bloom and have an adverse effect on the aquarium plants.*

Left: *Algae can build up on the inside of the aquarium glass and become difficult to clear. It is much better to use a scraper regularly to keep the surfaces clean.*

strong growth on plant leaves, it will also need to be removed. This should be done with extreme care so that the leaves are not damaged. A good method is to use cotton wool to wipe the leaves gently underwater. Brown algae is more common in aquariums with hard water and/or low light levels. This brown algae should not be confused with the "true" brown algae that include many complex saltwater seaweeds.

Brush algae Brush algae grows relatively slowly at first, but will soon begin to spread rapidly in most aquariums. It appears as small, furlike tufts, up to 0.4 in (1 cm) high and normally black or brown in color. The algae grows particularly well on bogwood, but will also flourish on the substrate and plant leaves, around filters, and in the corners of the aquarium glass. Unfortunately, the causes are largely unknown and therefore it is likely that there are no special conditions beyond those of a normal aquarium that encourage it to grow. Although there are some chemical treatments available to treat brush algae, their effectiveness is

wildly variable. The only way to ensure a reduction in growth is to remove any items on which the algae is growing. In some cases, the algae will continue to grow only at a slow rate and should not become a problem. It has been noted in a number of situations that the Siamese flying fox (*Crossocheilus siamensis*) may eat brush algae.

Using algae treatments
Chemical algae treatments should be used only as a last resort in aquariums, especially in planted aquariums, as the chemicals involved can be harmful to both fish and plants. Many algae treatments contain high levels of copper or flocculents (compounds that bind particles together), both of which can be toxic to fish either directly or indirectly. High copper levels also build up in plants and in many cases, in a well-planted aquarium, the copper will be taken up by plants before it begins to affect algae. In this instance it is possible that copper toxicity will occur in plants before the algae are greatly affected. Chemical treatments are only a temporary measure and will not eliminate the

causes of algae. If the cause of the algal bloom is not eradicated, the algae will simply grow back after treatment.

Natural prevention
The best way to prevent algae in a planted aquarium is to establish continued strong plant growth. Plants have many advantages over algae when it comes to collecting nutrients and utilizing sunlight, so good plant growth will often starve algae of nutrients. The allelochemicals produced by plants may also play a part in restricting algal growth. Whatever the reasons may be, a healthy, well-planted aquarium should rarely encounter harmful algal blooms. Algae-eating fish, such as many loaches and catfish, can also be introduced to the aquarium, as well as some snail and freshwater shrimp species. All these animals will browse on algae as part of their main diet and will prevent it from gaining a foothold in the aquarium. Do bear in mind, however, that algae-eating species are often selective and will eat only certain types of algae unless they are forced to do otherwise due to a lack of their preferred food.

Snails in the planted aquarium

Whether snails are useful or harmful in a planted aquarium depends largely on the number present and, to a lesser degree, the type of snails. Generally speaking, a small and controlled snail population is beneficial in a planted aquarium. Snails are scavengers, so as well as eating algae, they will also feed on any waste organic matter, be it in the form of fish waste and fish food or plant waste in the substrate. As they remove some of the organic debris found in the top layer of the substrate, which is not useful to plants, they reduce levels of harmful bacteria. In addition, they continually move the substrate about, preventing algal growth.

Unfortunately, most snail species rapidly breed in the aquarium environment and soon become unsightly. In large numbers, they may damage plants, although this is unlikely; the main reason for ridding an aquarium of snails is simply aesthetic. Any visible damage on plant leaves in an aquarium is far more likely to be nutrient- or water quality-related, rather than due to snail damage. Snails often eat "dead" areas of plant tissue, giving the impression of eating (and causing harm to) plants.

Snails are generally introduced into the aquarium by accident, often arriving on the leaves of plants. If snails are unwanted, the best time to remove them is before they enter the aquarium, so thoroughly check any new plants for snails before adding them to the tank. It is possible to buy solutions in which plants can be dipped for a short period to kill any snails that may be present. However, many of these treatments may not affect snail eggs, which appear as

Right: Larger snails, such as this Viviparus sp., normally found in garden ponds, can eat some delicate plant leaves and should be removed from the aquarium. Smaller species, such as trumpet or spire snails, are less harmful and sometimes useful in the aquarium.

small blobs of jelly on the stems and underside of plant leaves, and on the aquarium glass.

Snail populations already in the aquarium can be controlled by regularly cleaning the top layer of substrate, as well as by removing them. You can make a snail trap by placing a sinking food pellet (such as catfish food) underneath an upside-down saucer on the aquarium floor. Place this in the aquarium at night, when snails are more active, and the following morning there will be a congregation of snails underneath the saucer, which are easy to remove. Some fish, such as clown loach (Botia macrantha) or mollies (Poecilia sp.), will readily eat small snails, helping to keep populations to a minimum. Snail-killer treatments are available, but avoid them if possible as they can be very harmful to fish and plants if not added in the correct dosages. Much like algae treatments, chemicals used in snail killers are very potent and contain a number of toxic metals, including copper, which may harm many plant species, as well as some fish, including clown loach, which are very susceptible to strong treatments.

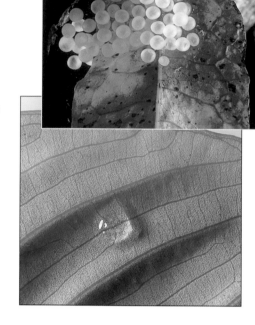

Above: The appearance of snail eggs varies. The eggs in the top picture are those of the large apple snail (Ampullarius sp.), while those in the lower picture are more likely to belong to a much smaller species.

Above: *The clown loach (Botia macracantha), a popular and attractive fish, relishes snails as a food source, just as it would in nature. In the aquarium, clown loaches will eat the younger snails, therefore preventing a population increase.*

Below: *Freshwater pufferfish (Tetraodon spp.), such as this Carinotetraodon lorteti remain small (less than 2.75–3.2 in/7–8 cm) but can easily crush snail shells with their teeth and welcome such a feed in the aquarium.*

Left: *If large snails are allowed to over-populate the aquarium, the damage can be quite significant, as seen on this previously healthy plant.*

Aquascaping

The difference between a well-planted aquarium and a stunning display aquarium lies in good aquascaping. Aquascaping is not just a matter of placing plants and decor in the right combinations or in the right places, it means being creative, imaginative – even inspired. There are certainly methods of planting and guidelines to positioning that will help you create a good display aquarium, but ultimately, the design should be the realization of your personal vision.

Suitable aquarium decor

These days, aquarists are faced with a wide range of rocks, wood, and other decor, but not all materials are suitable for a planted aquarium. When making a choice, it is often best to keep things simple and stick to, say, one or two types of rock, rather than crowd the aquarium with all manner of objects. All the decor should, of course, be bought and not collected from the wild. Clean it well before using it in the aquarium.

Rocks Be careful when choosing rocks; most are inert and suitable for the aquarium. They will have no effect on the environment, but others are calcareous and will adversely affect water quality by releasing calcium and carbonates that raise the pH and water hardness. There is a simple test that you can carry out on rocks to check whether they are suitable; simply put a few drops of vinegar on the rock, and if it fizzes or shows any kind of reaction do not use the rock. The fizzing is a result of the acidic vinegar reacting with the alkaline substances present in the rock. Calcareous rocks can be used in hardwater and marine aquariums, but not in planted or general community aquariums.

In the planted aquarium, rocks fulfill a number of roles, both practical and aesthetic. Smaller cobbles and pebbles can be used in the foreground, creating gaps between smaller plants and making open spaces more interesting. Larger rocks in the midground can also be used as breaks between planting areas and as bolsters to create raised substrate areas. Porous rocks, particularly lava rock, can be used as rooting media for plants such as Java fern *(Microsorium pteropus)* or *Anubias* species.

Granite pieces can be stacked or used individually.

Quartz is an interestingly colored rock.

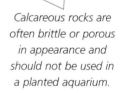

Calcareous rocks are often brittle or porous in appearance and should not be used in a planted aquarium.

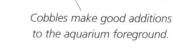

Cobbles make good additions to the aquarium foreground.

Once washed, coal is a striking rock that is safe to use in the aquarium.

ROCKS IN A PLANTED AQUARIUM

The following inert rocks are safe to use: coal, basalt, flint, granite, sandstone, quartz, slate, and lava rock.

Rocks to avoid include chalk, limestone, marble, and tufa rock.

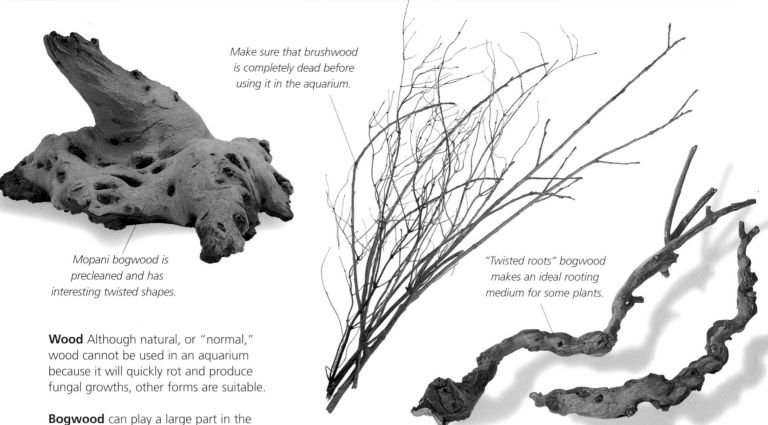

Make sure that brushwood is completely dead before using it in the aquarium.

Mopani bogwood is precleaned and has interesting twisted shapes.

"Twisted roots" bogwood makes an ideal rooting medium for some plants.

Wood Although natural, or "normal," wood cannot be used in an aquarium because it will quickly rot and produce fungal growths, other forms are suitable.

Bogwood can play a large part in the design of the planted aquarium. There are many different forms of bogwood, although these often arise from the different cleaning methods applied to the wood before it reaches the retailer. Some woods are precleaned using sand as an abrasive, which gives the wood a smoother and two-toned appearance.

Bogwood from aquatic retailers is safe to use in the aquarium without any prior treatment. This is because it has been dead and soaked for many years, during which time any harmful organisms will have been removed. Although you can safely place it directly into the aquarium, it is not inert. Various humic and tannic acids continually leach from it over a long period of time and although the effect is minimal, these acids will lower the pH and hardness of the aquarium water. This is not harmful to plants and may even benefit many species. Soaking bogwood for a week or two can help to remove some tannins.

The other side effect of using bogwood is that the tannic acids will color the water slightly, often making it a light "tea" color. This coloration can be removed using carbon or other absorptive media. However, these media should be used only temporarily in a planted aquarium, as they also remove nutrients vital to long-term plant health.

Bogwood is a good medium for planting up in the same way as porous rock and is suitable for mosses such as Java moss. Twisted roots, another form of bogwood, are particularly effective in the planted aquarium. Being long and thin, they do not take up too much space, but still become a dominant presence in the aquarium.

Cork bark can be used in some circumstances, as long as it is old and completely dry. The major problem with bark is that it is very buoyant and must first be fixed to a weight of some kind. It can be particularly effective if fixed to unsightly items such as bulky filters, or when used to hide inlet and/or outlet

Bark is highly buoyant and must be weighted down in the aquarium.

pipes. In this instance, the best method is to silicone the bark to the object while both are dry, before the aquarium is filled with water.

Brushwood is simply a term for the dead twigs and small branches from trees or bushes. Because the wood is very thin, it dies quickly and dries easily, making it safe for use in the aquarium.

Bamboo is available in several thicknesses, but bamboo canes are the easiest to find. Placing a number of canes among dense planting will create an interesting visual effect.

Above: *To ensure that woods such as bamboo last longer underwater, they can be varnished using a clear polyurethane varnish. Varnish both the inside and the outside of the wood.*

When using brushwood, it is important to make sure that it is completely dead, with no green areas present within the wood. If it is clearly dead and dried out, it should be brittle and will snap easily rather than bend when pressure is applied.

Bamboo is another form of wood with decorative possibilities in the aquarium. Various lengths of bamboo cane, placed randomly among dense planting, will add a natural and attractive element to many aquascapes. In time, it begins to rot and will need replacing, but this slow decay can be reduced – and in some cases prevented altogether – by coating the wood with a polyester resin or varnishing it before use.

Preparing wood
Woods such as bamboo, brushwood, and cork bark will need preparing before use. Dry woods such as these may contain fungal spores and are prone to rotting when wet. If they are placed in the aquarium without prior treatment they quickly decay, producing bacterial blooms that will appear as a slimy film over the wood and/or cloudy water. Fungal blooms (normally white or orange patches) may grow on the wood itself. To prepare brushwood and bamboo, coat the surface of the wood with a clear polyurethane varnish. It is important to use only clear varnish, as colored varnishes may contain chemicals harmful to aquatic life.

The inside of larger bamboo pieces contains a protective layer of film; remove this before varnishing. Also scrub the wood clean (using only water) and dry it before varnishing. Once the wood has been varnished and is dry, soak it for up to a week to make sure it is ready for the aquarium.

Bark does not normally need to be varnished as it is unlikely to rot underwater, but it will need to be cleaned and soaked before use. All dry woods will float and will take a long time before they are fully waterlogged and begin to sink. To solve this problem, the wood can be siliconed to rocks or to a flat piece of glass that will sit underneath the substrate, acting as an anchor to keep the wood down.

Over time, even well-prepared and varnished wood will rot and start to fall apart. When this begins to happen, the wood will need to be removed and replaced, although it normally takes at least a year for this to happen.

Fake or synthetic decor can also be used as part of the design, and many synthetic rocks, tree roots, and caves will look very realistic once they are established and a slight algal growth has lent them a weathered appearance.

Fake bark, ideal for hiding filters.

Below: *Artificial equivalents of natural decor make safe, although initially expensive, alternatives for planted aquariums. Once established, they can look very realistic.*

Natural-looking bogwood.

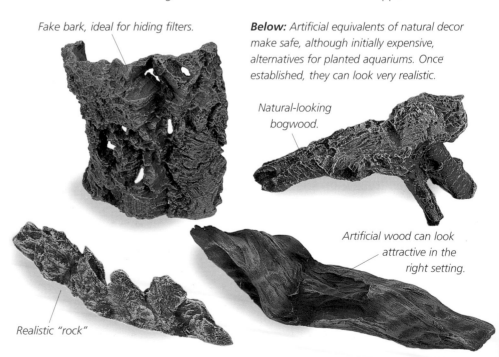

Realistic "rock"

Artificial wood can look attractive in the right setting.

Above: *Bloodfins and glowlight tetras will show better health and colors when kept in a well-aquascaped aquarium with plenty of places to hide, such as these granite rocks.*

Fixing items

Many types of decor, such as lava rock or cork bark, can be used to create a three-dimensional background in the aquarium. An almost vertical (rather than sloped) background will need to be firmly fixed in place to prevent any rocks from falling and damaging the glass panels of the aquarium. Silicone sealant is ideal for fixing items to glass and to each other, although the items must be fixed whilst the aquarium is dry. A good method to use for creating a backdrop is to carry out a dry run first and work out where you want each item of decor to be placed. Once this is done, clean and dry the individual items of decor to remove any dust before siliconing them securely in place.

In most cases, the silicone will be applied in areas that will not be visible, so it does not have to be very neatly done. It is usually better to use too much, rather than too little silicone. Any excess that can be seen from the front of the aquarium can be removed later with a sharp knife.

If the background is quite steep and likely to collapse until fully secured, place the empty aquarium on its back while you fix the rocks in position. It is a good idea to build up larger backgrounds in stages, allowing each stage to set so that you can check that everything is firmly secured before attaching another group of rocks. Placing the aquarium on its back while fixing rocks also gives you the opportunity to create overhangs and outcrops of rocks that can be used as planting areas and that also produce interesting shading effects in the lights.

Silicone sealant can also be used to fix together smaller individual rocks to create caves and hiding spots for the aquarium fish or to fix buoyant items to glass or rocks. Silicone sealant should be used only on dry items and you must wait for about three days before adding any water to the aquarium.

Laying out a design

Providing you have access to a good range of materials, it is sometimes possible to design and create a good display on impulse, but results are often far better if you do some preplanning. Sketching out a rough design for the aquarium allows you to assess the number of plants you will need and check the practical aspects of the display. Taking an overhead view, make a sketch of the aquarium, showing all the filtration, heating, and other equipment that will be present inside it and then divide the space into foreground, midground, and background areas. This sketch then becomes the framework on which you can build up the planting areas and position the decor.

When deciding where to place decor other than plants and designing the display as a whole, a good rule is to have one main focal point to attract interest and, using similar decor, a second, smaller area to provide a counterbalance. For example, you could complement a large, central group of cobbles and plants with a couple of smaller cobbles and plants elsewhere in the aquarium.

Simple or diverse?

There are many styles of aquarium design, from barren rockscapes to heavily and diversely planted "Dutch-style" aquariums. You could be inspired by such designs or simply use your own, but in either case it is important to stick to a single style within one aquarium. When using rocks, select one or two types and use them in various sizes, rather than mix several different types of rocks and individual pieces. The same applies to wood; it is usually better to use one type than many.

Plant species, on the other hand, can be used either singly, in small groups, or in large groups. A stunning aquarium can be created using one species, two species, or 30 species. A simple "lawn" aquarium can be created with only one or two plants, such as the pygmy chain sword (*Echinodorus tenellus*) or hairgrass

Below: Not all plants are restricted to the substrate. Plants that root on rocks or wood, such as this Anubias barteri, *can become a focal point in the aquarium and add welcome variety to the display.*

(*Eleocharis* sp.), which can be used to cover most of the aquarium floor. You can also add one or two pieces of bogwood with Java fern (*Microsorium pteropus*), Java moss (*Vesicularia dubyana),* or dwarf anubias (*Anubias barteri* var. *nana*) attached to them. Although simple in design, such an aquarium can provide a stunning display.

Grouping plants

Individual plant species all have a place in the aquarium. Taller stem plants and large-leaved species work well as background plants, while smaller plants can be used in the midground, with low-growing species in the foreground. However, there are no set rules for what constitutes a foreground or background plant and it is often better to mix up the areas a little. Generally speaking, a larger plant should be placed behind a

Above: An aquascape should be suited to the fish that inhabit the aquarium. These harlequins, gouramis, and kuhli loaches will all appreciate this heavily planted design.

smaller plant for obvious reasons, but plants can be grouped and placed in a number of different ways to create an interesting design. Although it is tempting to use many different species, it is often a lot easier and more effective to use a limited number of species in larger groupings.

Background planting The plants along the back of the aquarium should all be tall-growing species, and groups often look better than individual plants. In the larger aquarium, big-leaved plants, such as many of the larger *Echinodorus* species, can be used either singly or in well-spaced groups. As they can look quite imposing and often do not mix well with smaller-leaved stem plants, it may be better to complement them with large pieces of rock or wood. On the other hand, bushy stem plants, such as *Cabomba, Limnophila,* or *Myriophyllum* species, make good background plants when grouped together and combine well with adjacent, tall but small-leaved stem plants such as *Rotala, Egeria, Bacopa,* or *Ludwigia* species.

In areas of water flow, such as those near the filter outlet, the best background plants are those with long, narrow leaves. They are suited to the constant disturbance and create an element of movement in the aquarium. *Vallisneria* and *Crinum* species are ideal. Background planting can be extended around the sides of the aquarium to create a more enclosed environment and a "border" for the display.

Midground planting The "midground" is an undefined area – simply a mixing of the foreground and background. Plants that can be trimmed to variable heights are ideal here. Creating a "street" grouping of one particular plant, with taller specimens in the background, and others gradually becoming shorter toward the foreground is a very effective and visually appealing method of blending areas together. Stem plants with many large or long leaves are excellent for this purpose and include *Alternanthera, Bacopa, Heteranthera, Hygrophila,* and *Lysimachia* species. Plants that grow on wood and porous rocks also work well in the midground. *Anubias, Bolbitis, Fontinalis, Microsorium,* and *Vesicularia* can all be used in this way. "Specimen" plants can also look at home in the midground, providing they have sufficient space. In most average-sized aquariums, it is only practical to have a few specimen plants.

The midground is also the ideal spot for using decor other than plants. Rocks and wood can be used to create a divider between areas, but do not be tempted to make dividers throughout the aquarium display.

Foreground planting The foreground of the aquarium provides an open swimming area. So that it does not become an underwater jungle, it should occupy at least a third to half of the available space, assuming that the midground is an undefined area. Depending on the size of the aquarium, one or two "carpet-forming" species can cover an open substrate area without intruding on the swimming space. (You could use more in a larger tank.) Plant groups of *Cryptocoryne parva, C. willisii, Echinodorus tenellus,* and *Eleocharis* species here, leaving at least 3–4 in (7.5–10 cm) between plants for growth. The counterbalance rule can be applied here; create one large group of a particular plant and complement it with a smaller group elsewhere.

The foreground of the aquarium is a good site for individual specimen plants, either in their own space or among the "carpet-forming" species. Small pieces of bogwood or small stones and pebbles add interest to the foreground.

Raised areas We have seen how to create "streets" of plants graded in height from the taller background to the smaller mid-foreground specimens. A similar effect can be achieved using raised areas of substrate. Place large flat rocks upright in the substrate and build up substrate behind them to create a raised area. This allows you to use smaller plants toward the mid and background areas and helps to define plants in the foreground, in front of the rock. This "terrace" effect can be created a number of times in the same aquarium, providing there is sufficient space. The deeper substrate should consist of a mixture of various-sized cobbles, topped with the same substrate used elsewhere in the aquarium. The cobbles in the lower layers should help to prevent any major compaction and anaerobic conditions.

Below: The foreground, midground, and background plants are clearly defined in this attractive and carefully designed aquascape. The use of different and contrasting leaf shapes, along with sparingly used rockwork, help to define each area of the display.

Placing plants in the aquarium

BACKGROUND

Alternanthera reineckii
Ammannia gracilis
Anubias barteri var. barteri
Anubias congensis
Aponogeton ulvaceus
Bacopa caroliniana
Barclaya longifolia
Blyxa echinosperma
Bolbitis heudelotii
Cabomba aquatica
Cabomba caroliniana
Cabomba piauhyensis
Ceratophyllum demersum
Ceratophyllum submersum
Ceratopteris cornuta
Crinum natans
Crinum thaianum
Cryptocoryne balansae
Cryptocoryne undulata
Cryptocoryne wendtii
Echinodorus amazonicus
Echinodorus bleheri
Echinodorus cordifolius
Echinodorus grandiflorus
Echinodorus horemanii
Echinodorus macrophyllus
Echinodorus major
Echinodorus osiris
Echinodorus parviflorus
Echinodorus uruguayensis
Egeria densa
Eichhornia azurea
Elodea canadensis
Eusteralis stellata
Gymnocoronis spilanthoides
Heteranthera zosterifolia
Hygrophila corymbosa
Hygrophila corymbosa 'Crispa'
Hygrophila corymbosa 'Glabra'
Hygrophila corymbosa 'Gracilis'
Hygrophila corymbosa 'Strigosa'
Hygrophila difformis
Hygrophila guianensis
Hygrophila polysperma
Hygrophila stricta
Limnophila aquatica
Limnophila indica

Limnophila sessiliflora
Ludwigia arcuata
Ludwigia brevipes
Ludwigia glandulosa
Ludwigia repens
Ludwigia palustris
Microsorium pteropus
Myriophyllum aquaticum
Myriophyllum hippuroides
Myriophyllum scabratum
Myriophyllum tuberculatum
Najas indica
Nesaea crassicaulis
Nuphar japonica
Nymphaea lotus
Nymphaea lotus var. rubra
Potamogeton crispus
Potamogeton gayii
Rotala macrandra
Rotala rotundifolia
Rotala wallichii
Sagittaria subulata
Shinnersia rivularis
Spathiphyllum wallisii
Vallisneria americana
Vallisneria asiatica var. biwaensis

Vallisneria gigantea
Vallisneria spiralis

MIDGROUND

Alternanthera reineckii
Ammannia gracilis
Anubias angustifolia 'Afzelii'
Anubias barteri var. barteri
Anubias gracilis
Anubias lanceolata
Aponogeton boivinianus
Aponogeton crispus
Aponogeton elongatus
Aponogeton madagascariensis
Aponogeton ulvaceus
Aponogeton undulatus
Bacopa caroliniana
Bacopa monnieri
Bacopa rotundifolia
Barclaya longifolia
Blyxa echinosperma
Blyxa japonica
Bolbitis heudelotii
Cardamine lyrata
Ceratophyllum demersum
Ceratophyllum submersum
Cryptocoryne affinis

Cryptocoryne albida
Cryptocoryne balansae
Cryptocoryne beckettii
Cryptocoryne ciliata
Cryptocoryne cordata
Cryptocoryne lutea
Cryptocoryne moehlmannii
Cryptocoryne pontederiifolia
Cryptocoryne undulata
Cryptocoryne walkeri
Cryptocoryne wendtii
Didiplis diandra
Echinodorus amazonicus
Echinodorus cordifolius
Echinodorus horemanii
Echinodorus opacus
Echinodorus osiris
Echinodorus parviflorus
Echinodorus quadricostatus var. xinguensis
Echinodorus uruguayensis
Egeria densa
Eichhornia azurea
Eleocharis acicularis
Eleocharis parvula
Eleocharis vivipara
Eusteralis stellata
Fontinalis antipyretica
Gymnocoronis spilanthoides
Hemianthus micranthemoides
Heteranthera zosterifolia
Hydrocotyle leucocephala
Hydrocotyle sibthorpioides
Hydrocotyle verticillata
Hygrophila corymbosa
Hygrophila corymbosa 'Glabra'
Hygrophila corymbosa 'Strigosa'
Hygrophila guianensis
Hygrophila stricta
Lagarosiphon major
Limnophila indica
Limnophila sessiliflora
Lobelia cardinalis
Ludwigia arcuata
Ludwigia brevipes
Ludwigia repens
Ludwigia palustris
Lysimachia nummularia

Ludwigia repens *grows up to 20 in (50 cm) tall and makes an excellent background or midground plant.*

Microsorium pteropus
Myriophyllum aquaticum
Myriophyllum hippuroides
Myriophyllum scabratum
Myriophyllum tuberculatum
Najas indica
Nuphar japonica
Nymphaea lotus
Nymphaea lotus var. rubra
Nymphaea stellata
Nymphoides aquatica
Potamogeton crispus
Potamogeton gayii
Potamogeton mascarensis
Rotala macrandra
Rotala rotundifolia
Rotala wallichii
Sagittaria platyphylla
Sagittaria subulata
Saururus cernuus
Shinnersia rivularis
Spathiphyllum wallisii
Vallisneria americana
Vallisneria tortifolia

FOREGROUND

Anubias angustifolia 'Afzelii'
Anubias barteri var. nana
Anubias gracilis
Anubias lanceolata
Aponogeton crispus
Aponogeton madagascariensis
Aponogeton undulatus
Bacopa monnieri
Bacopa rotundifolia
Blyxa japonica
Cardamine lyrata
Cryptocoryne albida
Cryptocoryne affinis
Cryptocoryne balansae
Cryptocoryne beckettii
Cryptocoryne ciliata
Cryptocoryne cordata
Cryptocoryne lutea
Cryptocoryne moehlmannii
Cryptocoryne parva
Cryptocoryne pontederiifolia
Cryptocoryne siamensis
Cryptocoryne undulata
Cryptocoryne walkeri

Cryptocoryne willisii
Didiplis diandra
Echinodorus bolivianus
Echinodorus opacus
Echinodorus quadricostatus var.
   xinguensis
Echinodorus tenellus
Eleocharis acicularis
Eleocharis parvula
Eleocharis vivipara
Eusteralis stellata
Fontinalis antipyretica
Glossostigma elatinoides
Hemianthus callitrichoides
Heteranthera zosterifolia
Hydrocotyle leucocephala
Hydrocotyle sibthorpioides
Hydrocotyle verticillata
Lagarosiphon major
Lilaeopsis novae-zelandiae
Lobelia cardinalis
Lysimachia nummularia
Marsilea hirsuta
Micranthemum umbrosum
Nymphoides aquatica
Potamogeton mascarensis
Sagittaria platyphylla
Sagittaria pusilla
Samolus valerandi
Saururus cernuus

Vallisneria tortifolia
Vesicularia dubyana

SPECIMEN

Anubias barteri var. barteri
Anubias barteri var. nana
Anubias congensis
Anubias gracilis
Aponogeton boivinianus
Aponogeton crispus
Aponogeton elongatus
Aponogeton madagascariensis
Aponogeton ulvaceus
Aponogeton undulatus
Azolla filiculoides
Bolbitis heudelotii
Cardamine lyrata
Crinum natans
Cryptocoryne balansae
Cryptocoryne siamensis
Cryptocoryne undulata
Echinodorus amazonicus
Echinodorus bleheri
Echinodorus cordifolius
Echinodorus macrophyllus
Echinodorus major
Echinodorus osiris
Echinodorus uruguayensis
Eichhornia azurea
Eichhornia crassipes

Above: *A close view of the floating leaves of Salvinia natans.*

Eleocharis vivipara
Fontinalis antipyretica
Hydrocotyle leucocephala
Microsorium pteropus
Nuphar japonica
Nymphaea stellata
Vesicularia dubyana

FLOATING

Azolla caroliniana
Azolla filiculoides
Ceratophyllum demersum
Ceratophyllum submersum
Ceratopteris cornuta
Eichhornia crassipes
Hydrocotyle leucocephala
Lemna minor
Lemna trisulca
Limnobium laevigatum
Ludwigia helminthorrhiza
Micranthemum umbrosum
Najas indica
Nymphoides aquatica
Pistia stratiotes
Riccia fluitans
Salvinia auriculata
Salvinia oblongifolia
Salvinia minima
Salvinia natans
Trapa natans

Vallisneria tortifolia, a compact species that will provide interest in both the midground and foreground areas of a planted aquarium.

A paludarium

In a paludarium, the design focuses on a combination of above- and below-water environments. A typical paludarium will be no more than a third to half full, so you will need a relatively tall aquarium to ensure that there is enough space above and below the water. The plants can be a mixture of aquatic, terrestrial, and marsh species, but all should do well in moist conditions. Mosses and ferns are particularly suited to paludariums. This example features only aquatic and marsh plants. The most vital part of the construction is ensuring that the rockwork is secure, so anchor it all firmly with silicone sealant before filling the tank. Good ventilation is also important to prevent the air from overheating and damaging plant leaves. Use an air pump to create small currents of moving air above the water.

Below: *A palludarium focuses on decor and plants rather than fish, but the combination makes such displays extremely effective.*

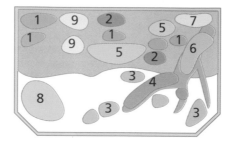

Plant list

1. *Acorus gramineus* var. *pusillus* (Dwarf Japanese rush)
2. *Anubias lanceolata* (Narrow-leaved anubias)
3. *Cryptocoryne* spp.
4. *Anubias barteri* var. *nana*
5. *Lysimachia nummularia* (Creeping Jenny)
6. *Microsorium pteropus* (Java fern)
7. *Ophiopogon japonicus* 'Variegatus' (Variegated fountain plant)
8. *Spathiphyllum wallisii* (Peace lily)
9. *Syngonium podophyllum* (Stardust ivy)

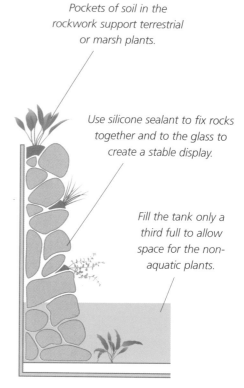

Pockets of soil in the rockwork support terrestrial or marsh plants.

Use silicone sealant to fix rocks together and to the glass to create a stable display.

Fill the tank only a third full to allow space for the non-aquatic plants.

Tank dimensions

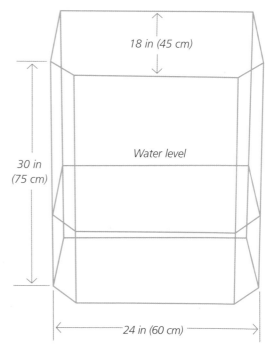

18 in (45 cm)

Water level

30 in (75 cm)

24 in (60 cm)

Acorus gramineus var. pusillus
(Dwarf Japanese rush)

Syngonium podophyllum
(Stardust ivy)

Anubias lanceolata
(Narrow-leaved anubias)

Ophiopogon japonicus 'Variegatus'
(Variegated fountain plant)

Lysimachia nummularia
(Creeping Jenny)

*Long, branch-style
bogwood adds to the
riverbank appearance
of the display and also
provides a medium for
growing plants.*

Microsorium pteropus
(Java fern)

*The water depth is only
a quarter to a third of
the aquarium depth,
but this is sufficient to
sustain emerging and
foreground plants.*

Anubias barteri
var. *nana*

*There are few plants in the
substrate so nutrient-rich
additives or heating cables
are not needed. A simple
pea-gravel or lime-free
substrate is adequate.*

Spathiphyllum wallisii (Peace lily)

Cryptocoryne spp.

Sphagnum moss covering the rocks

An open-topped aquarium

The water surface of an aquarium without a hood can be used as an extension of the display. Floating plants and leaves produced above the water add an extra element. If the aquarium is large enough, you can also include bogwood and houseplants. An open-topped aquarium must be illuminated with pendant-type lighting. If plants are to grow on or above the water surface, allow enough space (at least 18 in/45 cm) between the light and the water surface so that the leaves do not overheat. For the same reason, provide good ventilation. If the light source is very hot, it may be worth carefully positioning a small fan to create a cooling air current above the aquarium.

Recommended equipment

Because this aquarium is designed to be viewed from many angles, large and bulky internal filters may not be ideal. External filters will be far less restricting. Many of the plants (including the floating species) produce leaves above water and obtain carbon dioxide from the atmosphere, and the submerged plants are all relatively hardy species, so an elaborate carbon dioxide system is not essential. Carbon dioxide is still required, but a small, internal tablet or powder-based system will be adequate.

Tank dimensions

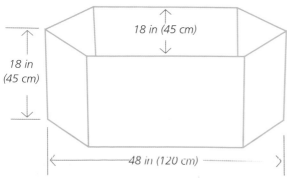

18 in (45 cm)

18 in (45 cm)

48 in (120 cm)

Echinodorus grandiflorus (Large-flowered Amazon swordplant)

Pistia stratiotes (Water lettuce)

Nymphaea lotus var. *rubra* (Red tiger lotus)

Echinodorus tenellus (Pygmy chain swordplant)

The substrate consists of a layer of sand, followed by a nutrient-rich layer and a lime-free top layer. A heating cable is ideal for the foreground "lawnlike" plants, which will spread rapidly with the aid of available nutrients in the substrate.

Anubias congensis (Congo anubias)

Salvinia auriculata (Salvinia)

Nuphar japonica (Spatterdock)

Cryptocoryne parva

Cabomba piauhyensis (Red cabomba)

Plant list

1. *Anubias congensis* (Congo anubias)
2. *Cabomba piauhyensis* (Red cabomba)
3. *Cryptocoryne parva*
4. *Echinodorus grandiflorus* (Large-flowered Amazon swordplant)
5. *Echinodorus tenellus* (Pygmy chain swordplant)
6. *Nuphar japonica* (Spatterdock)
7. *Nymphaea lotus* var. *rubra* (Red tiger lotus)

Floating plants

Pistia stratiotes (Water lettuce)
Salvinia auriculata (Salvinia)

SUITABLE FISH

Choose surface-dwelling fish for movement when seen from above. Floating plants and tiger lotus leaves provide cover for hatchetfish (Carnegiella, Gasteropelecus and Thoracocharax spp.), livebearers, and gouramis. Small algae-eating fish, such as Otocinclus, will browse on the leaves of Echinodorus tenellus. *(Larger algae-eaters may damage the thin tiger lotus leaves.) Small Corydoras catfish will remove debris from the smaller-leaved foreground plants. Tetras and small rasboras make good shoaling groups among the vegetation. For a more showy effect, choose larger fish, such as angelfish.*

A low-light aquarium

As we have seen, the correct lighting is vital for the continued growth and health of aquarium plants, but in some situations, providing suitably intense light may be costly or impractical. Luckily for the aquarist, there are plants that thrive in shady streams with little natural light, and these have adapted to grow in relatively dim conditions. Indeed, some of them will not do well if given too much light.

One limitation of low light conditions is that suitable foreground plants are hard to obtain. Because foreground plants are low growing, they do not receive as much light as taller plants nearer the water surface. This means that most foreground plants require a more intense light source in the aquarium. The exceptions to this rule are many *Cryptocoryne* species, which come from shallow streams, often shaded by terrestrial vegetation.

Many slow-growing plants, such as Java fern *(Microsorium pteropus)* or *Anubias* sp., can be kept in low-light conditions. Slow-growing plants generally have a slow metabolism, so they have less need of light energy. The plants in this display can be kept in a tank with one or two fluorescent tubes.

Salvinia auriculata (Salvinia). *Floating plants cast welcome shade on the plants positioned beneath them in the aquarium.*

Egeria densa (Elodea)

Hygrophila corymbosa

Cryptocoryne affinis

The background, floating, and wood-rooted plants take most nutrients from the water, and the foreground cryptocorynes will do well with liquid fertilizers and CO_2. Substrate is, therefore, relatively unimportant in this aquarium and a simple small-grade lime-free or pea gravel substrate will suffice.

Tank dimensions

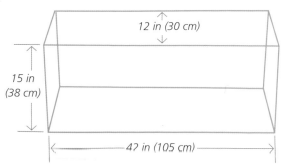

12 in (30 cm)

15 in (38 cm)

42 in (105 cm)

Most floating plants will thrive with only one or two fluorescent tubes. These run cool and do not overheat the delicate leaves.

Ceratophyllum demersum (Hornwort)

Microsorium pteropus (Java fern)

Cryptocoryne lutea

Anubias barteri var. *nana* (Dwarf anubias)

Cryptocoryne walkeri

Plant list

1. *Anubias barteri* var. *nana* (Dwarf anubias)
2. *Ceratophyllum demersum* (Hornwort)
3. *Cryptocoryne affinis*
4. *Cryptocoryne lutea*
5. *Cryptocoryne walkeri*
6. *Egeria densa* (Elodea)
7. *Microsorium pteropus* (Java fern)
8. *Hygrophila corymbosa*

Floating plant

Salvinia auriculata (Salvinia)

SUITABLE FISH

The smaller cryptocorynes should be kept free from algae and debris, so small algae-eaters, such as Otocinclus *spp., and scavengers, such as* Corydoras *spp., are fine. All the plants used here are quite hardy, so slightly boisterous fish can be added, such as barbs and danios. These fish will also appreciate the open swimming space in the center of the aquarium. Barbs, including the tiger barb (*Puntius tetrazona*), golden barb (P. sachsi), rosy barb (P. conchonius), black ruby barb (P. nigrofasciatus), and cherry barb (P. titteya), are all suitable.*

A *hardwater aquarium*

Depending on where you live, your water may be hard and alkaline (high pH). Although it is possible to remove hardness and soften water with proprietary chemicals and filtration systems, it can be costly and time consuming. Most plants do best in medium-soft water and although many will acclimatize to harder water for short periods, in the long-term, hard water will damage them and adversely affect their growth. However, there are hardwater areas in the wild where plants thrive, and the importance of soft water in planted aquariums is debatable as far as these species are concerned. A few plants survive notably better in harder water; a typical example is elodea or pondweed *(Egeria densa)*. Adding CO_2 in hardwater conditions is an excellent idea, as it will slightly acidify the water and compensate for the drop in available nutrients (see page 67).

Tall plants along the back of the aquarium will begin to grow around the sides to create a frame for the aquascape. Using smaller foreground plants or suitable decor in front of them helps to break up the solid appearance they create.

Tank dimensions

Vallisneria asiatica var. *biwaensis* (Twisted, or corkscrew, vallisneria)

Hygrophila stricta (Thai stricta)

Cryptocoryne wendtii

A mix of fine-grade pea gravel at the bottom and larger-grade toward the top will provide a good rooting medium. A layer of nutrient-rich substrate will boost plant growth.

Sagittaria pusilla (Dwarf sagittaria)

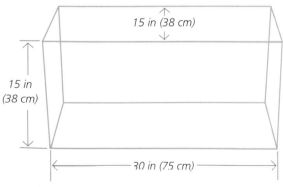

15 in (38 cm)

15 in (38 cm)

30 in (75 cm)

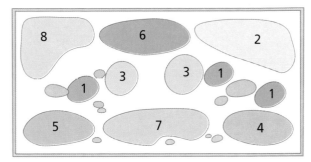

Cardamine lyrata
(Chinese ivy)

Cabomba caroliniana
(Green cabomba)

Aponogeton elongatus
(Elongated swordplant)

Cryptocoryne walkeri

Plant list

1. *Aponogeton elongatus* (Elongated swordplant)
2. *Cabomba caroliniana* (Green cabomba)
3. *Cardamine lyrata* (Chinese ivy)
4. *Cryptocoryne walkeri*
5. *Cryptocoryne wendtii*
6. *Hygrophila stricta* (Thai stricta)
7. *Sagittaria pusilla* (Dwarf sagittaria)
8. *Vallisneria asiatica* var. *biwaensis* (Twisted, or corkscrew, vallisneria)

SUITABLE FISH

Small, shoaling fish are ideal, although many tetras prefer softer water. Try danios, barbs, and some rasboras instead. Corydoras are useful for removing debris. Algae-eaters, such as Siamese flying foxes, Chinese hillstream loach, and the sucking loach, do well in harder water. Consider midwater shoaling fish, including White Cloud Mountain minnows, zebra danios, and giant danios. Many livebearers are also suited to this type of aquarium and to harder water. Common livebearers such as guppies, sailfin mollies, mollies, platies, and swordtails are all ideal additions.

A coldwater aquarium

The greatest variety of commonly available aquarium plants originate from tropical waters. This is good news for the majority of fishkeepers who keep tropical freshwater fish, but not for those with coldwater aquariums. Well-planted coldwater aquariums are rarely seen, although there are plenty of plants available that prefer colder water. Many of these are sold alongside tropical plants and also do well in warmer water. Another place to look for suitable plants for an unheated aquarium is among submerged or marginal pond plants. If you do use these, be sure to remove the aquatic soil they are planted in, as it will muddy the aquarium water.

An unheated or coldwater aquarium kept indoors rarely becomes very cold, often stabilizing at about 64–72°F (18–22°C), and should more accurately be described as a temperate aquarium. It may be worth investing in a heaterstat for a coldwater aquarium to prevent temperatures from fluctuating, which can adversely affect both fish and plants.

Tank dimensions

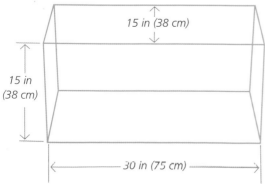

15 in (38 cm)

15 in (38 cm)

30 in (75 cm)

Vallisneria spiralis

Nuphar japonica (Spatterdock)

Egeria densa (Elodea)

Gymnocoronis spilanthoides (Spadeleaf plant)

Hydrocotyle verticillata (Whorled umbrella plant)

Eleocharis parvula (Dwarf hairgrass)

Lysimachia nummularia (Creeping Jenny)

Ludwigia palustris
(Broad-leaf
ludwigia)

Myriophyllum hippuroides
(Green milfoil)

*Potamogeton
crispus*

*Sagittaria
platyphylla*
(Giant sagittaria)

A bottom layer of soil-like, nutrient-rich substrate will satisfy the background plants, many of which are faster growing and nutrient hungry. (Potting soil would also be a suitable lower substrate for this type of aquascape.) This is covered by a deeper, lime-free rooting substrate. The smaller foreground plants are bog plants that prefer a dense and compact substrate.

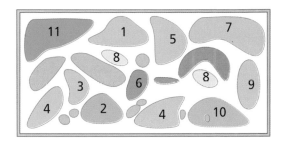

Plant list

1. *Egeria densa* (Elodea)
2. *Eleocharis parvula* (Dwarf hairgrass)
3. *Gymnocoronis spilanthoides* (Spadeleaf plant)
4. *Hydrocotyle verticillata* (Whorled umbrella plant)
5. *Ludwigia palustris* (Broadleaf ludwigia)
6. *Lysimachia nummularia* (Creeping Jenny)
7. *Myriophyllum hippuroides* (Green milfoil)
8. *Nuphar japonica* (Spatterdock)
9. *Potamogeton crispus*
10. *Sagittaria platyphylla* (Giant sagittaria)
11. *Vallisneria spiralis* (Straight vallis)

SUITABLE FISH

Coldwater aquariums are not limited to common and fancy goldfish, which may damage some plants when they are large enough. Instead, consider some common "temperate fish" that may prefer the cooler water. Good algae-eaters and scavengers include the Chinese hillstream loach, the sucking loach, and the weather loach. Some Corydoras spp. can also be kept in cooler water. Midwater swimmers, such as White Cloud Mountain minnows, zebra danios, golden and rosy barbs, will also enjoy cooler water. Beware of certain tropical fish, such as livebearers and plecs (Hypostomus spp.), which may become prone to disease if not acclimatized properly to coldwater aquariums.

An African pool

Two main styles of aquarium can be recreated here. The fast, open waters of the Zaire River, for example, are home to few plants, since the high oxygen levels and rapid waters make conditions unsuitable for many species. This type of display would resemble a mountain stream biotope. By contrast, the lowland swamps, pools, and slow-moving streams found in many places, often by the sides of faster moving waters, are filled with aquatic plants. Along the muddy banks, species of *Azolla, Eleocharis acicularis,* and *Ceratopteris* grow in dense clumps in the nutrient-rich water and substrate. Temperatures in these areas can approach 86°F (30°C), although these need not be recreated in the aquarium. For best results, provide soft water with a pH between 6 and 6.8.

   This aquarium represents the deeper area of a pool. The lack of water movement and large fish makes it a suitable environment for delicate-leaved species, such as *Ammannia* and *Barclaya* spp. The broken branches and wood often found in these pools can be represented by bogwood, which also releases tannic acids, helping to keep the pH level low. Many of the plants used here may need good lighting and a supply of liquid fertilizer.

Crinum natans (African onion plant) *needs plenty of space, as it will quickly grow upward and along the surface.*

Barclaya longifolia (Orchid lily) *will add a little color to the aquarium display.*

Tank dimensions

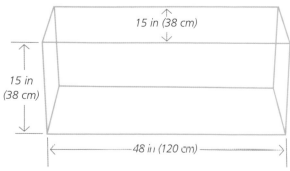

15 in (38 cm)

15 in (38 cm)

48 in (120 cm)

The substrate includes a nutrient-rich layer. A heating cable on the base creates currents to circulate a good supply of nutrients to the plants. A darker top layer of pea gravel or a dark lime-free substrate enhances the color of plants and fish.

Bacopa monnieri (Dwarf bacopa). *In open areas with bright light, the plant grows short and compact.*

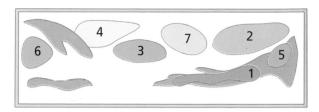

Lagarosiphon major (African waterweed) grows quickly and rapidly assimilates nutrients from the water.

Ammannia gracilis (Delicate ammannia). Bright lighting intensifies the leaf color.

Plant list
1. *Anubias barteri* var.*nana*
2. *Ammannia gracilis* (Delicate ammannia)
3. *Bacopa monnieri* (Dwarf bacopa)
4. *Barclaya longifolia* (Orchid lily)
5. *Bolbitis heudelotii* (African fern)
6. *Crinum natans* (African onion plant)
7. *Lagarosiphon major* (African waterweed)

Bolbitis heudelotii (African fern) should be placed in the top half of the display.

SUITABLE FISH
The waterways of Africa are home to many species of fish, including a large number of characins. This display has a large, open area toward the front, which is ideal for active, shoaling fish such as the Congo tetra. Many catfish also come from African regions, including many of the Synodontis group, but some grow too large for a well-planted aquarium. Smaller catfish will enjoy the hiding places provided by the bogwood. Active, open-water-swimming catfish, such as the African glass catfish, can be kept in shoals. Larger midwater swimmers, such as many anabantids, are also suitable. Many of the killifish family also originate from African pools, although there are far too many similar varieties to pick individual fish, and availability is often scarce.

Anubias species are tolerant of a wide range of conditions. Virtually any variety is suitable for this display, such as this short Anubias barteri var. nana.

Bogwood plays a significant part in this display. It provides a rooting medium for the bolbitis and for the anubias, which can be planted in any area of the aquarium.

An Indonesian stream

In the rain forests of Indonesia there are many small tropical streams, often slow moving and swamplike, with overhanging vegetation creating light and dark patches. A number of aquatic plants flourish in the iron-rich reddish substrate, which is interspersed with small pebbles and stones. Many of the species for this biotope are slow growing and do not require strong light, making this biotope an ideal one for beginners to attempt. However, not all the plants from this region will do well without strong lighting. Many are found in areas with little overhanging vegetation, where intense sunlight penetrates the shallow waters.

The red substrate often found in these types of streams is the result of iron, and can be recreated using a reddish brown gravel. Water quality should be neutral to soft (pH 6.8–7.2), with a temperature of 77–80°F (25–27°C). Provide additional CO_2.

Blyxa echinosperma
(Giant Japanese rush)

Hygrophila corymbosa
'Crispa'

Rotala wallichii
(Whorly rotala)

The close planting of the fine-leaved blyxa and broadleaved cryptocorynes provides a striking contrast in texture, especially as the two groups intermingle with each other.

Cryptocoryne affinis

An ideal substrate should consist of a fine or sandy medium, with an additional iron-rich planting substrate.

Tank dimensions

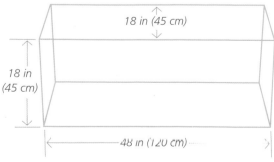

18 in (45 cm)

18 in
(45 cm)

48 in (120 cm)

Rotala rotundifolia

Bamboo canes and bogwood create good focal points in the display.

Microsorium pteropus (Java fern)

Cryptocoryne moehlmannii (Moehlmann's cryptocoryne)

Vesicularia dubyana (Java moss)

Cryptocoryne balansae

Plant list

1. *Blyxa echinosperma* (Giant Japanese rush)
2. *Cryptocoryne affinis*
3. *Cryptocoryne moehlmannii* (Moehlmann's cryptocoryne)
4. *Hygrophila corymbosa* 'Crispa'
5. *Microsorium pteropus* (Java fern)
6. *Vesicularia dubyana* (Java moss)
7. *Cryptocoryne balansae*
8. *Rotala wallichii* (Whorly rotala)
9. *Rotala rotundifolia*

SUITABLE FISH

Many aquarium fish come from the Indonesian region, including some loaches, anabantoids (gouramis), and barbs. Bottom-dwellers for this aquarium include clown, horse-face and kuhli loaches, and algae-eaters, such as the flying fox. For midwater swimmers, try tiger, checkered, five-banded or cherry barbs, and dwarf, harlequin, or scissortail rasboras. Some gouramis are also suitable and will do well in the hiding places provided by the plants and bamboo. Suitable anabantoids include Siamese fighting fish, three-spot, opaline and gold gouramis, pearl or chocolate gourami, paradise fish, and the kissing gourami.

A mountain stream

The mountain streams found at the source of many rivers are inhospitable places for aquatic plants. Fast-moving water constantly batters the leaves and removes useful nutrients, while high oxygen levels make life hard for many plants. However, a few are highly adaptable and, although sparse, are readily found in such environments. To imitate this biotope, use large, rounded gravel for the top layer of the aquarium substrate, plus a number of cobbles or rocks. Overpowered filtration or additional pumps will recreate the fast-flowing water.

CO_2 systems would be ineffective in this type of aquarium, as the increased air/water exchange would remove much of the CO_2 as soon as it was introduced. Instead, use liquid fertilizers to replace any substrate fertilization. Water quality is relatively unimportant to both fish and plants in this biotope. Recreating this type of environment in the aquarium results in a poor environment for most aquatic plants, but providing you choose the correct group of plants, you can be successful and achieve dramatic results.

Fontinalis antipyretica
(Willow moss)

Microsorium pteropus
(Java fern)

Bolbitis heudelotii
(African fern)

Tank dimensions

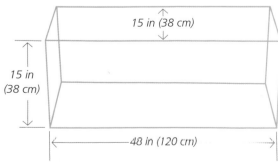

15 in (38 cm)

15 in
(38 cm)

48 in (120 cm)

Sagittaria pusilla
(Dwarf sagittaria)

*The bogwood looks like a
sunken tree root trapped
among the rocks.*

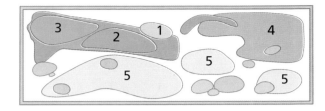

Plant list
1. *Bolbitis heudelotii* (African fern)
2. *Fontinalis antipyretica* (Willow moss)
3. *Microsorium pteropus* (Java fern)
4. *Vallisneria gigantea* (Giant vallisneria)
5. *Sagittaria pusilla* (Dwarf sagittaria)

Vallisneria gigantea
(Giant vallisneria)

Install powerheads or filter returns to produce strong currents across the tank. This will simulate the fast-flowing waters of the natural environment. Tall plants with flexible leaves emerging from the base will sway in the flow, enhancing the aquarium display.

Rounded cobbles and a large-grade top substrate will imitate the stream bed. For the best effect, use only one type of rock.

A smaller-grade substrate toward the bottom would provide a better rooting area for the plants. Pea gravel imitates the substrate of a fast-flowing stream, although an iron-rich nutrient substrate could be added underneath the main substrate for additional fertilization.

SUITABLE FISH
The fast-flowing nature of the aquarium can be enhanced by the use of fast-moving, active fish species. Fish with a "streamlined" torpedo body shape (long and thin) are often from fast-flowing areas, as are algae-eaters with flat, compressed bodies. Midwater swimmers include White Cloud Mountain minnows, zebra and leopard danios, pearl danios, giant danios, glass catfish, and silver-tip tetras. Some smaller catfish will also do well in this aquarium; a few interesting varieties include the striped talking catfish, royal panaque, upside-down catfish, and any of the shoaling Corydoras spp.

Fish for the planted aquarium

Some aquarium fish can be damaging to plants, although nearly all will appreciate a well-planted aquarium. Healthy plants provide hiding places, food, territories, and also help to make an aquarium a much better environment, in terms of water quality and aesthetics, for the fish. Many fish are also beneficial to plants, removing debris and cleaning the leaves of algae. A good selection of plants and fish will benefit each other and create a lively and interesting aquarium display.

Algae-eating fish

The leaves of aquatic plants are ideal surfaces on which algae can grow and if such algae is not removed from large-leaved or slow-growing plants, it can hinder photosynthesis (see pages 89–91). Removing algae growth by hand is tricky and usually results in damage to the leaves, so you need to find an alternative method of dealing with it. Most types of algae have high levels of protein and are very nutritious, making them an ideal food source for fish. Not all fish will eat large amounts of algae, but over many years, specific fish have adapted and evolved into excellent algae-eaters. Most of these fish are in the catfish group, although some loaches and livebearers are also good algae-eaters.

In a planted aquarium, it is important to use only smaller fish as algae-eaters; many algae-eaters grow quite large and then the damage they cause to plants outweighs their useful role in removing algae. Small catfish, such as *Otocinclus* and *Peckoltia* species, are excellent algae-eaters that can be kept in small groups in a planted aquarium. They will constantly graze algae from plants without damaging the leaves and will not grow too big. Loaches, such as red-tailed black sharks *(Epalzeorhynchus bicolor)* or ruby sharks *(E. frenatus)*, do attain about 6 in (15 cm), but are

normally delicate feeders. They are ideal for tanks with larger and tougher-leaved plants, such as some *Echinodorus* species. Siamese flying foxes *(Crossocheilus siamensis)* and sucking loaches *(Gyrinocheilus aymonieri)* are particularly good at eating algae; some flying foxes even eat brush algae, which many other algae-eating fish avoid. Guppies and mollies are also good algae-eaters and mollies also eat snails.

USEFUL ALGAE-EATING FISH FOR THE PLANTED AQUARIUM

Crossocheilus siamensis (Siamese flying fox)
Epalzeorhynchus bicolor (red-tailed black shark)
Epalzeorhynchus frenatus (ruby shark)
Farlowella acus (twig catfish)
Gastromyzon borneensis (hillstream loach)
Gyrinocheilus aymonieri (sucking loach)
Otocinclus affinis (dwarf otocinclus)
Peckoltia pulcher (dwarf plec)
Poecilia reticulata (guppy)
Poecilia sphenops (molly)
Poecilia velifera (sailfin molly)
Rineloricaria hasemania (whiptail catfish)

Scavenging fish

Many fine-leaved, grasslike, foreground plants will trap debris between their leaves. In nature, this debris would be

Above: *Although the popular red-tailed black shark* (Epalzeorhynchus bicolor) *can get quite large, it is a useful addition to a planted aquarium. This attractive, lively, and strikingly colored fish spends most of its time grazing algae from rocks and plant leaves.*

swept away by water currents and scavenging fish. Small scavenger fish can be introduced to a planted aquarium for the same purpose. Removing trapped debris will allow the plants to receive more light and the foraging activity also helps to move debris toward the filter, where it can be trapped and removed from the aquarium. Corydoras catfish are ideal scavengers and can be kept in small groups in the planted aquarium. Although scavengers will find many food items among the substrate, you should also feed them on sinking pellet or wafer foods to ensure that they receive the correct diet.

Some loaches, such as kuhli loaches *(Pangio kuhlii)*, or horse-face loaches *(Acanthopsis choirorhynchus)*, are excellent scavengers that also bury themselves and move underneath the top layer of substrate. This helps to turn over the top layer of substrate constantly, preventing algae growth and removing trapped debris. Fish like these spend most of their time hidden under the substrate, under wood and rocks or between fine-leaved plants. Although they may not be seen very often, they are doing an important job in maintaining the aquarium.

USEFUL SCAVENGERS FOR THE PLANTED AQUARIUM

Acanthopsis choirorhynchus (horse-face loach)
Botia lohachata (Pakistani loach)
Botia macrantha (clown loach)
Botia striata (banded loach)
Corydoras spp. (corydoras catfish)
Pangio kuhlii (kuhli loach)

Surface swimmers

Floating plants are useful as well as aesthetic in a planted aquarium. Surface-swimming fish, such as gouramis, livebearers, and hatchetfish, will welcome the hiding places provided by floating plants and their roots. Many anabantoids (which includes the gouramis), make bubblenests on the surface of floating plants in which to lay their eggs. This rarely happens in a crowded community aquarium, but if the water conditions are correct and the fish stocking level is low, a well-planted display aquarium with many floating plants provides an ideal environment in which many anabantoids can breed.

SURFACE SWIMMERS FOR THE PLANTED AQUARIUM

Betta splendens (Siamese fighting fish)
Carnegiella strigata (marbled hatchetfish)
Colisa lalia (dwarf gourami)
Colisa sota (honey gourami)
Kryptopterus bicirrhis (glass catfish)
Macropodus opercularis (paradisefish)
Poecilia reticulata (guppy)
Poecilia sphenops (molly)
Poecilia velifera (sailfin molly)
Thoracocharax stellatus (silver hatchetfish)
Trichopsis vittatus (croaking gourami)
Xiphophorus maculatus (platy)

Below: *Corydoras catfish are useful shoaling fish that will gently disturb the substrate in their constant search for food. These are* Corydoras trilineatus.

Above: *The beautifully patterned sailfin molly* (Poecilia velifera) *enjoys grazing on algae as part of its diet and may also eat some small snails. This confident fish will actively display its finnage in a planted aquarium.*

Above: *The hatchetfish group of fish will spend virtually all their time at the top of the aquarium, looking for items of food on the surface. These fish will appreciate the cover provided by tall or floating plants.*

Midwater shoaling species

Small tetras and rasboras make excellent, lively additions to planted aquariums. They swim in groups among the plant leaves and aquarium decor, often chasing each other to establish hierarchies within a group. Most tetras also prefer slightly soft and acidic water, which suits most plants, and are often the conditions found in aquariums with CO_2 fertilization. Since most tetras and small rasboras remain quite small, they

caring for those eggs and defending the young. Watching this process in the aquarium can be a very rewarding experience for the fishkeeper. Large plant leaves such as those of *Echinodorus* spp. make ideal locations for egg laying. Angelfish *(Pterophyllum scalare)* and discus *(Symphysodon* spp.*)* are particularly likely to use large leaves for laying eggs.

Dwarf cichlids display similar behavior in the aquarium, although many lay their eggs in natural caves as well as on plant leaves. These fish are ideal additions to planted aquariums with some open areas around the substrate, and display many more behavioral and personality traits than other fish.

can be kept in large groups and are unlikely to damage any plants. Some rasboras and danios are very active and prefer a moderate current in the aquarium water, with plenty of swimming space. These fish are more suited to a fast-flowing aquarium with robust plants and may not do well in a slow-current, low-oxygen, heavily planted aquarium.

SMALL SHOALING FISH FOR A PLANTED AQUARIUM

Hemigrammus bleheri (rummy-nose tetra)
Hemigrammus erythrozonus (glowlight tetra)
Megalamphodus megalopterus (black phantom tetra)
Megalamphodus sweglesi (red phantom tetra)
Nematobrycon palmeri (emperor tetra)
Paracheirodon axelrodi (cardinal tetra)
Puntius titteya (cherry barb)
Rasbora heteromorpha (harlequin rasbora)

SMALL SHOALING FISH THAT PREFER A CURRENT

Brachydanio sp. (danios)
Hasemania nana (silver-tip tetra)
Tanichthys albonubes
(White Cloud Mountain minnow)

Above: *A group of small, colorful fish, such as these harlequins* (Rasbora heteromorpha), *are visually interesting in any aquarium, but a well-planted environment will provide them with many places to dart in and out of.*

Larger midwater swimmers

Some larger fish can be used in the planted aquarium without risking damage to the plants and many will make a bold and welcome addition to a display. The most popular fish in this category are the angelfish *(Pterophyllum scalare)*, which will gracefully glide between taller plants such as *Vallisneria* spp. Although when fully grown, these fish will become large enough to eat smaller fish, such as young cardinal tetras *(Paracheirodon axelrodi)* or young harlequins *(Rasbora heteromorpha)*, they can normally be kept with significantly smaller fish.

Many anabantoid species can become quite large, including the popular gouramis, which can reach 4–6 in (10–15 cm), although they appear larger because of their rounded shape. Some larger fish, mainly some cichlids, will use flat surfaces on which to lay eggs. They then spend considerable time

LARGER FISH SUITABLE FOR A PLANTED AQUARIUM

Ctenopoma maculata (marbled ctenopoma)
Mesonauta festivus (festive cichlid)
Pterophyllum scalare (angelfish)
Symphysodon discus (discus)
Trichogaster leeri (pearl gourami)
Trichogaster microlepis (moonlight gourami)
Trichogaster trichopterus (three-spot gourami)

OTHER SMALL FISH OF INTEREST

Apistogramma agassizi (Agassiz's dwarf cichlid)
Apistogramma borellii (yellow dwarf cichlid)
Apistogramma cacatuoides (cockatoo dwarf cichlid)
Apteronotus albifrons (white-tip black ghost knifefish)
Papiliochromis ramirezi (ram)
Pelvicachromis pulcher (kribensis)

Large fish and plant-eaters

There are many fish that cannot normally be kept with plants. Some of the larger characins are herbivorous and quickly consume plants; aggressive cichlids also destroy plants, although this is a consequence of their territorial behavior, and not because they are searching for food; and large barbs, such

as tinfoil or spanner barbs, will destroy plants through sheer boisterous clumsiness. However, a few plants are robust enough to be kept with such fish and can be used to add a little vegetation to an otherwise barren aquarium containing these fish.

Java fern *(Microsorium pteropus)* is a robust plant with a bad-tasting toxin in its leaves that normally prevents fish from eating it, although most fish will make a few attempts first. Despite the taste, some large cichlids will tear chunks off Java fern, but herbivorous fish can normally be kept safely with Java fern.

Most *Anubias* species have thick, leathery leaves that are strong enough to survive a little abuse by larger fish. The same is often true of semiaquatic species, which have thicker leaves due to a waxy surface that prevents them from drying out above water.

Above: *Keep gouramis such as these pearl, gold and opaline varieties, in groups to avoid dominant aggression from individuals. These larger fish are graceful and slow-moving and will not damage plants.*

Below: *Very few cichlids are suitable for a planted aquarium, but this cockatoo dwarf cichlid* (Apistogramma cacatuoides) *will not grow large and will use plants to establish small territories and may even breed.*

Part Two
Plant profiles

Aquarists are lucky in that there are literally hundreds of plant species suitable for aquarium conditions. Not all these plants are found in nature; many are cultivated varieties developed by plant growers, wholesalers, and, in some cases, individual aquarists. As a result of crossbreeding and selective propagation, we can now choose from a wide range of plants with varied and interesting leaf shapes, colors, growth patterns, and care requirements. Many plants also have subspecies, which are usually slightly different in height or leaf shape. Whatever type of aquarium design you are aiming for, there will be a good choice of plants to suit those conditions. Most aquatic outlets stock a good selection of aquarium plants, which should vary slightly from week to week. But what happens if you are looking for a certain species or type of plant? If you are having difficulty obtaining a particular plant, you may find that one of the many mail-order suppliers will stock it, or something similar. Alternatively, your local retailer may be able to locate it from one of their suppliers. Whichever method you use to obtain plants, you should never be short of choices.

Although welcome, this wide selection of aquarium plants can be quite daunting. Where do you start? In the aquascaping chapter of this book, we looked at using plants in

Hemigraphis colorata

Aponogeton boivinianus

various areas of the tank: background, midground, foreground, etc. However, there are many other ways of grouping plants and drawing up a "short list" of suitable species by a process of elimination. For example, plants can be selected for suitability by their height, spread, lighting and nutrient requirements, temperature, as well as by location in the aquarium. A welcome challenge for aquarists is a biotope aquarium, where the fish and plants featured represent a natural habitat. In this case, plants can be chosen by their geographical origin. Or you can simply choose plants based on their colors, size, and leaf shapes. Plants in the aquarium should both contrast and complement each other, although choosing plants in this way is purely down to the artistic taste of the individual. However, a planted aquarium is not a static display and over time, plants can be moved around, swapped around, trimmed, propagated, or removed as required. A planted aquarium is quite literally, a living picture, and as such, it has a somewhat magical property. Choosing the right plants needs time and thought, although mistakes are easily remedied. In this part of the book over 150 plants are featured, along with detailed descriptions of their environmental requirements, growth patterns, origins, and recommended locations. We conclude with a brief review of some non-aquatic species that you can include in an aquarium. Using this guide, you will find it easy to select a range of plants to create your own "living picture."

Hydrocotyle verticillata

Cryptocoryne walkeri var. lutea

DIFFICULTY GUIDE

1 Suitable for beginners
These plants should do well in most aquariums. Fertilizer is not vital and most water conditions, including harder water, are suitable for them. Fluorescent lighting will be adequate. To ensure good health, use CO_2.

2 Hardy and adaptable
These plants will do well in most conditions, but some species may need brighter lighting. Provide CO_2 and fertilizer. Propagation should be easy. Soft water is best, but if adequate CO_2 is used, the plants should do well in harder water.

3 More challenging
These plants will need bright light, regular fertilization, CO_2, and a good-quality substrate. Propagation may be difficult and the plants may take time to become established. Generally speaking, they will do better in softer water.

4 Difficult to care for and propagate.
These plants must have strong lighting (use alternatives to fluorescent tubes, such as metal-halide and mercury vapor lamps). Provide a good-quality, iron-rich substrate, regular fertilizer, and CO_2 for best results.

Scientific name:
Ammannia gracilis

Common name: Delicate ammannia, Red ammannia

Origin: Africa

With its unusual leaf shape, *Ammannia gracilis* can look very effective when planted in groups and set against other plants with light green leaves. For the best effect, use shorter foreground plants around the base. The leaves vary in length depending on aquarium conditions. In good conditions, they may reach 4–4.7 in (10–12 cm) long, but 3.2–4 in (8–10 cm) is more usual. For the best results, provide bright lighting and a nutrient- and iron-rich, loose substrate. Under moderate lighting the leaves may appear thin and/or weak. Bright lighting intensifies the leaf color.

Maximum height: 10–20 in (25–50 cm)

Growth rate: Medium to Fast, depending on conditions

Area: Background, Midground

Light: Very Bright

Temperature: 72–82°F (22–28°C)

Propagation: From cuttings and side shoots

Difficulty: 2, 3

Scientific name:
Alternanthera reineckii

Synonym: *Alternanthera rosaefolia*

Origin: South America

This red-leaved stem plant can be found in many different leaf forms and shades of color. The top leaf surface may vary from olive-green to brown, while the underside is pink-red. A good source of iron will help to intensify the red color. The plant is easy to care for if given the right conditions, which include strong lighting and a good iron-rich substrate. In larger aquariums, plant *A. reineckii* in small, well-spaced groups around the center of the aquarium. The red leaves make the plant a good contrasting and focal specimen.

Maximum height: Up to 20 in (50 cm), usually less

Growth rate: Medium to Fast depending on conditions

Area: Background or Midground

Light: Bright to Very Bright. More light will increase health and color

Temperature: 72–82°F (22–28°C)

Propagation: From cuttings

Difficulty: 2

Anubias *species*

Anubias plants are a highly robust, undemanding, and adaptable group that can be used in a number of ways in the aquarium. The plants come from various river and stream areas in Africa and are usually found on the edges of waterways and in marsh conditions. They have an adapted rhizome and roots that will attach to solid objects, such as wood or rocks, so substrate conditions are unimportant. With the minor exception of Anubias gracilis, *lighting is unimportant; indeed, bright lighting may even slow plant growth. In open-topped aquariums, anubias can be grown out of water, providing the root is either submerged or in very wet conditions. This makes it ideal for use in bog aquariums or paludariums. Some anubias will produce flowers and fruit on long stalks.*

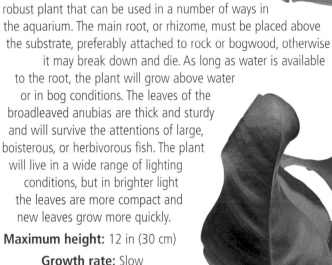

Above: *Anubias sp. can be planted on rocks, wood, or in the substrate but the rhizome (the thicker root) must be in open water, otherwise it may die.*

Scientific name:

Anubias barteri var. barteri

Common name: Broadleaved anubias

Origin: West Africa

This common *Anubias* species is an adaptable and robust plant that can be used in a number of ways in the aquarium. The main root, or rhizome, must be placed above the substrate, preferably attached to rock or bogwood, otherwise it may break down and die. As long as water is available to the root, the plant will grow above water or in bog conditions. The leaves of the broadleaved anubias are thick and sturdy and will survive the attentions of large, boisterous, or herbivorous fish. The plant will live in a wide range of lighting conditions, but in brighter light the leaves are more compact and new leaves grow more quickly.

Maximum height: 12 in (30 cm)

Growth rate: Slow

Area: Background, Midground, Specimen, or unusual

Light: All light conditions.

Temperature: 72–82°F (22–28°C)

Propagation: From side shoots or by dividing the rhizome

Difficulty: 1

The leaves of this Anubias *sp. are tough and will withstand many conditions.*

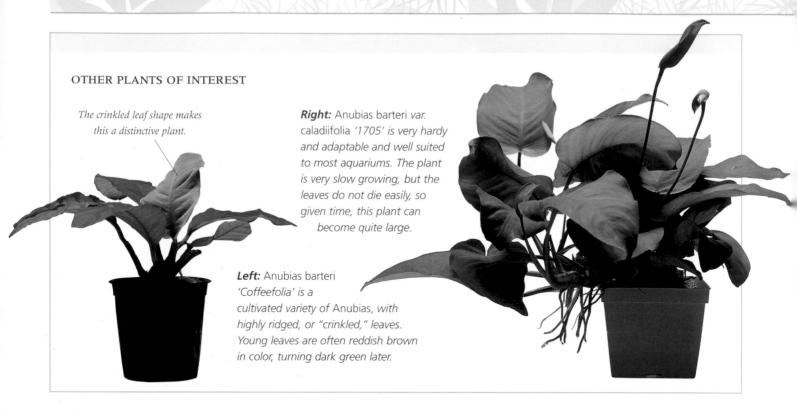

The crinkled leaf shape makes this a distinctive plant.

Right: Anubias barteri *var.* caladiifolia '1705' is very hardy and adaptable and well suited to most aquariums. The plant is very slow growing, but the leaves do not die easily, so given time, this plant can become quite large.

Left: Anubias barteri 'Coffeefolia' is a cultivated variety of Anubias, *with highly ridged, or "crinkled," leaves. Young leaves are often reddish brown in color, turning dark green later.*

Scientific name:

Anubias barteri var. *nana*

Synonym: *Anubias nana*

Common name: Dwarf anubias

Origin: West Africa

This is one of the smallest *Anubias* species and makes an ideal foreground plant. The leaves are dark green, robust both physically and in appearance, and grow to about 3.2 in (8 cm) on the end of short stems. The plant will produce side shoots and grow horizontally, producing stems and leaves from a central root, or rhizome. It is highly adaptable, sturdy, and well suited to any aquarium. This and other *Anubias* species can be grown on rocks and wood (see page 18).

Maximum height/spread: 4.7 in (12 cm)

Growth rate: Slow

Area: Foreground, Specimen, or unusual

Light: Undemanding

Temperature: 72–82°F (22–28°C)

Propagation: From side shoots or by dividing the rhizome

Difficulty: 1

Anubias congensis

Common name: *Congo anubias*
Origin: *West Africa*
Maximum height: *18 in (45 cm)*
Growth rate: *Slow*
Area: *Background, Specimen or unusual*
Light: *Undemanding; avoid very bright light.*
Temperature: *72–82°F (22–28°C)*
Propagation: *From side shoots or by dividing the rhizome*
Difficulty: *1, 2*
This adaptable and undemanding anubias has become more widely available in recent years. It will grow quite tall, so is best suited to the background of the aquarium. The thick, leathery leaves are terrestrial in appearance. The Congo anubias can be used in bog or marsh conditions or in an open-topped aquarium, where it may produce leaves above the surface.

Scientific name:

Anubias gracilis

Origin: Africa

The spade-shaped 3.2–4.7 in (8–12 cm) leaves and longer stalks give this anubias a much tidier appearance than smaller anubias, which may grow in seemingly random directions, but it is harder to care for than other anubias species. This plant does best when allowed to grow above the water surface and given plenty of nutrients. The substrate should be fairly loose and contain iron-rich fertilizer. In good conditions, this is an attractive and dominant plant that makes an excellent addition to any planted aquarium. For the best effect, give it plenty of room among smaller foreground plants.

Maximum height: 10–12 in (25–30 cm)

Growth rate: Slow, Medium

Area: Midground, Foreground, Specimen, or unusual

Light: Moderate or Bright

Temperature: 72–79°F (22–26°C)

Propagation: By rhizome division

Difficulty: 2, 3

This plant can be used in tanks with boisterous or herbivorous fish, which usually ignore it.

Scientific name:

Anubias angustifolia 'Afzelii'

Common name: Narrow-leaved anubias, Small anubias

Origin: West Africa

This anubias is often sold as *A. barteri* var. *angustifolia* and *A. afzelii*, although *A. afzelii* is taller. The elongated leaves resemble those of *A. lanceolata*, which has slightly longer leaves and grows to about 10–12 in (25–30 cm). This attractive, thick-leaved plant is tough and adaptable and suitable for aquariums with boisterous or herbivorous fish.

Maximum height: 8 in (20 cm)

Growth rate: Slow

Area: Foreground, Midground

Light: Moderate

Temperature: 68–82°F (20–28°C)

Propagation: Division, side shoots

Difficulty: 1, 2

Aponogeton *species*

The aponogetons are a group of more than 40 species from Africa, Asia, and Australia. The plants are found both in fully aquatic and terrestrial forms, as marsh or bog plants. In nature, many aponogetons occur in specialized habitats, adapted to the local environment. This specialization limits the number of plants suited to the broad-based conditions of the aquarium. However, about 15 varieties are suitable for the aquarium and around half of these are readily available. Many aponogetons are found in shallow bog or marginal areas that dry up annually. The plants found in these areas have a growth period that coincides with natural rainy seasons and a rest period during dry seasons. In the aquarium, these plants may grow well for a number of months and follow this with a period of little or no growth. Normally, growth is resumed if conditions are adequate. Conditions for good growth vary with individual plants, but a fine, nutrient-rich and warm substrate will benefit all aponogetons. Some varieties will do well in harder water, while others must be kept in soft water. Most aponogetons will produce stalks with flowers and produce fruit in the aquarium.

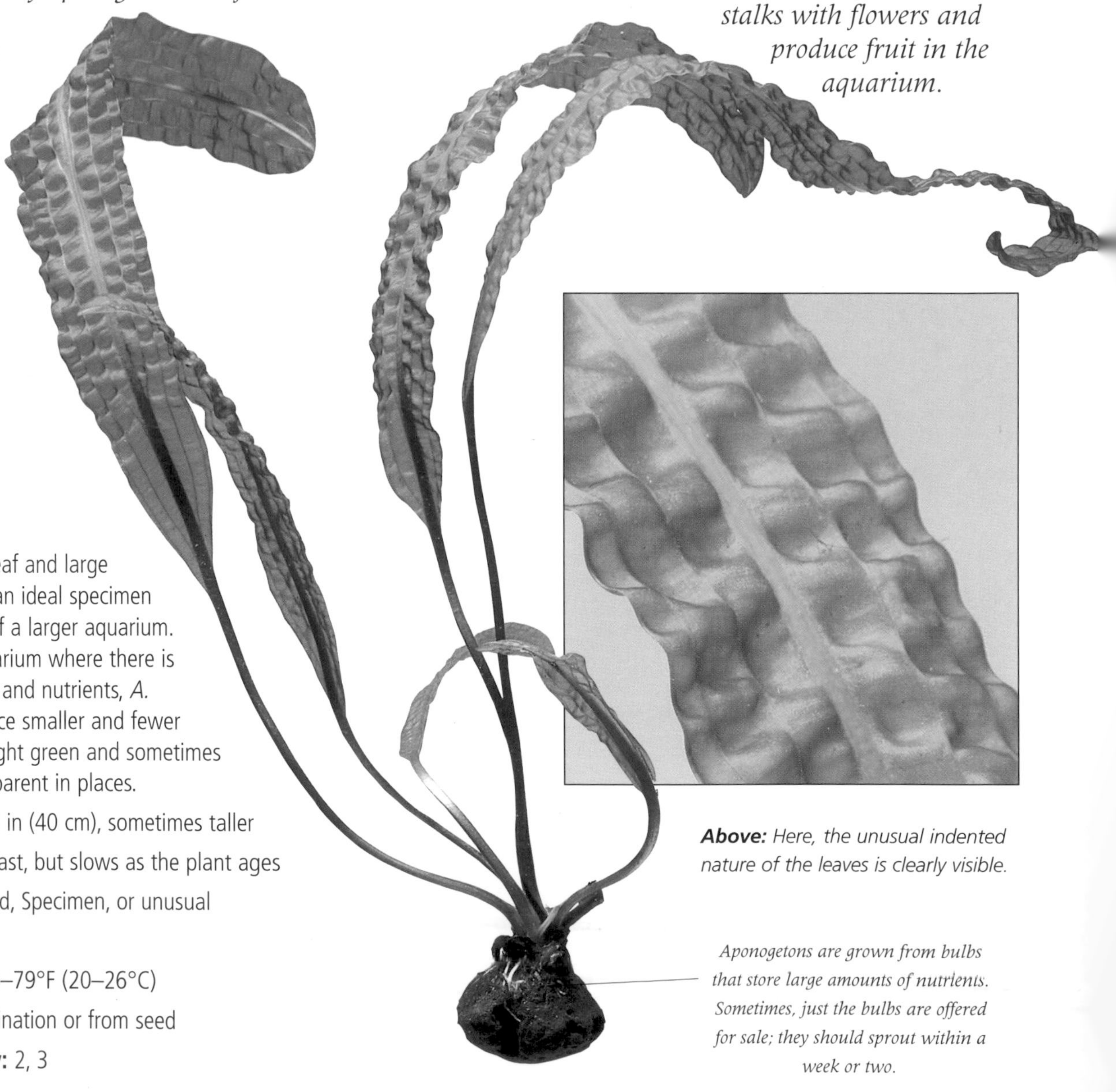

Scientific name:

Aponogeton boivinianus

Origin: Madagascar

The attractive crinkled leaf and large size of this plant make it an ideal specimen plant for the midground of a larger aquarium. In a heavily planted aquarium where there is competition for light and nutrients, *A. boivinianus* may produce smaller and fewer leaves. The leaves are bright green and sometimes slightly transparent in places.

Maximum height: 16 in (40 cm), sometimes taller

Growth rate: Initially fast, but slows as the plant ages

Area: Midground, Specimen, or unusual

Light: Bright

Temperature: 68–79°F (20–26°C)

Propagation: By pollination or from seed

Difficulty: 2, 3

Above: *Here, the unusual indented nature of the leaves is clearly visible.*

Aponogetons are grown from bulbs that store large amounts of nutrients. Sometimes, just the bulbs are offered for sale; they should sprout within a week or two.

Scientific name:

Aponogeton crispus

Common name: Crinkled or ruffled aponogeton

Origin: Sri Lanka

This popular, attractive and adaptable plant is readily available in the aquarium trade. Once settled into an aquarium and given all the right growing conditions, it will grow quickly, producing numerous olive green-brown ruffled leaves. These are normally up to 1.6 in (4 cm) wide and 8–14 in (20–35 cm) long. In weak light, the leaves are produced on longer stems that may spread across the water surface in search of more illumination. *A. crispus* may flower in the aquarium.

Maximum height: 14 in (35 cm), sometimes taller

Growth rate: A period of strong growth, followed by very slow growth

Area: Midground, Foreground, Specimen, or unusual

Light: Bright

Temperature: 72–86°F (22–30°C)

Propagation: By pollination or from seed

Difficulty: 1, 2

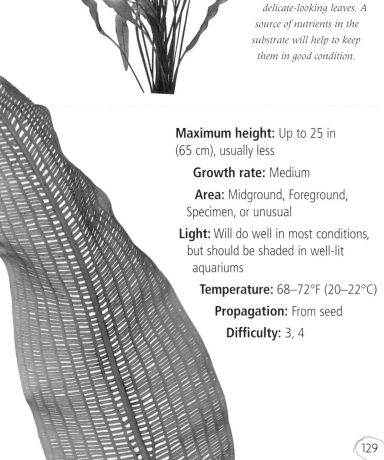

Many aponogetons have delicate-looking leaves. A source of nutrients in the substrate will help to keep them in good condition.

Scientific name:

Aponogeton madagascariensis

Synonym: *A. fenestralis*

Common name: Madagascan lace plant, Laceleaf

Origin: Madagascar

The laceleaf has become a popular aquarium plant, mainly due to its novel "skeletonlike" appearance. This is due to a lack of leaf tissue; only the interconnecting veins are visible. It is not an easy plant to care for and requires clean and clear water conditions. Any algae or debris will clog the leaves and undermine the health of the plant. Be sure to keep it in soft water with a pH of 7 or lower. Narrow and wider leaf varieties are also available.

Maximum height: Up to 25 in (65 cm), usually less

Growth rate: Medium

Area: Midground, Foreground, Specimen, or unusual

Light: Will do well in most conditions, but should be shaded in well-lit aquariums

Temperature: 68–72°F (20–22°C)

Propagation: From seed

Difficulty: 3, 4

Scientific name:

Aponogeton ulvaceus

Common name: Compact aponogeton

Origin: Sri Lanka

This aponogeton sports the common wavy-edged leaves of the genus, although the light green 1.6–2.4 in (4–6 cm)-wide leaves often appear smooth, shiny, and slightly fleshy. The plant often grows in spurts, producing numerous new leaves before slowing down and eventually shedding the old ones. In bright light it will grow taller.

The highly ruffled leaves of Aponogeton ulvaceus may vary in color and sometimes appear pale green-yellow. This is a natural coloration and should not be confused with a nutrient deficiency. Given time, the plant will produce many leaves and become a good showpiece.

Maximum height: 14–16 in (35–40 cm)

Growth rate: Medium

Area: Background, Midground, Specimen, or unusual

Light: Moderate to bright

Temperature: 72–82°F (22–28°C)

Propagation: From seed

Difficulty: 2, 3

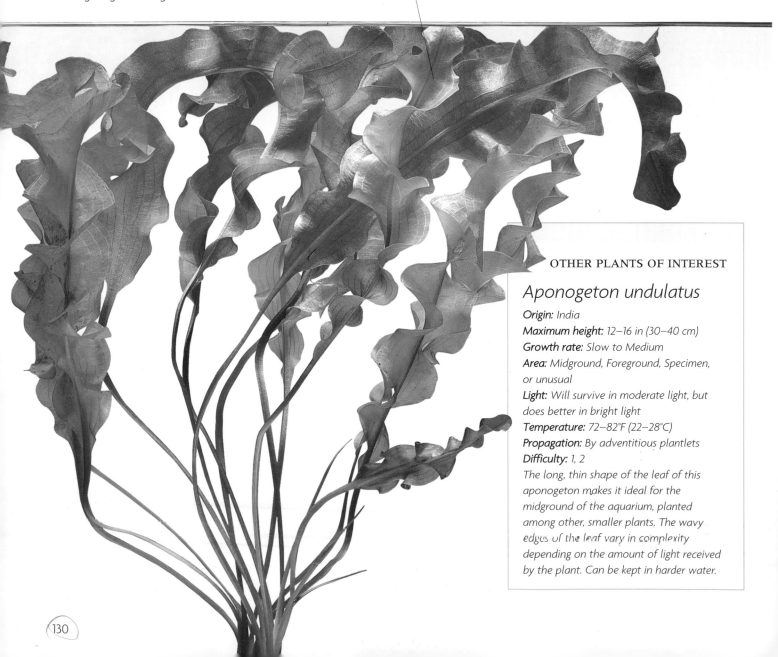

OTHER PLANTS OF INTEREST

Aponogeton undulatus

Origin: *India*
Maximum height: *12–16 in (30–40 cm)*
Growth rate: *Slow to Medium*
Area: *Midground, Foreground, Specimen, or unusual*
Light: *Will survive in moderate light, but does better in bright light*
Temperature: *72–82°F (22–28°C)*
Propagation: *By adventitious plantlets*
Difficulty: *1, 2*
The long, thin shape of the leaf of this aponogeton makes it ideal for the midground of the aquarium, planted among other, smaller plants. The wavy edges of the leaf vary in complexity depending on the amount of light received by the plant. Can be kept in harder water.

Scientific name:

Azolla caroliniana

Common name: Water velvet

Origin: North America

Water velvet is a small (0.8–1.2 in/2–3 cm diameter) floating plant that can be used in tropical and unheated aquariums and even in outdoor ponds (although in ponds it may die back in winter). In good conditions, the plant will spread rapidly and may need to be thinned regularly. It does not produce trailing roots, but will provide cover for some fish. In brighter lighting, the plant sports an attractive rusty red coloration. Provide adequate ventilation in the aquarium to prevent condensation on the leaves or overheating.

Growth rate: Fast

Area: Floating

Light: Moderate to Bright

Temperature: 64–75°F (18–24°C)

Propagation: By division

Difficulty: 1

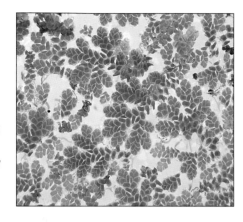

Above: The small leaves of Azolla sp. have a velvety appearance, as a result of many fine hairs, which help to resist water and keep the plant afloat.

Small, surface-dwelling fish such as this honey gourami (Colisa sota) appreciate the cover provided by floating plants.

OTHER PLANTS OF INTEREST

Azolla filiculoides

Common name: *Azolla, Moss fern*
Origin: *America, Asia*
Growth rate: *Medium, Fast*
Area: *Floating, Specimen, or unusual*
Light: *Moderate to Bright*
Temperature: *64–75°F (18–24°C)*
Propagation: *From side shoots*
Difficulty: *1*

This attractive and popular floating plant will do well in most aquariums, providing adequate ventilation is provided. The leaves vary in color from a light green to a rusty red-brown, depending on conditions. Natural sunlight often causes the leaves to turn red. Azolla is sometimes sold as a pond plant, although it usually dies off during winter. The plant provides useful cover for surface-dwelling fish species.

Scientific name:

Bacopa caroliniana

Synonym: *B. amplexicaulis*

Common name: Giant bacopa

Origin: Central America

Given good lighting, a fine substrate and regular fertilization, this plant will prove a highly adaptable and hardy variety, ideal for most aquariums. It does better in clean, clear water. The small (1 in/2.5 cm) light green, oval leaves contrast well with other leaf shapes. Plant giant bacopa in groups, roughly 1.2–2 in (3–5 cm) apart.

The small, fleshy, pale-colored leaves of this bacopa contrast well with other plants in the aquarium.

Maximum height: 8–16 in (20–40 cm)

Growth rate: Medium

Area: Background, Midground

Light: Bright

Temperature: 72–82°F (22–28°C)

Propagation: From cuttings

Difficulty: 1, 2

Scientific name:

Bacopa monnieri

Common name: Dwarf bacopa, Baby tears

Origin: West Africa

This plant makes an ideal foreground plant for more open areas, where it can be kept short and compact with good lighting. The leaves are thick, oval, and roughly 0.8 in (2 cm) long. In low light conditions, the plant will grow taller with wider spaces between the leaves, which can look messy and unattractive.

Too much pruning will also create an untidy-looking plant. Dwarf bacopa is tolerant of water conditions, hardness, and substrate, but will look its best only under ideal conditions.

Maximum height: 20 in (50 cm)

Growth rate: Slow to Medium

Area: Midground, Foreground

Light: Bright, Very Bright

Temperature: 72–86°F (22–30°C)

Propagation: From cuttings and side shoots

Difficulty: 2

Above: Good lighting will allow Bacopa monnieri *to grow compactly, with smaller spaces between the leaves. This often produces a better-looking plant and reduces the need for regular pruning.*

In low light some stems will grow rapidly, with larger spaces (nodes) between the leaves.

OTHER PLANTS OF INTEREST

Bacopa rotundifolia

Common name: *Round bacopa*
Origin: *Southern United States*
Maximum height: *16 in (40 cm)*
Growth rate: *Medium*
Area: *Midground, Foreground*
Light: *Bright*
Temperature: *72–79°F (22–26°C)*
Propagation: *From cuttings*
Difficulty: *3*

Although commonly available, this is not an easy aquarium plant to care for. Good lighting is essential for good health, as is iron fertilization, both in the substrate and by adding liquid fertilizer. The light-green, 1.2 in- (3 cm-) long leaves are round-oval in shape. Both the leaves and stem are delicate and should be handled with care, particularly during transport. Damaged areas will simply rot away; if just one part of the stem is damaged, the rest will also die.

Scientific name:

Barclaya longifolia

Common name: Orchid lily

Origin: East Africa

This attractive plant has long, wavy leaves with a reddish underside and olive-green topside, although the colors do vary across the leaf. The plant is demanding and requires soft water with plenty of nutrients, both in the substrate and in the water. High oxygen levels may cause it to deteriorate quickly. However, if it is properly cared for, it can become a very fine display specimen for the midground or background of smaller aquariums.

Maximum height: 14 in (35 cm)

Growth rate: Slow to Moderate

Area: Background, Midground

Light: Bright

Temperature: 72–79°F (22–26°C)

Propagation: By seed only

Difficulty: 3, 4

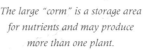

The large "corm" is a storage area for nutrients and may produce more than one plant.

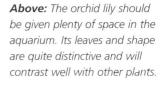

Above: *The orchid lily should be given plenty of space in the aquarium. Its leaves and shape are quite distinctive and will contrast well with other plants.*

Scientific name:

Blyxa japonica

Common name: Japanese rush

Origin: Asia

Blyxa japonica is similar to *B. echinosperma*, but much shorter and harder to care for. In nature the leaves may grow fairly tall, but in aquarium conditions they rarely reach more than 2–3.2 in (5–8 cm). Even in the best conditions this plant may have a limited life span in the aquarium. For optimum care, provide very bright lighting and a soft water environment.

Maximum height: 3.2 in (8 cm)

Growth rate: Slow to Medium

Area: Midground, Foreground

Light: Bright, Very Bright

Temperature: 72–79°F (22–26°C)

Propagation: From side shoots

Difficulty: 3, 4

Special note:

Acorus gramineus is similar in appearance and has the same common name, but is not a true aquatic plant (see page 193).

Scientific name:

Bolbitis heudelotii

Common name: African or Congo fern

Origin: Africa

This slow-growing fern produces large, stalked, dark-green leaves with a very solid structure. The plant will attach itself to solid objects, such as rocks and bogwood, and prefers to live in areas of flowing water. The plant is otherwise undemanding and can be kept in a wide range of water conditions.

Maximum height: 14–20 in (35–50 cm)

Growth rate: Slow

Area: Background, Midground, Specimen, or unusual

Light: Bright

Temperature: 72–82°F (22–28°C)

Propagation: By cuttings from the rhizome

Difficulty: 2, 3

Bolbitis heudelotii is often sold already attached to bogwood. Place it in areas of water movement.

Scientific name:

Cabomba aquatica

Common name: Yellow cabomba, Giant cabomba

Origin: Central America

This attractive plant produces many fine, feathery leaves. The yellow-green coloration is unusual and makes for an interesting ornamental plant. Due to the very fine nature of the leaves, it is vital that the water is clean and free from floating debris, and that algae is not allowed to form on the plant. Strong lighting is required to keep it looking healthy and compact. Stems should be planted in small groups in open areas, and at least 2–2.4 in (5–6 cm) apart, so that light can reach the lower leaves. The plant prefers water with a low pH (6–7).

Maximum height: 16 in (40 cm)

Growth rate: Medium

Area: Background

Light: Very Bright

Temperature: 75–86°F (24–30°C)

Propagation: From cuttings

Difficulty: 3

Scientific name:

Cabomba caroliniana

Common name: Green cabomba

Origin: Central and South America

This plant is the most commonly available *Cabomba* species, and the easiest to keep. The plant is highly adaptable to various aquarium conditions and does well in harder water and aquariums with moderate light. However, brighter lighting will make the plant appear healthier and more attractive.

Maximum height: 20 in (50 cm)

Growth rate: Fast

Area: Background

Light: Bright

Temperature: 72–82°F (22–28°C)

Propagation: From cuttings and side shoots

Difficulty: 1

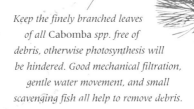

Keep the finely branched leaves of all Cabomba *spp. free of debris, otherwise photosynthesis will be hindered. Good mechanical filtration, gentle water movement, and small scavenging fish all help to remove debris.*

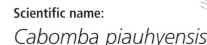

Scientific name:

Cabomba piauhyensis

Common name: Red cabomba

Origin: Central and South America

The red cabomba is a demanding subject, but if given the correct conditions and care, the result is a stunning aquarium plant that creates a strong impact in any planted aquarium. As with other fine-leaved plants, clear, well-filtered water is essential. To keep this plant at its best, it must have a good, preferably iron-rich substrate, strong lighting, regular fertilization, additional CO_2, and, ideally, a low pH (6–7).

Maximum height: 16 in (40 cm)

Growth rate: Medium

Area: Background

Light: Very Bright

Temperature: 75–82°F (24–28°C)

Propagation: From cuttings

Difficulty: 3, 4

Scientific name:

Cardamine lyrata

Common name: Chinese ivy, Japanese cress

Origin: China, Japan, Korea

This unusual plant can be placed in the foreground, even though it reaches up to 14 in (35 cm) in height. It has a messy appearance and unusual leaf shape and often looks best when planted in small groups of three or four stems in between smaller, low-growing foreground plants. At higher temperatures and without adequate lighting, leaf growth may be stunted and stems will become weaker. Ideal conditions include a low temperature, bright lighting, and a pH of 7–7.5. The plant is sensitive to many chemicals and does not do well in very soft water.

Maximum height: 14 in (35 cm)

Growth rate: Medium to Fast

Area: Midground, Foreground, Specimen, or unusual

Light: Bright

Temperature: 59–72°F (15–22°C)

Propagation: By cuttings, self-propagation

Difficulty: 1, 2

Scientific name:

Ceratophyllum demersum

Common name: Hornwort

Origin: Worldwide

Hornwort can be used either as a floating plant or as an upright stem plant. Although it has no roots, in nature it produces rootlike rhizoids that anchor it to the substrate. This fragile plant breaks easily and any sizable pieces will grow into individual plants. Side shoots are produced regularly and if left unattended, the plant becomes a dense mass of tangled vegetation. Hornwort can be used in coldwater and tropical tanks and provides good hiding areas for fry and young fish.

Maximum height: 20 in (50 cm)

Growth rate: Fast

Area: Background, Midground, Floating

Light: Moderate

Temperature: 64–82°F (18–28°C)

Propagation: From cuttings and side shoots

Difficulty: 1

Hornwort provides valuable cover for fry.

The leaves of Ceratopteris cornuta *vary in shape depending on various environmental conditions and the original plant. The leaves may be finely branched or more "whole" in appearance.*

Scientific name:

Ceratopteris cornuta

Synonym: *C. thalictroides*

Common name: Floating fern

Origin: Africa

The leaves of *C. cornuta* are an unusual shape and the plant varies in size, depending on aquarium conditions. It does well if given good lighting and plenty of space for growth. Can be used as a floating plant. Plantlets are frequently produced along older leaves.

Maximum height: Up to 20 in (50 cm), usually 14–16 in (35–40 cm)

Growth rate: Medium

Area: Background, Floating

Light: Bright

Temperature: 64–86°F (18–30°C)

Propagation: By adventitious plantlets

Difficulty: 1, 2

Scientific name:

Crinum natans

Common name: African onion plant

Origin: West Africa

This dominant, long-leaved plant can also be found in a narrow-leaved form, which is a very attractive plant in any display. The wider-leaved form needs bright lighting and adequate nutrients, but the narrow-leaved one is less demanding. Both forms will reach up to 39 in (1 m) in length and trail along the water surface. Some herbivorous fish will not eat this plant. Provide medium-soft water and a good substrate.

Maximum height: 39 in (1 m)

Growth rate: Medium to Fast

Area: Background, Specimen, or unusual

Light: Moderate to Bright

Temperature: 75–82°F (24–28°C)

Propagation: From daughter plants

Difficulty: 1

The long, highly indented leaves will trail on the water surface.

The tough leaves of Crinum thaianum *will survive the attentions of boisterous and herbivorous fish, so the plant is suitable for aquariums with larger fish where other plants would be quickly eaten or destroyed.*

Scientific name:

Crinum thaianum

Common name: Onion plant

Origin: Thailand

This large plant will produce leaves up to 60 in (150 cm) long, so although established plants can be cut back occasionally without any harm, use it carefully. The ribbonlike leaves are 0.8 in (2 cm) wide. Once they reach the surface, they will float horizontally on the water. The onion plant adapts well to the aquarium environment and is an undemanding species.

Maximum height: 60 in (150 cm)

Growth rate: Medium

Area: Background

Light: Moderate, Bright

Temperature: 72–86°F (22–30°C)

Propagation: From daughter bulbs

Difficulty: 1

The common name, "onion plant," comes from the onion-shaped bulb from which the plant sprouts and where it stores nutrients.

Cryptocoryne *species*

These are some of the most popular and widely available aquarium plants. There are over 60 species and about half of these are relatively easy to keep in the aquarium. In nature, cryptocorynes come from a wide range of habitats, including shallow, fast-flowing rivers, marsh areas, bogs, and swampy conditions. The plants in this group are either amphibious bog plants or true aquatic plants, but all will adapt to fully submerged aquarium life. Cryptocorynes are not easy to acclimatize to an aquarium, but the plants are relatively hardy once settled, providing conditions are stable. Constant changes in water temperature and lighting will make them susceptible to cryptocoryne rot, a disease where numerous holes form in the leaves and the plant slowly deteriorates. A fine, heated substrate will improve plant health and encourage growth. Lighting requirements vary with each species, but many cryptocorynes are suited to aquariums with low light or subdued light conditions.

Above: *Cryptocorynes are largely used for the foreground of the aquarium, where they will spread and cover a large area if regularly propagated and/or divided (see page 83).*

Scientific name:

Cryptocoryne albida

Synonym: *Cryptocoryne costata*

Origin: Thailand

A few leaf varieties are available and the color varies from light green to a reddish brown, occasionally with dark mottled leaves. The plant does not move well and will take time to acclimatize, but once settled, and if provided with suitable lighting and a nutrient-rich substrate, it should grow well. Very strong light can reduce leaf size.

Maximum height: 10–12 in (25–30 cm)

Growth rate: Slow

Area: Midground, Foreground

Light: Bright

Temperature: 68–82°F (20–28°C)

Propagation: Runners, division

Difficulty: 3, 4

The very attractive elongated leaf shape looks best in large groups along the foreground.

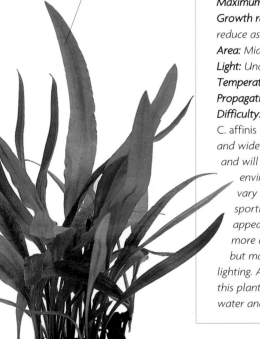

OTHER PLANTS OF INTEREST

Cryptocoryne affinis

Synonym: *C. haerteliana*
Origin: *Malaysia*
Maximum height: *10 in (25 cm)*
Growth rate: *Medium to Fast, but will reduce as the plant ages*
Area: *Midground, Foreground*
Light: *Undemanding*
Temperature: *72–82°F (22–28°C)*
Propagation: *By runners*
Difficulty: *1, 2*

C. affinis is one of the most popular and widely available cryptocorynes and will adapt well to a stable environment. The crinkled leaves vary in color and shade, usually sporting a light green glossy appearance. The plant will grow more quickly with increasing light, but may not appreciate very bright lighting. As with many cryptocorynes, this plant is sensitive to changes in water and environmental conditions.

Scientific name:

Cryptocoryne balansae

Origin: Thailand

This plant is similar to *C. affinis* but its leaves are much longer, elongated, and highly indented. They may grow up to 16 in (40 cm), although 12 in (30 cm) is more usual. The plant does well in moderate lighting and hard water and is easier to care for as it becomes established.

Maximum height: 14 in (35 cm)

Growth rate: Medium

Area: Midground, Foreground, Specimen, or unusual

Light: Undemanding, but does better in bright light

Temperature: 77–82°F (25–28°C)

Propagation: From runners

Difficulty: 2, 3

Scientific name:

Cryptocoryne beckettii

Common name: Beckett's cryptocoryne

Origin: Sri Lanka

The large leaves of this cryptocoryne are an interesting olive-green color that contrasts well with other plants. Once established, the thick, bushy plant produced from adventitious plantlets often looks best on its own in the foreground or with other cryptocorynes. A nutrient-rich and heated substrate will improve growth.

Maximum height: 6 in (15 cm)

Growth rate: Medium

Area: Midground, Foreground

Light: Moderate to Bright

Temperature: 77–82°F (25–28°C)

Propagation: Adventitious plantlets

Difficulty: 1, 2

The leaves and stems have a solid appearance and provide hiding spots for small, bottom-dwelling fish.

Above: The more compact cryptocorynes are ideal midground and foreground subjects. With olive-green above and red beneath, the leaves of these cryptocorynes are a good foil for the bright green foliage of other plants.

OTHER PLANTS OF INTEREST

Cryptocoryne cordata

Synonym: *C. blassii, C. kerrii*
Common name: *Giant cryptocoryne*
Origin: *Thailand*
Maximum height: *16 in (40 cm)*
Growth rate: *Slow*
Area: *Midground, Foreground*
Light: *Moderate*
Temperature: *72–82°F (22–28°C)*
Propagation: *Plantlets and runners*
Difficulty: *3*

The large leaves of Cryptocoryne cordata vary in color from light green to reddish brown and look effective when used in large, well-spaced groups. The plant requires a good substrate – preferably nutrient-rich and heated – to stay healthy. When moved, the plant is vulnerable and takes time to acclimatize. It is not easy to care for, but once established in the right environment it should grow well.

Scientific name:

Cryptocoryne walkeri var. *lutea*

Origin: Sri Lanka

This popular cryptocoryne is commonly available and easy to care for. The plant often only looks its best once it has spread, creating a dense group of plants. Individual plants may look a little "weak" on their own. A few leaf varieties are available, some of which produce brown veins and a reddish brown underside. The plant adapts to a wide range of conditions and should do well in any aquarium with stable conditions.

Maximum height: 4.7 in (12 cm)

Growth rate: Moderate

Area: Midground, Foreground

Light: Undemanding

Temperature: 72–86°F (22–30°C)

Propagation: From shoots

Difficulty: 1

Leaves and/or stems that grow away from the main plant are an indication that the plant is large enough to be divided at the center and replanted as two separate plants.

Cryptocoryne ciliata

Origin: Southeast Asia
Maximum height: 12 in (30 cm)
Growth rate: Slow
Area: Midground, Foreground
Light: Bright
Temperature: 72–82°F (22–28°C)
Propagation: By runners, shoots
Difficulty: 2

This olive green-leaved cryptocoryne looks best when planted in dense groups. Different leaf shape varieties are available. Most leaves are between 1.2–2 in (3–5 cm) wide. A slow-growing and undemanding plant, given the correct lighting.

Cryptocoryne moehlmannii

Common name: Moehlmann's cryptocoryne
Origin: Sumatra
Maximum height: 6–8 in (15–20 cm)
Growth rate: Medium
Area: Midground, Foreground
Light: Bright
Temperature: 77–82°F (25–28°C)
Propagation: Adventitious plantlets
Difficulty: 1, 2

The green leaves of this easy-to-keep cryptocoryne vary in shape from oval to almost round and have a dimpled surface. If given plenty of room and good conditions, the plant produces a number of leaves, creating a compact plant that is ideal for the midground or foreground of the aquarium. Although adaptable, C. moehlmannii may not do well in very hard water. Ideally, provide soft-medium water, strong lighting, and adequate CO_2.

Scientific name:

Cryptocoryne parva

Common name: Tiny cryptocoryne

Origin: Sri Lanka

This little plant will look very effective when used in groups along the foreground. With good growth, it is possible to achieve a lawn effect. However, the plant is not easy to care for unless you provide very good lighting, along with a reasonably good substrate. Well-established plants will spread relatively quickly through the production of daughter plants on runners. Can also be used as a bog or marsh plant.

Maximum height: 2 in (5 cm)

Growth rate: Slow to Medium

Area: Foreground

Light: Very Bright

Temperature: 77–82°F (25–28°C)

Propagation: From runners

Difficulty: 3

When kept in large groups, the leaf shape of this plant will create a grasslike appearance.

Scientific name:

Cryptocoryne pontederiifolia

Origin: Sumatra, Borneo

This cryptocoryne has a bold leaf shape that gives it a dominant appearance in the aquarium. Once established, this undemanding plant is hardy and can grow quite large in good conditions. Moderate lighting is sufficient, although bright light combined with good fertilization will increase its growth rate and overall size. The plant is similar in appearance to *C. moehlmannii.*

Maximum height:
Normally about 8–10 in (20–25 cm), but can grow larger

Growth rate: Moderate

Area: Midground, Foreground

Light: Moderate

Temperature: 68–82°F (20–28°C)

Propagation: Runners

Difficulty: 1, 2

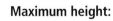

Larger-leaved cryptocorynes can be used in the midground or around the edges of the aquarium.

Scientific name:

Cryptocoryne undulata

Common name: Undulate cryptocoryne

Origin: India

This attractive cryptocoryne produces long, dark green, highly ruffled leaves, which make it a good display plant. As it ages it may produce leaves capable of reaching more than 14 in (35 cm) in length. Low light levels may cause the plant to produce light green leaves. It does well in hard water.

Maximum height: 12 in (30 cm)

Growth rate: Slow to Medium

Area: Background, Midground, Foreground, Specimen, or unusual

Light: Bright

Temperature: 72–82°F (22–28°C)

Propagation: By adventitious plantlets

Difficulty: 2, 3

OTHER PLANTS OF INTEREST

Cryptocoryne siamensis

Origin: *Thailand*
Maximum height: *4 in (10 cm)*
Growth rate: *Medium*
Area: *Foreground, Specimen, or unusual*
Light: *Bright*
Temperature: *77–82°F (25–28°C)*
Propagation: *From runners*
Difficulty: *2, 3*
Use this small reddish brown-leaved cryptocoryne to contrast with green-leaved plants in the aquarium foreground. Additional substrate fertilization will help it to acclimatize and spread quickly. In good conditions, C. siamensis will produce numerous daughter plants through runners and create a dense group.

Scientific name:

Cryptocoryne wendtii

Origin: Sri Lanka

This tall cryptocoryne can be used as a background or midground plant and adapts easily to a wide range of conditions. The leaf color depends on a number of factors, including lighting, and varies from an olive-green to green and slightly brown. The underside is usually a light orange-brown color. Plant it in spaced groups, allowing it to spread and create a dense clump.

Maximum height: 14 in (35 cm)

Growth rate: Medium to Fast

Area: Background, Midground

Light: Moderate to Bright

Temperature: 75–82°F (24–28°C)

Propagation: From shoots and runners

Difficulty: 1, 2

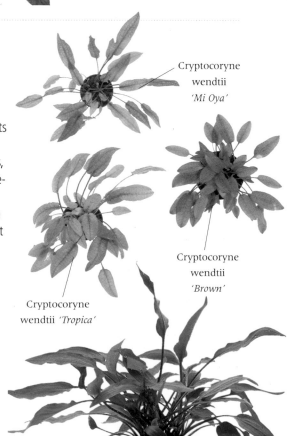

Cryptocoryne wendtii 'Mi Oya'

Cryptocoryne wendtii 'Brown'

Cryptocoryne wendtii 'Tropica'

Scientific name:

Cryptocoryne willisii

Synonym: *C. nevillii*

Origin: Sri Lanka

This tiny cryptocoryne may reach no more than 1.6–2 in (4–5 cm) in the aquarium and is often confused with similar species, such as *C. parva*. Its small size makes it ideal for the foreground area. If given adequate conditions, it will spread across an open area well. Adaptable and easy to care for if given adequate lighting and stable conditions.

Maximum height: 2–3.2 in (5–8 cm)

Growth rate: Medium

Area: Foreground

Light: Bright

Temperature: 68–84°F (20–29°C)

Propagation: From shoots

Difficulty: 1, 2

Cryptocoryne willisii *'Lucens'*

Scientific name:

Didiplis diandra

Synonym: *Peplis diandra*

Common name: Water hedge

Origin: North America

If planted in groups, this attractive and interesting aquatic plant will take on a hedgelike appearance. Good lighting and an available source of iron are essential if it is to remain healthy. In very strong lighting, the uppermost leaves will turn red, giving the plant an attractive rusty look. It prefers a fine substrate. Place any cuttings in sand or a small-grade, lime-free substrate. Once cuttings have been taken, the plant produces side shoots that increase its bushy appearance. The plant does not do well in hard water.

Maximum height: 10–14 in (25–35 cm)

Growth rate: Medium to Fast

Area: Midground, Foreground

Light: Very Bright

Temperature: 75–82°F (24–28°C)

Propagation: From cuttings, side shoots

Difficulty: 3

Echinodorus *species*

These American plants belong to one of the most common groups of aquarium subjects. There are more than 45 species in the wild and many of these are available for aquariums. Although there are a few solely aquatic species, echinodorus are predominantly amphibious bog plants that produce an aquatic form if kept submerged for long periods. The larger species are ideal for the background of spacious aquariums, and if given enough space and an open top, will quickly produce leaves above the surface. If the plants become too tall, you can keep them in check by occasionally trimming the roots and removing the taller leaves. Echinodorus species will propagate readily by producing numerous daughter plants on runners. Leave them in place until each plantlet has four or five leaves, then separate and plant them individually. Provide a nutrient-rich substrate, regular iron fertilization, and bright lighting. Given these conditions, echinodorus is one of the easiest plant groups to care for in the aquarium.

Scientific name:

Echinodorus bleheri

Synonym: *E. paniculatus, E. rangeri*

Common name: Broadleaved Amazon swordplant

Origin: South America

The broadleaved Amazon swordplant is the most widely available Amazon sword, partly due to its durability and ease of care. When established, the plant can take up a fair amount of space, so use it only in groups in larger aquariums or in tanks containing just a few plant species. Provide a good source of iron, both in the substrate and through liquid fertilizers. Does well in hard water.

Maximum height: 20 in (50 cm)

Growth rate: Moderate

Area: Background, Specimen, or unusual

Light: Bright

Temperature: 75–82°F (24–28°C)

Propagation: By adventitious plantlets

Difficulty: 1, 2

OTHER PLANTS OF INTEREST

Echinodorus amazonicus

Synonym: E. brevipedicellatus
Common name: Amazon swordplant
Origin: Brazil
Maximum height: 14 in (35 cm)
Growth rate: Slow to Medium
Area: Background, Midground, Specimen, or unusual
Light: Bright
Temperature: 75–82°F (24–28°C)
Propagation: From shoots
Difficulty: 1, 2
The thin leaves of the Amazon swordplant grow up to 14 in (35 cm) long. Use groups of plants in the background or plant it singly in the midground. It prefers a fine, iron-rich substrate and medium-soft water. Remove older leaves to keep the plant looking fresh.

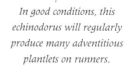

In good conditions, this echinodorus will regularly produce many adventitious plantlets on runners.

OTHER PLANTS OF INTEREST

Echinodorus bolivianus

Common name: *Bolivian swordplant*
Origin: *Brazil*
Maximum height: *4.7 in (12 cm)*
Growth rate: *Medium*
Area: *Foreground*
Light: *Bright*
Temperature: *64–82°F (18–28°C)*
Propagation: *From runners*
Difficulty: *1, 2*

This small plant has few demands and will do well in medium light, making it a good foreground alternative to similar, small, yet light-demanding foreground plants. The leaves are light green, 4–4.7 in (10–12 cm) long and up to 0.4 in (1 cm) wide. An individual plant will produce many leaves and runners, eventually creating a carpet effect. An iron-rich substrate and additional CO_2 fertilization will help to keep it in good condition.

Echinodorus grandiflorus

Common name: *Large-flowered Amazon swordplant*
Origin: *Central America*
Maximum height: *32 in (80 cm)*
Growth rate: *Medium*
Area: *Background, Specimen, or unusual*
Light: *Bright*
Temperature: *72–79°F (22–26°C)*
Propagation: *By seed*
Difficulty: *2*

Its size and leaf shape make the Amazon swordplant an imposing specimen, best suited to spacious aquariums. The oval leaves are up to 6 in (15 cm) long, but given the chance, the plant will also produce larger leaves above the water surface. This tendency makes it ideal for the background of large, open-top tanks. To keep the leaves submerged, regularly remove larger or taller leaves. Provide a deep, iron-rich substrate and plenty of growing room.

Echinodorus horemanii

Common name: *Black-red Amazon swordplant*
Origin: *Brazil*
Maximum height: *10 in (25 cm)*
Growth rate: *Medium*
Area: *Background, Midground*
Light: *Bright*
Temperature: *68–77°F (20–25°C)*
Propagation: *By shoots from the rhizome*
Difficulty: *1, 2*

Despite its common name, the leaves of this plant remain light green. The common name comes from a color variation that is sometimes available in which the leaf is a dark red-green. E. horemanii is adaptable and hardy and best planted in the background or singly in the midground of larger aquariums. A good nutrient- and iron-rich substrate will ensure continual good health.

Scientific name:

Echinodorus cordifolius

Synonym: *E. radicans*

Common name: Radicans swordplant

Origin: North America, Mexico

The leaves of this attractive swordplant are almost circular in shape, making the plant a dominant presence in a well-planted aquarium. Some color forms are available with attractive red-brown mottled leaves. To keep the plant short and tidy, remove large and older leaves and trim the roots occasionally. Provide plenty of iron-based fertilizers. An undemanding and relatively easy-to-keep species.

Maximum height: 16 in (40 cm)

Growth rate: Medium

Area: Background, Midground, Specimen, or unusual

Light: Undemanding, but does better in good lighting

Temperature: 72–82°F (22–28°C)

Propagation: From adventitious shoots

Difficulty: 1, 2

The unusual leaf shape of this plant makes it a good addition to a larger aquarium.

The large veins that transport gas and liquids can be clearly seen on many Echinodorus *species.*

Scientific name:

Echinodorus macrophyllus

Common name: Large-leaved Amazon swordplant

Origin: Guyana, Brazil

This Amazon sword produces large leaves for its size, hence its common name. The leaves are typically up to 12 in (30 cm) long and 8 in (20 cm) wide, light green, and robust in appearance. If given adequate conditions, it will produce a number of larger leaves above the water surface. Because of the substantial size of this Amazon sword, it works best as an individual specimen background plant in spacious aquariums. Ideal conditions for growth include a good iron- and fertilizer-rich substrate and plenty of light. However, the plant is adaptable and should survive well in most aquariums. Removing larger or older leaves and occasionally trimming the roots will prevent the plant from growing too large.

Maximum height: 20 in (50 cm)

Growth rate: Medium, Fast

Area: Background, Specimen, or unusual

Light: Moderate, Bright, Very Bright

Temperature: 72–80°F (22–27°C)

Propagation: By adventitious plantlets

Difficulty: 1, 2

Scientific name:

Echinodorus major

Synonym: *E. martii, E. leopoldina*

Common name: Ruffled Amazon swordplant

Origin: Brazil

This large Amazon swordplant is similar in appearance to *E. amazonicus* and *E. bleheri*, although the leaves will grow much larger and are slightly ruffled around the edges. An ideal plant for use singly in larger aquariums. Provide a fine, iron-rich substrate and allow room for growth.

The unusually ruffled leaves of E. major *can grow quite large and are best suited to a spacious aquarium.*

Maximum height: 20 in (50 cm)

Growth rate: Medium

Area: Background, Specimen, or unusual

Light: Bright

Temperature: 75–82°F (24–28°C)

Propagation: Adventitious plantlets

Difficulty: 1, 2

Although large, the leaves of this echinodorus are formed close together, creating a compact appearance. This impressive species makes an ideal specimen plant.

Scientific name:

Echinodorus osiris

Synonym: *E. osiris rubra, E. aureobrunata*

Common name: Red Amazon swordplant

Origin: Brazil

The clearly visible veins and ruffled leaf edges make this swordplant more interesting than some others. The common name is a little misleading, as only the new, young leaves sport a slightly red-brown colour. *E. osiris* is relatively easy to care for and ideal as a feature plant in a larger aquarium. It does better in hard water than in soft. Provide plenty of iron, especially if the plant is kept in bright light.

Maximum height: 16–20 in (40–50 cm)

Growth rate: Medium

Area: Background, Midground, Specimen, or unusual

Light: Bright

Temperature: 72–82°F (22–28°C)

Propagation: By adventitious plantlets

Difficulty: 2

Scientific name:

Echinodorus parviflorus

Synonym: *E. peruensis, E. tocantins*

Common name: Black Amazon swordplant

Origin: South America

This adaptable and hardy Amazon swordplant is a popular, commonly available species. As the plant will reach only 10 in (25 cm) in height, it is an ideal alternative to many of the larger Amazon swordplants when used in a smaller aquarium. The substrate should be fine and iron-enriched. Remove older leaves if they become tatty and covered with algae.

Maximum height: 10 in (25 cm), sometimes taller

Growth rate: Medium

Area: Background, Midground

Light: Bright

Temperature: 72–82°F (22–28°C)

Propagation: From adventitious plantlets

Difficulty: 1

Scientific name:

Echinodorus quadricostatus var. *xinguensis*

Synonym: *E. intermedius*

Common name: Dwarf swordplant

Origin: Brazil

This short, thin-leaved plant is ideal for use in the foreground. It will adapt to different levels of light and the leaf length will change according to light intensity. Given good conditions, the plant will grow and spread quickly, so initial planting should be well spaced. Yellowing of the leaves indicates a lack of iron.

Maximum height:
3.2–6 in (8–15 cm)

Growth rate: Medium to Fast

Area: Midground, Foreground

Light: Bright

Temperature:
72–82°F (22–28°C)

Propagation: From runners

Difficulty: 1, 2

OTHER PLANTS OF INTEREST

Echinodorus opacus

Common name: *Opaque Amazon swordplant*
Origin: *Southern Brazil*
Maximum height: *10 in (25 cm)*
Growth rate: *Slow to Medium*
Area: *Midground, Foreground*
Light: *Bright*
Temperature: *68–82°F (20–28°C)*
Propagation: *Side shoots from the rhizome*
Difficulty: *2, 3*
The darker green leaves of this species make a welcome change from the more common light-green color of most Amazon swordplants. It is adaptable and hardy, but can be slow growing when established and does not like to be moved. As with other Amazons, good fertilization of the substrate and water, combined with good lighting, should ensure continued health.

This is the aquatic leaf form of E. tenellus, but many plants are sold with the terrestrial leaf form.

Scientific name:

Echinodorus tenellus

Common name: Pygmy chain swordplant

Origin: Northern and southern America

In good conditions, this tiny *Echinodorus* species will spread and create a lawnlike appearance across the foreground of the aquarium. Provide medium-bright lighting, a fine substrate, and medium-soft water. When you buy them, many specimens exhibit the terrestrial leaf form, which is more oval shaped and on short stems. When placed underwater, the terrestrial form will lose all the existing leaves before growing new aquatic ones.

Maximum height: 3.2 in (8 cm)

Growth rate: Variable, depending on conditions

Area: Foreground

Light: Bright

Temperature: 72–86°F (22–30°C)

Propagation: From runners

Difficulty: 2, 3

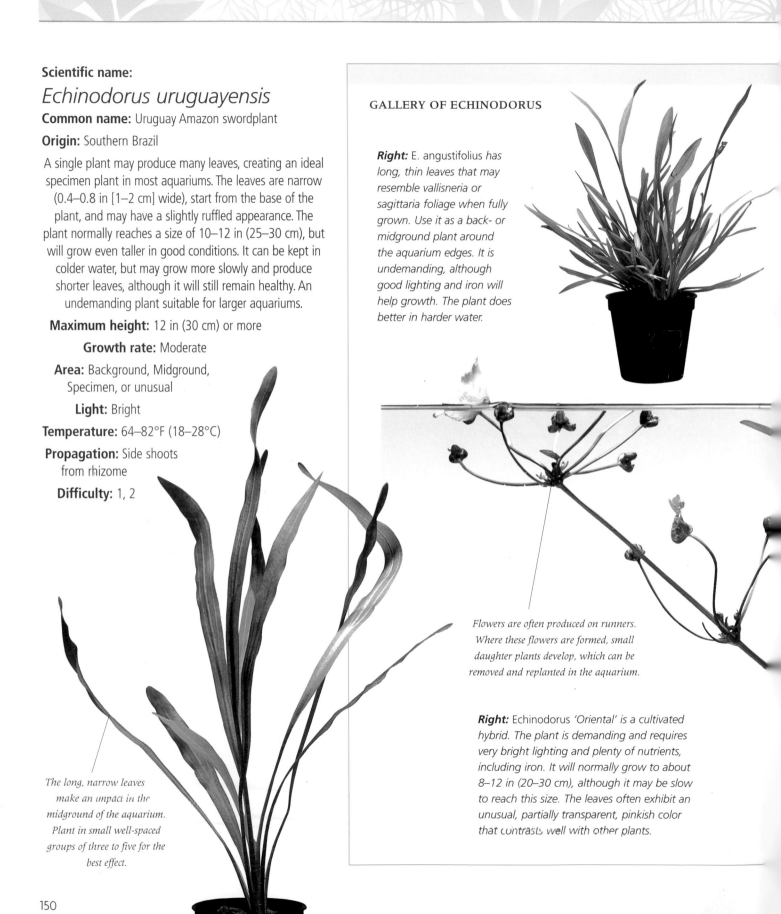

Scientific name:

Echinodorus uruguayensis

Common name: Uruguay Amazon swordplant

Origin: Southern Brazil

A single plant may produce many leaves, creating an ideal specimen plant in most aquariums. The leaves are narrow (0.4–0.8 in [1–2 cm] wide), start from the base of the plant, and may have a slightly ruffled appearance. The plant normally reaches a size of 10–12 in (25–30 cm), but will grow even taller in good conditions. It can be kept in colder water, but may grow more slowly and produce shorter leaves, although it will still remain healthy. An undemanding plant suitable for larger aquariums.

Maximum height: 12 in (30 cm) or more

Growth rate: Moderate

Area: Background, Midground, Specimen, or unusual

Light: Bright

Temperature: 64–82°F (18–28°C)

Propagation: Side shoots from rhizome

Difficulty: 1, 2

The long, narrow leaves make an impact in the midground of the aquarium. Plant in small well-spaced groups of three to five for the best effect.

GALLERY OF ECHINODORUS

Right: E. angustifolius *has long, thin leaves that may resemble vallisneria or sagittaria foliage when fully grown. Use it as a back- or midground plant around the aquarium edges. It is undemanding, although good lighting and iron will help growth. The plant does better in harder water.*

Flowers are often produced on runners. Where these flowers are formed, small daughter plants develop, which can be removed and replanted in the aquarium.

Right: Echinodorus 'Oriental' *is a cultivated hybrid. The plant is demanding and requires very bright lighting and plenty of nutrients, including iron. It will normally grow to about 8–12 in (20–30 cm), although it may be slow to reach this size. The leaves often exhibit an unusual, partially transparent, pinkish color that contrasts well with other plants.*

Left: Echinodorus barthii (double-red osiris) slowly grows to 8–10 in (20–25 cm). In good light, it will exhibit an attractive golden-red coloration.

Right: Some cultivars, such as this E. 'Gabrielii', can be kept short by continually removing the larger leaves. This method is particularly useful in a small aquarium where a compact plant is required.

A daughter plant develops on a runner at the water surface.

Most echinodorus plants have bold, oval leaves that create a striking display feature in the aquarium. Some are smooth-edged, while others have distinctive wavy margins.

Left: Echinodorus 'Ozelot Green', a fine specimen plant that will reach 16 in (40 cm) tall in the aquarium. It is easy to grow and tolerant of a wide range of water conditions.

Left: Echinodorus palaefolius *var.* latifolius originates from the rivers and lakes of Brazil. It will thrive in standard aquarium conditions and reach 16 in (40 cm) or more in height and width. An excellent specimen plant.

Below: With its red-dappled leaves and bold shape, Echinodorus 'Red Flame' lives up to its name in providing a colorful focal point in any planted display. Easy to grow, it will reach 16 in (40 cm) and more.

Green leaves splashed with burgundy red catch the eye in any planted aquarium.

GALLERY OF ECHINODORUS

Below: Echinodorus 'Rubin' is a cultivated variety of echinodorus. Many aquarium plants are "manmade" varieties, created by crossing separate species, which results in attractive, new hybrid plants.

The leaves of Echinodorus 'Rubin' vary in color. A mixture of red and green areas, combined with visible veins, creates a distinctive plant.

The red edging of this leaf is unusual and creates a good contrasting effect when viewed against other leaves and plants.

Right: The narrow-leaved form of E. 'Rubin' is equally stunning, with the same unusual reddish coloration. These plants are relatively easy to care for, although they require very bright lighting and may grow to more than 20 in (50 cm).

Below: E. schlueteri *is an ideal specimen plant for a small aquarium. Although it produces large leaves, it will grow no taller than 10–12 in (25–30 cm). Given strong lighting and a nutrient-rich substrate, the plant will develop attractive pale red-brown markings.*

Below: Echinodorus *'Tricolor' is another cultivated variety, with bold, oval leaves. In common with most large* Echinodorus *species, it needs good lighting and an iron-rich substrate for strong growth.*

Special note:

Nearly all *Echinodorus* sp. require a good source of iron. Without it, the leaves become thin and lacking in color, eventually breaking down and dying off. Iron can be added by regularly dosing plants with liquid fertilizers, although a good-quality, nutrient-rich or clay-based substrate additive will provide a long-term solution to iron fertilization.

The leaves are attractive shades of green, which add variety to the aquarium display.

155

Scientific name:

Egeria densa

Synonym: *Elodea densa*

Common name: Elodea, pondweed

Origin: USA, now worldwide

This is one of the best-known and popular aquatic plants. Elodea is highly adaptable, fast growing, and one of the easiest aquatic plants to keep. Ideally, it prefers harder water, but will adapt to a wide range of water conditions and temperatures. With good lighting, elodea can be kept in aquariums with higher temperatures.

Maximum height: 20 in (50 cm) or more

Growth rate: Fast

Area: Background, Midground

Light: Moderate

Temperature: 64–79°F (18–26°C)

Propagation: From cuttings

Difficulty: 1

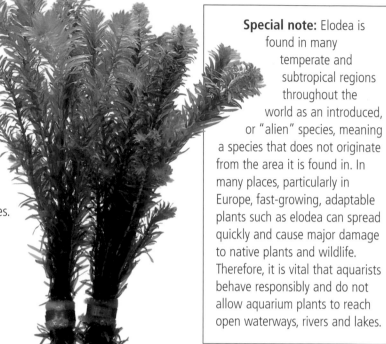

Special note: Elodea is found in many temperate and subtropical regions throughout the world as an introduced, or "alien" species, meaning a species that does not originate from the area it is found in. In many places, particularly in Europe, fast-growing, adaptable plants such as elodea can spread quickly and cause major damage to native plants and wildlife. Therefore, it is vital that aquarists behave responsibly and do not allow aquarium plants to reach open waterways, rivers and lakes.

Left: An overhead view shows the amount of cover provided by the plant, which is very welcome to the fish beneath the surface.

Plantlets are often produced from shoots and in good conditions, these may need regular thinning.

Scientific name:

Eichhornia crassipes

Common name: Water hyacinth

Origin: Throughout tropical regions

This potentially large floating plant can be kept in an open-top aquarium with reasonably bright lighting. The leaves are thick and waxy in appearance and may reach up to 6 in (15 cm) in length. The plant will spread rapidly and needs regular thinning. Water hyacinth is usually sold as a pond plant and does well in colder climates during the summer, but will die off during winter.

Maximum spread: 12 in (30 cm)

Growth rate: Fast

Area: Floating, Specimen, or unusual

Light: Bright, Very Bright

Temperature: 68–79°F (20–26°C)

Propagation: From shoots

Difficulty: 1, 2

OTHER PLANTS OF INTEREST

Eichhornia azurea

Common name: *Blue water hyacinth*
Origin: *Tropical and subtropical America*
Maximum height: *18–24 in (45–60 cm)*
Growth rate: *Medium*
Area: *Background, Midground, Specimen, or unusual*
Light: *Very Bright*
Temperature: *75–82°F (24–28°C)*
Propagation: *From cuttings*
Difficulty: *3, 4*
The leaf shape of this plant makes a good contrast with many other aquatic plants. The leaves are long (4–6 in/10–15 cm) and thin (0.3 in/0.7 cm). To minimize the need for frequent cutting back, keep it in a fairly deep aquarium so that it does not reach the water surface. It also requires a strong source of light and a low carbonate hardness to keep it in perfect health. Plant it in small groups of three or more, allowing plenty of room between the stems.

Eleocharis parvula

Common name: *Dwarf hairgrass*
Origin: *Cuba, Europe, Africa*
Maximum height: *6 in (15 cm)*
Growth rate: *Medium*
Area: *Midground, Foreground*
Light: *Strong lighting*
Temperature: *68–82°F (20–28°C)*
Propagation: *From runners*
Difficulty: *2*

This foreground plant has an attractive grasslike appearance and under ideal conditions will spread across the substrate, creating a "lawn" effect. As with other fine-leaved, foreground plants, bright lighting is required for healthy growth. A taller variety, Eleocharis acicularis (hairgrass), is also readily available in the aquarium trade.

Eleocharis vivipara

Synonym: *Eleocharis prolifera*
Common name: *Umbrella grass*
Origin: *Eastern United States*
Maximum height: *20 in (50 cm)*
Growth rate: *Fast*
Area: *Midground, Foreground, Specimen, or unusual*
Light: *Bright*
Temperature: *72–82°F (22–28°C)*
Propagation: *By adventitious plantlets*
Difficulty: *2*
This grasslike plant can be used as a specimen or midground plant and may reach up to 20 in (50 cm) in length. New plantlets are created at the top of the leaf, giving the plant its "umbrella" appearance. Good lighting and soft water will both prove beneficial when caring for this plant. In the best conditions it may spread quickly, so allow plenty of room for growth.

Scientific name:

Eleocharis acicularis

Common name: Hairgrass

Origin: Worldwide

This commonly available grasslike plant will vary in height depending on light conditions; brighter lighting will produce a shorter plant. Although easy to care for, good fertilization and a clear, debris-free environment will prevent the plant from dying back. Dense plants can be separated and replanted, which will encourage new growth.

Maximum height: 10 in (25 cm), but usually 6–8 in (15–20 cm)

Growth rate: Medium

Area: Midground, Foreground

Light: Bright

Temperature: 64–82°F (18–28°C)

Propagation: From runners

Difficulty: 2

The fine grasslike leaves collect undesirable floating waste from the aquarium water, but scavenging fish, such as corydoras catfish or kuhli loaches, will disturb the plant leaves and remove the debris.

Scientific name:
Elodea canadensis
Common name: Canadian pondweed

Origin: North America

Elodea canadensis is very similar in appearance to *Egeria densa*, and often sold as such, but does not tolerate warmer water as well as *E. densa*. Use it in groups of five or more for the best display. In good conditions, the plant will grow rapidly and may need regular pruning. Cutting will also result in the production of side shoots, creating a denser, bushier display. The plant is a good coldwater and pond subject; in tropical aquariums it may become weak over time. An adaptable specimen with no special requirements.

Maximum height: 20 in (50 cm) or more

Growth rate: Medium to Fast

Area: Background

Light: Moderate to Bright

Temperature: 50–68°F (10–20°C)

Propagation: From cuttings

Difficulty: 1, 2

Scientific name:
Eusteralis stellata
Common name: Star rotala

Origin: Australia, Asia

Used in well-spaced groups and given good conditions, this plant can become part of a stunning midground display. Unfortunately, it is not too easy to care for. A softwater, nutrient-rich environment, combined with strong lighting and a good supply of CO_2, will help to keep it in good condition. Taking cuttings will result in side shoots and a bushier plant. Even with the best care, growth may slow down or even stop.

Maximum height: 12–16 in (30–40 cm)

Growth rate: Varies depending on conditions

Area: Background, Midground, Foreground

Light: Bright to Very Bright

Temperature: 72–82°F (22–28°C)

Propagation: From cuttings

Difficulty: 3, 4

The star rotala is a very attractive plant, although it is not easy to keep. A good specimen will make a fine addition to any display.

Scientific name:

Fontinalis antipyretica

Common name: Willow moss

Origin: North America, Europe, Asia, North Africa

This unusual little plant has numerous dark green leaves roughly 0.2 in (0.5 cm) in length, and spreads over rocks and wood in the aquarium. It does not produce normal roots but attaches itself to any permanent object. Willow moss prefers moving water and does not appreciate hard water conditions. Ideally, keep it at a lower temperature; it is suitable for an unheated aquarium. Over time, the plant has a tendency to die off, even in the best conditions. In this instance, replace it or separate the newer shoots from the main plant.

Maximum spread: Continuous

Growth rate: Medium

Area: Midground, Foreground, Specimen, or unusual

Light: Bright to Strong

Temperature: 59–72°F (15–22°C)

Propagation: From shoots

Difficulty: 1, 2

Scientific name:

Glossostigma elatinoides

Origin: Australia, New Zealand

This tiny foreground plant usually reaches a height of only 0.6 in (1.5 cm) and once established, will spread to form a dense carpet across the substrate. Its only major requirement is strong lighting; as long as other conditions are adequate, the plant should do well once established. Avoid placing it in shaded or covered areas. It can be used as a bog/marsh plant in damp situations. If conditions in the aquarium are relatively good, this is an excellent foreground plant.

Maximum height: 0.4–0.8 in (1–2 cm)

Growth rate: Medium

Area: Foreground

Light: Bright to Very Bright

Temperature: 72–82°F (22–28°C)

Propagation: From shoots

Difficulty: 2, 3

Scientific name:
Gymnocoronis spilanthoides
Common name: Spadeleaf plant

Origin: South America

This plant is often confused with *Hygrophila corymbosa*, although the leaves are fleshier and less rigid than those of *H. corymbosa*. The leaves of the spadeleaf can be up to 4.7–5.5 in (12–14 cm) long, so allow adequate space between the stems when planting. New shoots will rapidly grow to the surface, where they may produce leaves above water. Airborne leaves are thinner, more robust, and jagged along the edges. The plant is relatively adaptable and easy to care for. Can be kept in an unheated aquarium.

Maximum height: 20–24 in (50–60 cm)

Growth rate: Medium to Very Fast

Area: Background, Midground

Light: Bright

Temperature: 64–79°F (18–26°C)

Propagation: From cuttings, side shoots

Difficulty: 1, 2

The common name of this plant comes from the spade or spoonlike shape of its leaves.

Scientific name:
Hemianthus callitrichoides
Common name: Dwarf helzine

Origin: Central America

Apart from good lighting and nutrients, this plant has little requirements and will adapt to most water conditions. Many specimens are grown floating before being sold to create a dense mat of leaves and a short appearance, providing the plant is regularly pruned, this appearance can be maintained. Without nutrients and strong light, the plant will quickly die.

Maximum height: 1.2–6 in (3–15 cm)

Growth rate: Medium

Area: Foreground

Light: Bright

Temperature: 68–82°F (20–28°C)

Propagation: From runners and cuttings

Difficulty: 2, 3

Scientific name:

Hemianthus micranthemoides

Synonym: *Micranthemum micranthemoides*

Common name: Pearlweed

Origin: Cuba, Southeast United States

Pearlweed has a delicate appearance, with small (0.4 in/1 cm), light green, oval leaves, and is an ideal plant for the midground area of the aquarium. It adapts to varying temperatures and water hardness, but may be sensitive to some chemical treatments. Cuttings will often form side shoots, creating a dense appearance. Pearlweed is best planted in small groups.

Maximum height: 6–8 in (15–20 cm)

Growth rate: Moderate

Area: Midground

Light: Bright

Temperature: 72–82°F (22–28°C)

Propagation: From cuttings and runners

Difficulty: 2, 3

Left: For the best effect, plant Heteranthera zosterifolia in groups, with taller specimens toward the back and shorter plants toward the front. Bright light will keep plant growth compact.

Scientific name:

Heteranthera zosterifolia

Common name: Stargrass

Origin: Brazil

Stargrass is so called because of the starlike arrangement of leaves when viewed from above. This tall, bushy plant is ideal for background planting, or if regularly trimmed, the midground. The leaves are roughly 1.6–2 in (4–5 cm) long and 0.2 in (0.5 cm) wide. With good lighting, the plant is relatively easy to keep. Once the stems reach the surface the plant will produce numerous side shoots. If planted in bright, open areas, it will grow short and compact, creating a bushy effect.

Maximum height: 16–20 in (40–50 cm)

Growth rate: Medium

Area: Background, Midground

Light: Bright to Very Bright

Temperature: 75–82°F (24–28°C)

Propagation: From cuttings; self-propagation

Difficulty: 2

Prune any extended stems to maintain a dense appearance.

Scientific name:

Hydrocotyle leucocephala

Common name: Brazilian pennywort

Origin: Brazil

This plant is similar in appearance to *Cardamine lyrata* although the leaves are much larger, reaching 1.2–2 in (3–5 cm) in diameter. It adapts to most aquarium conditions, although it does appreciate good lighting. The shoots quickly reach the surface, where the leaves spread rapidly, cutting out light to the aquarium. To prevent other plants from losing light, be sure to prune Brazilian pennywort regularly. It will also grow in damp bog conditions.

Maximum height: 20–24 in (50–60 cm)

Growth rate: Fast

Area: Midground, Foreground, Floating, Specimen, or unusual

Light: Bright

Temperature: 68–82°F (20–28°C)

Propagation: From cuttings; self-propagation

Difficulty: 1

The unusual "branching" appearance of the leaves and stems makes this a distinctive plant in any aquarium.

Scientific name:

Hydrocotyle sibthorpioides

Origin: Southeast Asia

This small Hydrocotyle species (up to 4 in/ 10 cm) requires very bright light and may be difficult to care for. In nature, it is normally found above water.

Maximum height: 4.7 in (12 cm)

Growth rate: Medium to Fast

Area: Foreground, Midground

Light: Bright to Very Bright

Temperature: 68–82°F (20–28°C)

Propagation: From cuttings and side shoots

Difficulty: 1, 2

Scientific name:

Hydrocotyle verticillata

Common name: Whorled umbrella plant

Origin: North and Central America

Apart from good lighting, this plant has no specific requirements and should do well in most aquariums. It can be used as a foreground or midground plant and also as a bog plant. It is often sold for ponds during the summer months, but in most temperate climates it will die during the winter. Careful and continual pruning will eventually produce a densely packed spread of individual stems with variable leaf shapes. The leaves are light green and 1.2 in (3 cm) in diameter.

Maximum height: 6–10 in (15–25 cm)

Growth rate: Medium to Fast

Area: Midground, Foreground

Light: Bright to Very Bright

Temperature: 68–77°F (20–25°C)

Propagation: From side shoots

Difficulty: 2

From above, it is possible to see that the arrangement of the leaves allows the plant to use as much light as possible.

Hygrophila *species*

Several varieties of hygrophila are available for aquariums and some of the common species have different leaf forms. This group of plants is highly adaptable and will do well in most aquariums. Growth rates vary between species, but most are fast growing and will need regular pruning and/or thinning to keep them tidy. Cuttings can be replanted in the substrate and should quickly produce roots. Good lighting, plus CO_2 and iron fertilization are important for good growth. In the wild, Hygrophila species grow in shallows above the water surface. If plants are allowed to grow above the surface in an aquarium, they may produce flowers.

Taking cuttings from taller stems will produce a more "bushy" plant.

The rigid stems and leaves of this plant appear terrestrial in origin.

Scientific name:

Hygrophila corymbosa

Synonym: *Nomaphila stricta*

Common name: Giant hygrophila

Origin: India, Indonesia

Hygrophila corymbosa, a very popular, readily available, and well-known aquarium plant, is highly adaptable and relatively fast growing. It is tolerant of a wide range of aquarium conditions, but may not do well in softer water. An ideal plant for any aquarium, it is not fussy about substrates or water quality. The plant can be grouped, but allow at least 2–2.4 in (5–6 cm) between shoots. It looks best when well spaced out and is ideal for the edges and corners of the aquarium. If the leaves begin to yellow, add more iron or CO_2. Can be kept in cooler water.

Maximum height: 20 in (50 cm)

Growth rate: Medium to Fast

Area: Background, Midground

Light: Moderate to Bright

Temperature: 68–82°F (20–28°C)

Propagation: From cuttings and side shoots

Difficulty: 1

Scientific name:

Hygrophila difformis

Synonym: *Synnema triflorum*

Common name: Water wisteria

Origin: India, Thailand, Malaya

This unusually shaped aquarium plant does well in bright light and looks best when kept in well-spaced groups of four or five stems. The leaf shape is dictated by aquarium temperature; at lower temperatures the leaves are thicker and smaller, at higher temperatures they are larger and more divided. The leaves are large – up to 4 in (10 cm) long – so adequate space is a must. If the plants receive too little light, the lower leaves may drop off and the spacing between the leaves increases.

Maximum height: 20 in (50 cm)

Growth rate: Medium

Area: Background

Light: Bright to Strong

Temperature: 75–82°F (24–28°C)

Propagation: From cuttings and side shoots

Difficulty: 2

OTHER PLANTS OF INTEREST

Hygrophila corymbosa 'Gracilis'

Origin: *Asia*
Maximum height: *20 in (50 cm)*
Growth rate: *Medium to Fast*
Area: *Background*
Light: *Bright*
Temperature: *72–82°F (22–28°C)*
Propagation: *From cuttings, shoots*
Difficulty: *1, 2*

This is one of the most attractive hygrophila variants, but the full leaf shape and bronze-red leaf color can be achieved only if the plant is given sufficient room and strong lighting. The elongated, oval leaves will grow to 6 in (15 cm) under normal circumstances. In exceptional conditions, the leaves may grow to more than 8 in (20 cm). It is quite normal, and sometimes unavoidable, for the leaves to revert to a green form. The plant has no special demands apart from good lighting, and is a good choice for any planted aquarium.

Hygrophila corymbosa 'Crispa'

Origin: *Indonesia*
Maximum height: *20–24 in (50–60 cm)*
Growth rate: *Medium to Fast*
Area: *Background*
Light: *Bright to Very Bright*
Temperature: *72–82°F (22–28°C)*
Propagation: *From cuttings and side shoots*
Difficulty: *2, 3*

Although not as commonly available as other types of hygrophila, in the right conditions this species can make a worthy addition to any planted display. As the leaves are long (up to 6 in/15 cm) and thin (0.6 in/1.5 cm), they require plenty of open space and unobstructed light. You can plant this hygrophila singly or in well-spaced groups, although this may require a larger aquarium. Not as easy to keep as other Hygrophila *species, but well worth trying.*

Hygrophila corymbosa 'Strigosa'

Origin: *Asia*
Maximum height: *24 in (60 cm)*
Growth rate: *Moderate to Fast*
Area: *Background, Midground*
Light: *Bright to Strong*
Temperature: *72–82°F (22–28°C)*
Propagation: *From cuttings, side shoots*
Difficulty: *1, 2*

The leaves of this hygrophila are almost upright and will grow up to 10 in (25 cm) tall. They have an unusual tendency to bend, giving a mature plant a "goblet" shape. The plant is best placed on its own in the midground of a larger aquarium. Apart from a strong light requirement, it has no special needs and will adapt to most aquariums.

The finely branched leaves of H. difformis *are delicate and can quickly degenerate in poor aquarium conditions.*

Hygrophila corymbosa 'Glabra'

Synonym: *Nomaphila stricta 'Glabra'*
Common name: *Broadleaf giant stricta*
Origin: *Asia*
Maximum height: *20 in (50 cm)*
Growth rate: *Fast*
Area: *Background, Midground*
Light: *Bright*
Temperature: *72–82°F (22–28°C)*
Propagation: *From cuttings and shoots*
Difficulty: *1*

This is one of the most adaptable hygrophilas and will do well in almost any aquarium. Depending on light intensity, the leaves vary in color from green to a light pinkish brown and will grow to 6 in (15 cm) long and up to 1.6 in (4 cm) wide. The lower leaves often turn green, regardless of light conditions. In a good environment, the plant will grow rapidly and may need regular thinning. It can be used singly among foreground plants or grouped as a background plant.

Hygrophila stricta

Synonym: *Hygrophila guianensis*
Common name: *Thai stricta, Green stricta*
Origin: *Southeast Asia, Thailand*
Maximum height: *20 in (50 cm)*
Growth rate: *Medium*
Area: *Background, Midground, Foreground*
Light: *Bright to Very Bright*
Temperature: *75–82°F (24–28°C)*
Propagation: *From cuttings*
Difficulty: *1, 2*

In an aquarium with good lighting, this plant – which is very similar in shape to H. corymbosa – will have an attractive, solid, and bushy appearance. It has a thick stalk and a pleasing green color. Plant it in groups of varying height for best effect. Thai stricta is highly adaptable and tolerant of aquarium conditions.

Scientific name:

Hygrophila guianensis

Common name: Guiana hygrophila

Origin: South America

This shorter hygrophila is readily available but does not do as well in the aquarium as other hygrophilas. For best results, provide bright lighting, plenty of room, and a nutrient-rich substrate. The light green leaves are fairly large — 4 x 0.8 in/10 x 2 cm — compared to the height of the plant and have a delicate appearance.

Maximum height: 10 in (25 cm)

Growth rate: Medium

Area: Background, Midground

Light: Bright to Very Bright

Temperature: 72–82°F (22–28°C)

Propagation: From cuttings and shoots

Difficulty: 2, 3

Hygrophila polysperma *'Big-leaf'*   Hygrophila polysperma *'Rosenverig'*

Scientific name:

Hygrophila polysperma

Common name: Dwarf hygrophila

Origin: India

A commonly available and popular aquarium plant that is tolerant and adaptable. The leaves are shorter (1.6 in/4 cm) and narrower (0.4 in/1 cm) than *H. stricta* and *H. corymbosa* and sport a light green, sometimes reddish-brown color. Regular pruning will keep the plant healthy. When it reaches toward the surface, the leaves become red and compact. Ideal conditions include strong lighting and an iron-rich, fine substrate.

Maximum height: 20 in (50 cm)

Growth rate: Medium to Fast

Area: Background

Light: Bright

Temperature: 68–86°F (20–30°C)

Propagation: From cuttings and side shoots

Difficulty: 1

The veins of Hygrophila polysperma varieties are often white in color.

Scientific name:

Lagarosiphon major

Synonym: *Elodea crispa*

Common name: African water weed

Origin: South Africa

This aquarium plant is often sold as a pond plant and does well in cooler water. The unusual curved leaves give the plant a unique appearance, which may prove a disadvantage when you come to find a suitable place for it in the aquarium. Good lighting and cool water are its only major requirements; otherwise it is hardy and adapts to most conditions.

Maximum height: 20 in (50 cm)

Growth rate: Medium

Area: Midground, Foreground

Light: Bright

Temperature: 64–72°F (18–22°C)

Propagation: From cuttings

Difficulty: 1

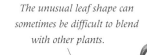

The unusual leaf shape can sometimes be difficult to blend with other plants.

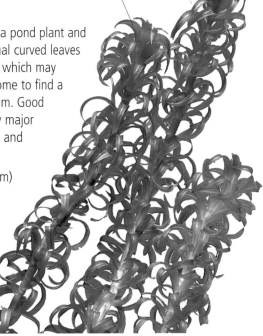

OTHER PLANTS OF INTEREST

Lemna trisulca

Origin: Widespread in subtropics
Maximum spread: Continuous, spreading
Growth rate: Moderate to Fast
Area: Floating
Light: Bright
Temperature: 50–82°F (10–28°C)
Propagation: By division
Difficulty: 1
Lemna trisulca *is more attractive than* L. minor *and not quite as fast growing, although in good conditions it will still need regular thinning. The leaves — typically 0.4 in (1 cm) long and 0.2 in (0.5 cm) wide — are connected by short stalks and spread to create a dense mat across the water surface. Provide adequate ventilation above them.*

Scientific name:

Lemna minor

Common name: Duckweed

Origin: Worldwide

Duckweed is adaptable, fast-growing, hardy, and has no specific requirements, but is often considered a pest. In good conditions it spreads rapidly, and a small group may develop to cover the surface of an average aquarium within a week. The light green, oval leaves are 0.12 in (3 mm) long. If regularly thinned, the plant can be very effective in an open-topped aquarium. Duckweed often looks better as an ornamental plant when kept together with other floating species, such as water lettuce (*Pistia stratiotes*), *Azolla* spp., or *Salvinia* spp.

Growth rate: Fast

Area: Floating

Light: Undemanding

Temperature: 50–86°F (10–30°C)

Propagation: By division

Difficulty: 1

Scientific name:

Lilaeopsis novae-zelandiae

Common name: New Zealand grassplant

Origin: Australia, New Zealand

This commonly available grasslike species produces thick, lush green groups of plants that will spread across the foreground. As long as a good substrate and strong lighting are provided, the plant will adapt well to most aquarium conditions. It can also be used as a bog/marsh plant out of water.

Maximum height: 3.2–4 in (8–10 cm)

Growth rate: Medium

Area: Foreground

Light: Strong

Temperature: 68–82°F (20–28°C)

Propagation: From side shoots

Difficulty: 2

Scientific name:

Limnobium laevigatum

Synonym: *L. stoloniferum, Hydromistria stolonifera*

Common name: Amazon frogbit

Origin: South America

The thick, waxy leaves of the frogbit are 0.8–1.2 in (2–3 cm) long and almost round in shape. This adaptable floating plant can be kept in open-topped aquariums or tanks with adequate ventilation. Given good conditions, it will spread rapidly and may need to be thinned occasionally.

Growth rate: Medium to Fast

Area: Floating

Light: Bright

Temperature: 72–75°F (22–24°C)

Propagation: From runners

Difficulty: 1, 2

Above: *Although the roots of this floating plant are not large and trailing compared to some floating species, they still provide welcome cover for surface-dwelling fish.*

Scientific name:

Limnophila aquatica

Common name: Giant ambulia

Origin: India, Sri Lanka

Once established, this attractive, fine-leaved bushy plant is relatively easy to look after. Any difficulties you experience in keeping it can usually be attributed to changing conditions or the lack of a particular nutrient. A readily available source of iron and fairly soft water (with a pH of 6–7) are particularly important. In good conditions and strong lighting, the plant will grow rapidly, producing noticeable growth almost daily. Stronger light will also ensure that the leaves are thicker and more compact. Do not take cuttings too often, as the original stem plant may begin to die back. Once cut back, the plant produces side shoots. Positioned in groups of individual stems placed slightly apart, giant ambulia makes an ideal background plant.

Maximum height: 20 in (50 cm)

Growth rate: Fast

Area: Background

Light: Bright to Very Bright

Temperature: 72–79°F (22–26°C)

Propagation: From cuttings and side shoots

Difficulty: 2, 3

Scientific name:

Limnophila sessiliflora

Common name: Dwarf ambulia

Origin: India, Indonesia, Sri Lanka

Dwarf ambulia is smaller, more robust in appearance, and hardier than the giant ambulia. The leaves are arranged in whorls along the stem and individual stems should be planted in groups about 1.2–1.6 in (3–4 cm) apart to create a dense, bushy appearance. When the plant reaches the surface it will grow horizontally across the water. It is adaptable to harder water and many aquarium conditions, making it an ideal plant for novices, although it does require a good source of iron.

Maximum height: 12–20 in (30–50 cm)

Growth rate: Moderate to Fast

Area: Background, Midground

Light: Bright to Strong

Temperature: 72–82°F (22–28°C)

Propagation: From cuttings, side shoots and runners

Difficulty: 1

OTHER PLANTS OF INTEREST

Limnophila indica

Synonym: L. gratioloides
Common name: Indian ambulia
Origin: Africa, Asia, Australia
Maximum height: 16–20 in (40–50 cm)
Growth rate: Medium to Fast
Area: Background, Midground
Light: Bright to Strong
Temperature: 72–82°F (22–28°C)
Propagation: From cuttings
Difficulty: 2

This is another appealing, fine-leaved plant. There are a few leaf varieties, but all are similar in appearance and requirements. Use them in groups in the background or midground of the aquarium, leaving at least 2 in (5 cm) between the stems. Apart from a high light requirement, the plant is adaptable and should do well in most aquariums.

The thick, fleshy leaves are hardy enough to withstand the attentions of some herbivorous or boisterous fish.

Scientific name:

Lobelia cardinalis

Common name: Scarlet lobelia, cardinal flower

Origin: North America

This plant is available in two distinctly different forms. The aquatic form featured here has short, thick stems with thick fleshy leaves that are often a deep scarlet-red on the underside. Color variations range from a light green on both leaf sides to a dark purple underside and dark green upper leaf. The plant is hardy and undemanding and able to tolerate a wide range of aquarium conditions. Due to its slow-growing nature, it requires little care. In its terrestrial form, the plant produces numerous purple-red flowers on stalks up to 36 in (90 cm) high. It is often sold as a marginal plant for ponds.

Maximum height Up to 12 in (30 cm)

Growth rate: Slow

Area: Midground, Foreground

Light: Bright

Temperature: 72–79°F (22–26°C)

Propagation: From cuttings and side shoots

Difficulty: 1, 2

Ludwigia brevipes

Origin: *North America*
Maximum height: *16 in (40 cm)*
Growth rate: *Moderate to Fast*
Area: *Background, Midground*
Light: *Bright to Very Bright*
Temperature: *64–73°F (18–23°C)*
Propagation: *From cuttings and side shoots*
Difficulty: *2, 3*

The small leaves of this plant can look very effective when used in a larger group toward the rear of the aquarium. L. brevipes is relatively hard to keep compared with other Ludwigia species, but strong lighting and a good substrate will help to maintain it in optimum health. The leaves are up to 1.2 in (3 cm) long and the uppermost or newer leaves may turn a yellow-pink color. Best kept in cooler water.

Ludwigia palustris

Common name: *Broadleaf ludwigia*
Origin: *United States*
Maximum height: *20 in (50 cm)*
Growth rate: *Medium*
Area: *Background, Midground*
Light: *Bright to Very Bright*
Temperature: *64–79°F (18–26°C)*
Propagation: *From cuttings and side shoots*
Difficulty: *2*

This undemanding ludwigia is a common aquarium plant that will adapt to most conditions if bright lighting is available. The reddish green leaves are formed close together, particularly near the surface, and vary in color throughout the plant. Regular pruning will cause it to produce side shoots, making the plant appear more bushy. If cared for correctly, L. palustris makes a good display plant.

Scientific name:

Ludwigia glandulosa

Common name: Glandular ludwigia, Red star ludwigia

Origin: Southern United States

In the right conditions, this ludwigia will grow quickly, producing intensely olive-green/pink leaves that stand out well in a planted aquarium. Regular trimming will keep the plant compact and tidy. Given very bright lighting and good all-round conditions, it is easy to care for and will adapt to most aquariums. The leaves will grow to 2 in (5 cm) long. Best planted in groups of five or more. With good care, this plant can be very attractive.

Maximum height: 8–12 in (20–30 cm)

Growth rate: Moderate to Fast

Area: Background

Light: Very Bright

Temperature: 72–82°F (22–28°C)

Propagation: From cuttings and side shoots

Difficulty: 2

The olive-green color of the elongated leaves is a subtle shade that will contrast well with more boldly colored plants.

Although the structure of this floating plant appears to be based on individual plants on runners, it is in fact a horizontally growing stem.

Left: Ludwigia helminthorrhiza *is an attractive floating plant that does well in bright conditions. It can also be planted in the substrate, although it will grow quickly to the surface, with large spaces between leaf nodes.*

Left: Ludwigia arcuata *is a narrow-leaved form of ludwigia. An ideal bushy plant for the mid- or background.*

Scientific name:

Ludwigia repens

Synonym: *Ludwigia natans*

Common name: Creeping ludwigia, Narrow-leaf ludwigia

Origin: North and Central America

This plant is found in a variety of forms that differ in leaf shape and color. The most commonly available is a wide, round-leaved form, that is light olive green-brown on the leaf surface and a reddish color on the underside. The plant is highly adaptable and fast growing. As it reaches the surface, the leaves become more compact and the stem grows horizontally across the water, creating an attractive overhead view. A number of rootlike shoots are produced from the leaf nodes. Regular pruning will keep the plant tidy and healthy.

Maximum height: 20 in (50 cm)

Growth rate: Fast

Area: Background, Midground

Light: Bright

Temperature: 68–82°F (20–28°C)

Propagation: From cuttings and side shoots

Difficulty: 1

Given good lighting, this plant is easy to grow and an excellent choice for beginners.

Scientific name:

Lysimachia nummularia

Common name: Creeping Jenny

Origin: Europe, Japan, North America

Creeping Jenny, an adaptable and commonly available species, is often sold as an aquarium plant as well as a marginal pond plant. In the wild it is found in ditches and marshy areas, where it is either partially submerged or growing in very damp ground. When kept in a tropical aquarium, growth may slow down and stop after a time. Replace the plant at this point. In the aquarium, good lighting is essential to keep the plant healthy. It tolerates a wide range of conditions and is ideal for the coldwater aquarium.

Maximum height: 16 in (40 cm)

Growth rate: Medium

Area: Midground, Foreground

Light: Bright to Very Bright

Temperature: 59–72°F (15–22°C)

Propagation: From cuttings

Difficulty: 1

Scientific name:

Marsilea hirsuta

Origin: Australia

This low-growing plant will spread via runners and shoots, creating an attractive display in the foreground of the aquarium. Although not always available, it is an attractive and adaptable plant and suited to a wide range of conditions. For best growth, provide a good substrate and bright light. Two similar varieties, *Marsilea drummondi* and *Marsilea crenata*, are also occasionally available.

Maximum height: 2 in (5 cm) or more

Growth rate: Moderate

Area: Foreground

Light: Bright

Temperature: 72–82°F (22–28°C)

Propagation: Runners

Difficulty: 2

Scientific name:

Micranthemum umbrosum

Synonym: *M. orbiculatum*

Common name: Helzine

Origin: Central America

This compact, small-leaved plant will grow in a messy yet attractive fashion, and is best situated to the foreground of the aquarium in front of larger plants. Regular pruning will keep it tidy. The tiny (0.2 in/5 mm) round leaves are numerous and light green in color. Although the plant needs very bright lighting when planted in the substrate, it can also be used as a floating plant and as a bog plant. Apart from good lighting, it has no special requirements.

Maximum height: 12 in (30 cm)

Growth rate: Medium

Area: Foreground, Floating

Light: Bright to Very Bright

Temperature: 75–86°F (24–30°C)

Propagation: From cuttings

Difficulty: 2

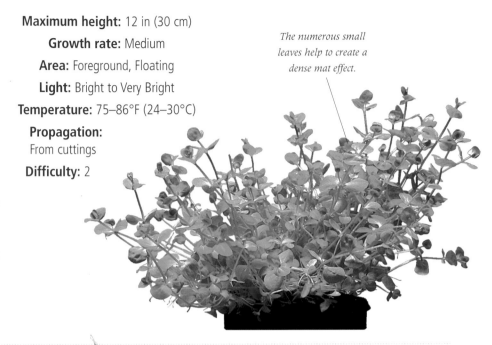

The numerous small leaves help to create a dense mat effect.

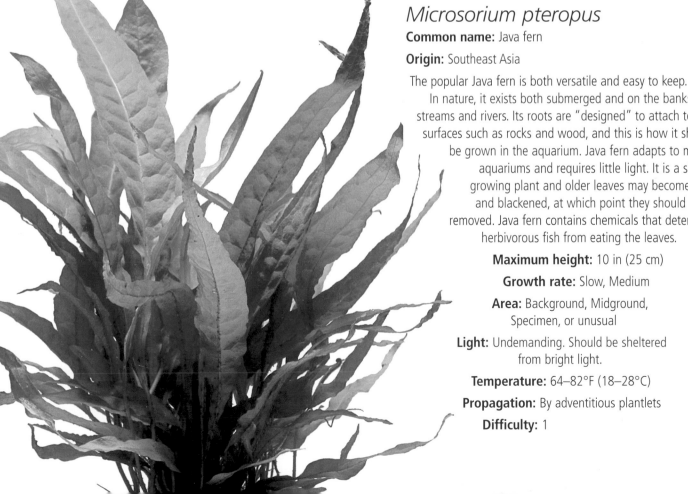

Scientific name:

Microsorium pteropus

Common name: Java fern

Origin: Southeast Asia

The popular Java fern is both versatile and easy to keep. In nature, it exists both submerged and on the banks of streams and rivers. Its roots are "designed" to attach to hard surfaces such as rocks and wood, and this is how it should be grown in the aquarium. Java fern adapts to most aquariums and requires little light. It is a slow-growing plant and older leaves may become tatty and blackened, at which point they should be removed. Java fern contains chemicals that deter most herbivorous fish from eating the leaves.

Maximum height: 10 in (25 cm)

Growth rate: Slow, Medium

Area: Background, Midground, Specimen, or unusual

Light: Undemanding. Should be sheltered from bright light.

Temperature: 64–82°F (18–28°C)

Propagation: By adventitious plantlets

Difficulty: 1

GALLERY OF JAVA FERN

Java fern (Microsorium pteropus) is a popular aquarium plant for many reasons: it is hardy and adaptable and can be kept in aquariums where other plants would not thrive; the tough leaves and slow growth are suited to low light and low nutrient conditions.

The leaves of Java fern contain a chemical that deters most herbivorous fish from eating it. However, large destructive fish, such as oscars (Astronotus ocellatus), or tinfoil barbs (Barbus schwanenfeldi) may still destroy leaves without eating

Black spots often form on the underside of the leaves. These are not damaged areas, but sporangia (spore cases), from which new daughter plants may develop.

Right: Microsorium pteropus 'Red' has the typical leaf form. Before planting, remove the pot and potting medium and tie the main root (rhizome) to a rock or piece of bogwood. You can place the plant in substrate, but the rhizome must be in open water.

Right: Microsorium pteropus 'Tropica' is a cultivated variety with a slightly "feathered" leaf. All varieties of Java fern require the same conditions, although this variety may grow slightly faster.

Left: Microsorium pteropus *'Windeløv'* is a finely branched, small leaf variety of Java fern and highly attractive in any display. The leaf size (4–8 in/10–20 cm) makes it ideal for the smaller aquarium.

Eventually, the leaves of Java fern will turn brown and die. When this starts to happen, they should be removed.

Right: This narrow-leaved variety of Java fern has a bushier appearance than the normal large-leaf form. All varieties of Java fern can be kept in cooler water (64°F/18°C) and even in slightly brackish conditions.

Scientific name:

Nymphaea lotus var. *rubra*

Common name: Red tiger lotus

Origin: East Africa, Southeast Asia

This color variety of the tiger lotus produces leaves that vary from a light green-red with reddish speckles to a darker green-brown with red speckles. It makes a good centerpiece and contrasts well with both tall, bushy, or small-leaved background plants and smaller foreground plants.

Maximum height: Will grow to the surface

Growth rate: Moderate to Fast

Area: Background, Midground

Light: Bright to Very Bright

Temperature: 72–82°F (22–28°C)

Propagation: From daughter plants on runners

Difficulty: 2, 3

Scientific name:

Nymphaea stellata

Common name: Red and blue water lily

Origin: India

Although sometimes sold as red tiger lotus (*Nymphaea lotus* var. *rubra*) this tropical lily has smaller, spade-shaped leaves and will grow more compact, sometimes creating a better effect in a well-planted aquarium than red tiger lotus. The leaves will grow up to 4.7 in (12 cm) long and are a brownish pink to red in color. If the light source is not bright, the plant will produce larger (8 in/20 cm) green floating leaves. As it ages it may die back naturally, even under the best conditions. Apart from a good light source and moderate fertilization, the plant has no special requirements.

Maximum height: 12–16 in (30–40 cm), sometimes to the surface

Growth rate: Medium

Area: Midground, Specimen or unusual

Light: Very Bright

Temperature: 72–82°F (22–28°C)

Propagation: From daughter plants produced on shoots

Difficulty: 2

The leaves of Nymphaea stellata *are more uniform in color than those of* N. lotus *varieties, and their growth pattern may be more suited to a well-planted aquarium. Nevertheless, pruning some larger leaves may be necessary to keep the plant tidy.*

Scientific name:

Nymphoides aquatica

Common name: Banana plant

Origin: Southern United States

This unusual little plant gets its name from the banana-shaped root sections that are used by the plant to store nutrients. These should be left above the substrate; the plant also produces "normal" roots that will bury themselves. The heart-shaped leaves on short stalks are 4–4.7 in (10–12 cm) long. In shallow areas, the leaves will reach the surface and grow to 6 in (15 cm). The plant is relatively easy to care for but may have a limited life span in the aquarium.

Maximum height: 6–8 in (15–20 cm)

Growth rate: Slow to Medium

Area: Midground, Foreground, Floating

Light: Bright to strong

Temperature: 68–86°F (20–30°C)

Propagation: By adventitious plantlets

Difficulty: 2, 3

Scientific name:

Caladium bicolor

Origin: Tropical jungles

This attractive plant produces spade-shaped leaves on long stems above the water surface. Many leaf forms are available, but most have a white or red center and green edging. This plant is commonly available, both as an aquatic and terrestrial garden plant, but will survive fully submerged for only six to eight weeks. It is better used above water, with the roots trailing into the aquarium. If it is kept in its original pot it will stay healthy, but grow very slowly and produce shorter stems, which may be an advantage in some situations.

Maximum height: Up to 16 in (40 cm) when grown above water

Area: Background, Specimen, or unusual

Light: Bright

Temperature: 72–82°F (22–28°C)

Propagation: From daughter plants produced from a bulb

Special note: If eaten, the plant is poisonous, but not normally deadly, to small animals (cats, dogs, etc.). Dangerous to humans if eaten in quantity.

OTHER PLANTS OF INTEREST

Acorus gramineus

Common name: *Japanese rush*
Origin: *East Asia*
Maximum height: *14 in (35 cm)*
Area: *Foreground, Midground, Specimen, or unusual*
Light: *Undemanding*
Temperature: *50–79°F (10–26°C)*
Propagation: *From cuttings at the base*
The numerous grasslike leaves of this plant are rigid, firm, and able to withstand fast-flowing water. Older leaves will begin to yellow before thinning and eventually dying, at which point they should be removed. Fully submerged, this plant may last many months, even a year in good conditions. It does not need much root space and is ideal for gaps in rockwork above the water or in marginal areas. When submerged, the plant does better at lower temperatures. A smaller variety, Acorus gramineus 'Pusillus' is also readily available and has a shorter (2–4 in/5–10 cm) dark green leaf.

Chlorophytum laxum 'Bichetii'

Common name: *Pongol swordplant*
Origin: *Gabon, Africa*
Maximum height: *6 in (15 cm)*
Area: *Foreground, Midground, Specimen, or unusual*
Light: *Strong lighting if grown submersed, otherwise moderate*
Temperature: *72–82°F (22–28°C)*
Propagation: *By adventitious plants or division of the rhizome*
This small plant produces many short (6 in/15 cm) curved leaves with white or yellow edging. The plant does not do well submerged and needs strong light if kept underwater. Used as a marginal or bog plant, it is hardy and requires only moderate lighting.

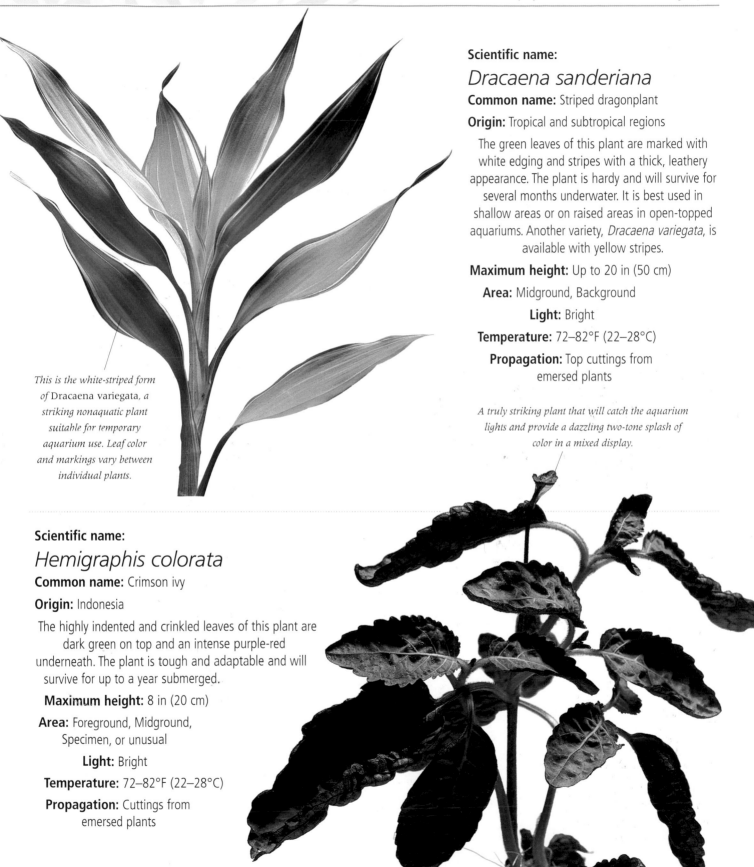

Scientific name:

Dracaena sanderiana

Common name: Striped dragonplant

Origin: Tropical and subtropical regions

The green leaves of this plant are marked with white edging and stripes with a thick, leathery appearance. The plant is hardy and will survive for several months underwater. It is best used in shallow areas or on raised areas in open-topped aquariums. Another variety, *Dracaena variegata*, is available with yellow stripes.

Maximum height: Up to 20 in (50 cm)

Area: Midground, Background

Light: Bright

Temperature: 72–82°F (22–28°C)

Propagation: Top cuttings from emersed plants

A truly striking plant that will catch the aquarium lights and provide a dazzling two-tone splash of color in a mixed display.

This is the white-striped form of Dracaena variegata, *a striking nonaquatic plant suitable for temporary aquarium use. Leaf color and markings vary between individual plants.*

Scientific name:

Hemigraphis colorata

Common name: Crimson ivy

Origin: Indonesia

The highly indented and crinkled leaves of this plant are dark green on top and an intense purple-red underneath. The plant is tough and adaptable and will survive for up to a year submerged.

Maximum height: 8 in (20 cm)

Area: Foreground, Midground, Specimen, or unusual

Light: Bright

Temperature: 72–82°F (22–28°C)

Propagation: Cuttings from emersed plants

Scientific name:

Ophiopogon japonicus

Common name: Fountain plant

Origin: Japan, Asia

The common name of this plant comes from the fountainlike appearance of the narrow leaves, which bend back and outward. For the best effect, group together a few well-spaced plants in the midground or at the edges of the aquarium. This is a particularly hardy variety that does well in most conditions. A dwarf variety, *Ophiopogon japonicus* var. *kyoto* grows to only 4 in (10 cm).

Maximum height: 8 in (20 cm)

Area: Foreground, Midground, Specimen, or unusual

Light: Undemanding

Temperature: 64–79°F (18–26°C)

Propagation: Cuttings from side sprouts

The flexible leaves bend over to create a fountain effect in the aquarium.

Scientific name:

Ophiopogon japonicus var. *giganteum*

Common name: Giant fountain plant

Origin: Japan, Asia

In this variety of *O. japonicus*, the leaves grow up to 14 in (35 cm) and are less rigid, but still bend back at the tips. The plant has a slightly "messy" appearance and is best placed in areas of water flow, where the leaves will create movement in the aquarium. It will survive for several months submerged and is hardy and undemanding.

Maximum height: 14 in (35 cm)

Area: Midground, Background, Specimen, or unusual

Light: Undemanding

Temperature: 64–79°F (18–26°C)

Propagation: Cuttings from side sprouts

Scientific name:

Ophiopogon japonicus 'Variegatus'

Common name: Variegated fountain plant

Origin: Japan, Asia

This plant has a dominant, imposing appearance. The leaves are up to 14 in (35 cm) long and 0.8 in (2 cm) wide, with white edging and smaller white stripes along the entire length of the leaf. The plant is relatively hardy and should survive for many months underwater, but should be removed and grown emersed if the leaves begin to deteriorate.

Maximum height: 14 in (35 cm)

Area: Midground, Background, Specimen, or unusual

Light: Undemanding

Temperature: 64–79°F (18–26°C)

Propagation: Cuttings from side sprouts

Scientific name:

Syngonium podophyllum

Common name: Stardust ivy

Origin: Jamaica

This climbing species is one of the most commonly available nonaquatic plants, and ideal for use on rockwork in a paludarium. However, it is not suited to life underwater and will quickly deteriorate if left submerged. It can be kept in small pots, with the roots trailing into the water. The three-lobed leaves are attractively patterned with white veins.

Maximum height: 12 in (30 cm)

Area: Specimen or unusual

Light: Bright

Temperature: 72–82°F (22–28°C)

Propagation: By division of the shoots

This is Syngonium *'White Butterfly', a popular variety of stardust ivy sold under the name of "lily leaf plant."*

General index

Page numbers in **bold** indicate major entries; *italics* refer to captions and annotations; plain type indicates other text entries.

A

Acidic compounds 18
Aeration 74, *74*
Air pump 36
Algae 11, 27, 44, 55, *57*, 59, 63, 74, 76, 84, 85, 87, 88, *88*, 89, *89*, *90*, 91, *91*, 107, 109, 111, 118, *118*, *119*, 129, 134, 148, 176, 177
  algal blooms 23, 63, 74, 88, *88*, 89, 90, 91, *91*
  growth 57, 59, *59*, 89, 92, 96, 118
  blanketweed 90
  blue-green 90
  brown 90, 91
  brush 91, *91*, 118
  filamentous 89, 90, *90*
  hair 90
  magnet 85
  marine 62
  pad 85, *89*, 90
  red *89*
  scraper 85, *91*
  single-celled 89, 90
  thread 90
  treatments 28, 88, 90, 91, 92
    liquid *90*
Alkaline substances 94
Allelopathy 88, 89
  allelochemical 88, 89, 91
Amino acids 75
Ammonia (NH$_3$) 27, 28, 30, 34, 37, 73, 76, 84, 86
  test kit 34
Ammonium (NH4+) 27, 28, 30, 66, 75, 77
Ampullarius sp. *92*
Aquarium/Tank
  African pool **112-113**
  bog aquarium 125, 188
  background 97
  biotope 22, 116, 123
  carbonator *70*
  coldwater aquarium **110-111**
  decor 94, 97, *102*, 119
    artificial *96*
    caves 96, 97, 120
    rocks 96
  synthetic 96
  tree roots 96
  design 97, 98, *98*
  equipment 104
  hardwater aquarium **108-109**
  Indonesian stream **114-115**
  low-light aquarium **106-107**
  mountain stream **116-117**
  open-topped aquarium **104-105**, 125, 126, 182, 193
  paludarium **102-103**, 125, 193, 197
  silicone sealant 97, 102, *102*
Aquascaping 11, **94-121**, 122

B

Bacteria 13, 26, 27, 28, 29, 30, *33*, 34, 45, 47, *47*, 70, 72, 73, 85, 86
  aerobic 30
  anaerobic 28, 30, 47, *67*, 84
  bacterial blooms 96
  bacterial disease 84
  bacterial organisms 17
  Nitrobacter 28
  Nitrosomonas 28
  substrate *28*
Bicarbonates 33, 34, 72
Biology of plants 10, **12-27**
Biotopes 22, 116
  African pool **112-113**
  coldwater aquarium **110-111**
  hardwater aquarium **108-109**
  Indonesian stream **114-115**
  low-light aquarium **106-107**
  mountain stream **116-117**
  natural 11
  open-topped aquarium **104-105**
  paludarium **102-103**
Borate (BO$_3$$^{3-}$) 76
Borax (sodium borate) 76
Boron (B) 66, 76
Breeding tanks 192
Buffering capacity 32, *32*, 35, 37
Bulbs *19*, *128*, *138*, 178
Buying plants 48
  mail order 48, 51, 122

C

Calcium (Ca) 31, 34, 40, 66, 67, 72, 73, 94
Carbohydrates *13*, 76

Carbon (C) *13*, 15, 66, 68, 72, 74, 95
Carbonates 15, 27, 32, *32*, *34*, 35, 37, 67, 94
  hardness (KH) 34, *36*
  testing *36*
Carbon dioxide (CO$_2$) 13, *13*, 14, *14*, 15, *15*, 17, *17*, 24, 31, 32, 33, *33*, 34, *34*, 36, 40, 44, 51, 55, 59, 67, 70, 71, 72, 74, 85, 104, 105, 108, 114, 116, 123, 135, 142, 158, 177
  fertiliser bubble counter *71*
  fertiliser cylinder 70, *70*, *71*
  fertiliser system 15, 68, 69, 70, *70*, *71*, 87, 104, 116
  fertiliser tablets 70, *70*, 104
Carbonic acid 32, 33, 34, *34*
Chelates 76
  EDTA 76
  natural organic 76
Chloramine 37, *37*
Chloride (Cl$^-$) 76
Chlorine (Cl) 30, 37, *37*, 66, 68, 76, 85, 86
Chlorophyll *13*, 15, 16, 17, *22*, 57, 58, 73, 75, 77
  synthesis 76
Chloroplasts 15, *22*
Chlorosis 77
Choosing and planting **48-55**, 123
Condensation cover 85, 86
Copper 66, 76, *77*, 92
  levels 91
Corm *133*
Coverglass 86

D

Dechlorinator *37*, 76, 86
Disease(s) and poisoning **88-93**
  allelopathy 88
  cryptocoryne rot 88, 139
  resistance 75
  treatments 88
    snail-killer 51, 88, 92
Diurnal fluctuations 33, 36

E

Environmental conditions 50, 55, 88, *137*, 139
  natural *117*

Enzyme 77
  production 76
  urease 76

F

Fast-flowing streams 24
Feeding 11, **66-77**
  fish 90, 118
Fertilization 11, 68, 73, 76, 77, 84, 87, *117*, 123, 131, 135, 142, 177, 188
  by insects *21*
  CO$_2$ 68, 69, 70, *70*, 87, 106, 119, 146, 164
  fertilizer 123
    iron-rich 127, 146, 176, 183
    multipurpose 176
  iron 69, *117*, 132, 145, 155, 164
    liquid 68, 132, 164
  liquid 40, 55, 66, 67, 69, *69*, 73, 75, 77, 84, 85, 87, 90, 106, 112, 116, 177, 186, 192
  substrate 67, 68, 77, 116, 143
  tablets 55, 69, 77
Filtration 10, **26-30**, 32, 51, 89, 97, 108, 116
  biological 26, 27, 28, 29, 66, 73, 85
  chemical 26, 27, 28, 29
    media 29, *29*, 37, *86*, 87, 95
    activated carbon 29, 37, 44, *86*, 87
    zeolite-based 29
  filter 30, *52*, 84, 85, 91, 95, 96, 118
    bacteria 85
    external 29, *29*, 30, 85, 104
    floss 85
    internal 29, *29*, 85, 104
    medium 85, 86
      fine floss 61
    sponge 29, *29*, 30, *30*, 85
  mechanical 26, 27, 29, 89, 90, *135*
  powerhead *117*
  pump 29, *29*, 102, 116
  returns *117*
  sterilization 26, 27
  UV clarifiers 90
  unit 29, *29*
Fish 91, *98*, 116, 123, 156, 182, *187*, 189
  algae-eating 90, 91, 105, 117, 118